A Is Amazing

The Ultimate Alphabet Resource Book

dayle m. timmons

D1275745

FEARON TEACHER AIDS

Simon & Schuster Supplementary Education Group

Acknowledgments

To Maree, my sister and my friend. To the children I have taught and loved in my classes, who have taught me that teaching can truly be fun! Also to their parents, who have encouraged me in this endeavor.

To my family . . . my children Wesley and Courtney, and my husband, Jimmy, who encouraged me to take a leave of absence from my work to write this text. To my many colleagues whose ideas were often the inspiration for these activities.

Editor: Marilyn Trow
Copyeditors: Sally Eve Criticos and Lisa Schwimmer
Cover and Inside Illustration: Tracy La Rue Hall
Design: Diann Abbott

ISBN 0-8224-0253-X

Printed in the United States of America
1. 9 8 7 6 5

Contents

Introduction

A Is Amazing is a teacher resource intended to be used as a base of inspiration for your own ideas. Every class is different and the children in each class have individual and unique needs. You are encouraged to explore and use your imagination and energy to adapt the activities included here to meet the diverse needs of the children in your classroom.

Each of the alphabet letter sections is a self-contained unit. How long you spend studying a particular letter depends entirely upon your class. Some kindergarten teachers do the entire alphabet before the spring holidays. Other teachers, in classes for the mentally and physically handicapped, take the entire extended year, including summer school. Some teachers like to do a letter until they feel the class has mastered the sound, whether it takes three days or two weeks, and others abide by a very strict rule of one week for each of the twenty-six letters. It is helpful to tentatively map out your preference on a calendar at the beginning of the school year.

Teach only one sound for each letter at a time, such as the k sound for c as in *cage* (and not the c in *cereal)* and the g as in *girl* (and not the g in *gingerbread*), so as not to confuse the children. Try to stay away from words that include blends, especially those that have entirely different sounds from the initial consonant, such as *sh* and *ch*.

The letter units may be taught in any sequence. If you are in a situation, such as a self-contained Special Education class, and work with the same children for several years, you might wish to use a different approach each year so your activities will naturally be varied and exact repetition will be kept to a minimum. Several suggestions for sequencing the presentation of the letters are provided.

❖ Start with the letter A and work sequentially through the letter Z.

❖ Follow a researched sequence, such as the sequence

recommended in the *Brigance Diagnostic Inventory of Early Development*—M B H J G R S D N F C P L T Y W Z V K Q X (A E I O U)—or the *Alpha Time Series* which introduces the letters in groups, teaching identification of the letters first and then the letter sounds. These groupings are included here for your convenience.

Group 1: M T F H N (A)

Group 2: B Z P S V (E)

Group 3: L D G C (I O)

Group 4: K W Y

Group 5: R J (U)

Group 6: X Q

❖ Integrate the teaching of the letters with the times and seasons of the year. A list of suggested letters to teach for each school month is also provided. Some letters appear more than once because they seem to fit well at several different times of the year. The letters not listed (Q, U, X, Y, Z) have no seasonal significance and may be introduced at any time. Consider your own local and school holidays as well.

September	S (September) L (Labor Day, leaves) F (Fall)	February	F (February) V (Valentine's Day) H (hearts)
October	O (October, orange) F (Fire Prevention Week) H (Halloween) J (jack-o'-lantern)	March	M (March) S (spring, St. Patrick's Day) K (kites) G (green)
November	N (November) I (Indians) P (pumpkins, pilgrims) T (turkeys)	April	A (April) E (Easter) B (bunnies) R (rain)
December	D (December) C (Christmas)	May	M (May, Mother's Day)
January	J (January) W (winter) S (snow)		

❖ Start with the initial letter of each child's name in your class. The names of classmates are words the children will quickly learn. After going through the letters of the names of all the children, use one of the other methods for choosing the remaining letters.

❖ Coordinate your efforts with other teachers in your school who might be using the letter-of-the-week approach. Plan a field trip, show a film, or prepare a snack that corresponds to the letters you are teaching.

Making the Connections

Some activities are intended to be ongoing throughout the study of the alphabet. This helps to reinforce letters already studied and encourages children to see the continuity and relationships between the various letters and their connections to other subject areas.

ABC Bulletin Board

Choose a bulletin board in your classroom to display pictures associated with each letter you introduce. Include the upper and lower case alphabet letter, pictures that begin with the initial consonant sound, and labels for each picture as well. Cut out pictures from old magazines (an excellent activity for a volunteer) or use picture cards from language kits. Simple pictures are most effective. If possible, laminate the pictures so they may be kept from year to year. Place a small table or shelf under the bulletin board to display objects for each featured letter—an ant farm for A; a real baby bottle and bobby pins for B; a can of corn, deck of cards, and cactus plant for C; and so on. Invite the children to bring items from home as well. Then include the objects in your daily discussion.

Review the pictures on the bulletin board with the children every day. When the children can name all of the pictures, begin to describe each picture and invite the children to guess the correct word label. For example, you might say, "This is what you use with a bow," and the children may guess "arrow." Make the clues harder as the children progress. Use the clues to focus the children's attention on specific words.

Alphabet Book

Make alphabet books when all of the letters of the alphabet have been studied or as a review after each letter. Give each child a sheet, like the one illustrated here, for each letter of the alphabet. Encourage the children to write the upper and lower case letters. Invite the children to draw a picture of an object that begins with the letter. Or suggest that children cut out a picture of an object that begins with that letter from a magazine and glue it to the paper. Help the children label each picture as well. (Or you may elect to label the pictures for the children.) Assemble each child's completed alphabet sheets to make individual alphabet books. Encourage the children to take their books home to share with their families.

Alphabet Review Game

At the beginning of each week (and possibly every day), show the children flash cards of the alphabet letters they have learned thus far. Invite the children to say each letter name and the sound each letter makes. The game may also be played by arranging the flash cards along the chalkboard ledge. Make a letter sound and invite the children to select the correct card. You might also give the children several word cards or picture cards (include both familiar and unfamiliar words) and encourage the children to give you the initial consonant sound. This is a good opening group activity to use each morning and takes only a few minutes.

Books

A Book Review section is provided for your convenience at the end of each letter unit. Most of the books may be found in the easy reading section of your library. Take the list with you to the library at the beginning of each week and check out as many of the listed books as possible. Keep a record of the books your library has and where each book may be found for future reference. Most libraries will not have all of the books listed. If there is a particular subject or book that you feel you need, ask your school librarian to order the book or provide a suggestion for another selection.

Set up a reading center to display all of the books you choose each week. Some of the books will be just for the children to browse through and some you will choose to read to the class during reading time. If possible, read two to three books each day to the class, possibly before quiet time, for about 15 minutes. Some books you will want to read while doing a mini-unit on a particular vocabulary word. For example, you might introduce the word *jam* with the book *Bread and Jam for Frances* by Russell Hoban. Or, after making jam with your class, culminate the activity by reading the book *The Giant Jam Sandwich* by John V. Lord and Janet Burroway.

Make storytime an exciting and much anticipated event. Consider telling a story with puppets, showing a filmstrip of a story you have just read, or invite the children to act out a story after you have read it. You may also use a flannelboard to tell a story or simply retell the story in your own words. Make every book an adventure—a fun and intriguing experience that teaches and helps the children remember the letters and sounds.

Invite a guest reader to school once a month or even once a week to share a book with the class. Encourage the reader to choose a book that reinforces the letter your class is studying. The reader may be a parent, the librarian, the principal, a teacher's assistant, a cafeteria worker, an older student, or someone from the community. It's important for the children to know that many different people enjoy reading a good book. Encourage parents to read to their children at home as well. You might wish to award certificates (or set up some other sort of reinforcement system) to both the children and their parents for this activity. Instill in your young students an excitement for reading.

Cooking

Most children enjoy learning by doing, experimenting, touching, smelling, and tasting. It is often through one of these alternate senses, or through a multisensory approach, that children will remember and thus learn the alphabet and alphabet sounds when all else has failed. Cooking projects provide lots of opportunities for children to explore using all of the senses. Whether a child watches as you make a recipe, performs one part (such as pouring or stirring), or does the entire project individually following your directions, it is an experience that totally involves the child. Even the most active child becomes miraculously attentive.

When you incorporate cooking as part of your total curriculum, consider your own facilities and equipment— it's hard to cook without a stove! However, be creative.

There may be a stove that you could use in another part of the building, or consider adapting recipes for toaster ovens, electric frying pans, hot plates, or microwaves. If none of these options is feasible, choose no-cook recipes or choose fresh fruit and vegetables as an alternative to cooking. Exploring a coconut, pineapple, or kiwi can be an intriguing lesson. Even carrots and cucumbers will be new to some children. Although you may not be cooking, the experience can be as rewarding.

Schedule the time for cooking when it is best for you. Once a week might not be feasible for you—maybe once a month or just when you find a recipe that particularly inspires you! Regardless, work out some kind of schedule early in the year. Talk with other teachers who might be working on the letter-of-the-week approach. You can plan the cooking one week and another teacher might plan the next. Or you might consider combining your classes for a particular experience or just share the cost of supplies.

It is often fun to choose a theme for cooking. Maybe you want your class to taste and experience vegetables, so you might cook when there's a vegetable recipe for the letter you are studying. You could do the same with fruit. Regardless, you will find that children will often eat what they cook— even when parents have said their children *hate* what you're cooking. You may also discover some interesting facts about the children's likes and dislikes. For example, many children who dislike cooked vegetables will simply love the same vegetables raw! Many children will try a food just because of their pride in having created it. Don't miss this wonderful opportunity to expand your students' taste horizons!

An extensive list of foods is provided at the end of each letter unit in the Food for Thought section. Many school programs offer daily snacks and this would be a wonderful opportunity to try foods starting with the letter of the week every day—or maybe once a week. The food list and recipes are not inclusive. Think of some of your own favorite recipes. Encourage all of the adults working in your class, including parents of the children, to contribute ideas for cooking. The recipes in this section were chosen because they are easy to prepare. You can and should add to them, substituting ingredients that may be more available or less expensive to make each recipe your own. Use fresh fruits and vegetables that are grown in your area. Take advantage of *anything* and *everything* in your area.

Probably the biggest deterrent to using cooking as a part of your curriculum is money! You might consider these options:

❖ Ask parents to make a financial contribution. A few dollars from each child goes a long way.

❖ Request parents to contribute one ingredient for each cooking project.

❖ Ask parents to contribute one often-used item at the beginning of the year, such as peanut butter, flour, dry milk, confectioners' sugar, vanilla flavoring, honey, salt, brown sugar, vegetable oil, granulated sugar, and so on. These should be stored in airtight containers or in the refrigerator. These items will take care of a large portion of the expense.

❖ Take advantage of "freebies." Let everyone know what letter you are working on. When we studied the letter B, for instance, the foster grandmother in my class wanted to demonstrate making homemade biscuits and brought in all the ingredients. Even the director of the school cafeteria sent extras, such as eggs and butter, when the cafeteria refrigerator had to be cleaned out before the holidays.

❖ Let everyone know that you want to cook in your class, but you need money. The principal may think of you when an extra $20 is found in the budget. The PTA might be willing to find a small amount. The curriculum specialist might think of you when small grants are being applied for. Talk with other teachers in your school who need the same kind of funding and discuss the possibility of long-term school or district funding. If administrators see the educational benefit of cooking and realize that it's goal-directed, they'll usually try to find a way to partially fund it.

Before you begin, check with parents about any food allergies their children may have. There may be children on special diets, children who can't have sugar or food additives, and children with medical or religious considerations. Be considerate of these children. Try to cook foods that every child can eat or choose recipes that can easily be adapted to meet individual needs.

Cooking provides great opportunities for children to practice fine motor skills and increase their attention span and concentration, but every cooking experience is a valuable language experience as well. Suggestions for language "games" are provided below.

❖ Set out all of the cooking utensils, pans, and so on, that you will be using for your cooking project. Then choose different children to get the items you need as you call for them. Help the children describe how and why each utensil and piece of equipment is used.

❖ Leave the ingredients in their original containers. Help the children find the ingredient's name on each container by using initial consonant sounds.

❖ Encourage the children to predict what each recipe ingredient is. When all of the ingredients have been identified, ask the children to show you the ingredients you ask for by name. For example, you might say, "Show me which box contains brown sugar."

❖ When appropriate, invite the children to taste the food ingredients raw. Then discuss how the ingredients are alike and how they are different once they are cooked.

❖ Blindfold the children and see if they can guess what each ingredient is by tasting, touching, or smelling.

This is a wonderful way of experiencing each of the senses.

❖ Ask the children as many questions as possible about each ingredient you use. For example, you might ask these questions about a cup of milk: "What color is milk? What letter does the word *milk* start with? Name some other words that start with the letter M. What sound does the letter M make? What is brown milk called? Where does milk come from? Is milk good for your body? What other foods are made from milk?" Practice sequencing and discuss the concepts *before* and *after*. After each step, ask "Now what did we do first? Second? What did we do before we put in the milk? What did we do after we mixed the flour and eggs?"

❖ Arrange frequently used utensils on a table in the classroom, such as cookie sheets, spatulas, muffin tins, a vegetable peeler, a colander, graters, pot holders, a can opener, an ice-cream scoop, cake pans, a mixer or blender, measuring cups, and spoons. Then help the children label each item. This is a good filler activity as you wait for a cake to bake or for gelatin to gel. You might even take a photograph of each kitchen item and make a set of flash cards for labeling. Challenge the children to match the photographs with the actual items. When the children are competent with the labels, describe how each item is used and then encourage children to guess which item you are describing. Invite the children to provide descriptions for some of the items as well.

Drawing

Throughout this text, you will note very simple drawing exercises relating to the letter sound that is being taught. All of the activities were chosen because simple strokes and basic shapes reinforce prewriting skills. The drawing activities may be completed in five minutes or less. And you don't have to be an artist to teach these activities. You are not teaching art per se, although more advanced children might take the simple pictures and use their creativity to add additional detail. Adapt the drawings to your group. You may think of other pictures that might be drawn as well. You might want to add more sophisticated lines for more advanced children or eliminate lines for other children. Don't be afraid to try something different. The worst that can happen is that nobody can guess what you've drawn when you're finished! If that happens, at least the children have had practice making the strokes.

Draw each picture on the chalkboard or on a large sheet of newsprint. Then invite the children to copy the pictures stroke-for-stroke at their desks. This is a perfect time to teach left-right and top-bottom concepts. Describe every stroke you make as you make it. For example, if you are drawing a lollipop, you might say, "Start with a circle in the middle of your paper" as you draw the circle. As you draw the stick, you might say, "Start at the bottom of the circle and make a straight line, top to bottom." You have incorporated the concepts *middle, top*, and *bottom* and have drawn a circle and straight line in this very simple activity. Encourage the children to color their pictures as well. Label each picture. Encourage more advanced children to copy the word under their pictures as you write it on the chalkboard. Less experienced children may only copy the upper case letter.

Letter Display

Designate a specific place in your classroom, preferably near the doorway, to prominently display the letter of the week. Some type of permanent, laminated picture would be nice with a place to change the letter each week, or you may wish to develop a different eye-catching display for each letter.

Music

It has been said that music is an international language. It is often through music that we reach children who seem unreachable. Children who often have difficulty in other aspects of the academic curriculum come to life when they hear the beat of the music. Even children who seem uncoordinated sometimes have unbelievable rhythm and children who can't remember their own addresses can remember every word to a simple song or fingerplay. It is for these reasons that it is important to include music as an integral part of your curriculum.

Become involved with the existing music program in your school and reinforce the skills that the music teacher presents to the children. Make it a point to speak with the music teacher early in the school year about your letter-of-the-week approach and see if he or she might be willing to teach the children songs and musical activities appropriate to the letter sound you are teaching. Or invite a musical person to the classroom who would be willing to share or teach some music lessons occasionally. Identify these people in your school and use them as resources. Ask the music teacher for assistance in locating records and tapes, getting the words to songs, borrowing music books, learning simple music games and dances, identifying other people in school who might assist you in music, or borrowing instruments. Continue to teach the children songs and use rhythm instruments regularly, even if the children have access to a regular music program.

If you tend to skip music because you feel you aren't musical, reconsider. Children don't seem to care if you're off-tune! Try to use your own voice as a musical instrument. It's always available and doesn't need a cassette recorder, plug, or record player to work. It doesn't have any trouble starting at the beginning or repeating over and over, either. Best of all, it's free! If you're hesitant, practice. The more you practice, the more confidence you'll have. Take that first step and lead a song. You might be surprised at how easy it is and how accepting your class will be! If you absolutely cannot see yourself leading a song, get involved with fingerplays. The students will benefit from hearing the same sing-song rhyming sounds—and fingerplays can be lots of fun!

The *Wee Sing* series by Pamela Beall and Susan Nipp is a great musical resource for the curriculum. These songs stimulate the memory and help children learn and remember the different letter and letter sounds. The series includes several titles and each title comes with a cassette tape and a songbook. You may order individual titles in the series by contacting the publisher directly at the address provided below. The cassettes and books are available in many toy and bookstores as well.

Price Stern Sloan Publishers, Inc.
360 North La Cienega Boulevard
Los Angeles, California 90048

Parent Newsletter

It is important to stay in touch with parents. One way is with a parent newsletter. You may wish to send a one-page memo home with the children at the end of each week, highlighting the past week's activities. Or you may choose to send out a memo when special events occur. I prefer a monthly letter which includes highlights of the children's activities during the previous month, special acknowledgment of accomplishments by individual students, a thank-you note to parents for their contributions, a calendar of special events and announcements, a preview of the letters of the alphabet to be studied next month, and, whenever possible, drawings by the children. The newsletter serves as a wonderful way of keeping parents involved with what their children are studying at school and encourages them to reinforce these same concepts at home.

Show and Tell

Try structuring your sharing time around the featured letter of the alphabet for that week. Choose one particular day, such as Friday, and encourage the children to bring something from home that starts with the letter you are studying. When studying the letter B, for example, a child might bring an empty box of brownie mix and talk about making brownies with his mom. Another child might bring a brown bag each Friday filled with everything she and her dad could find around the house that started with the letter for that week. This type of activity gives the letter and letter sound you are studying real meaning to the children. This is a marvelous way of reinforcing the letters for children and promoting the home/school connection as well.

Storing the Materials

As you begin to accumulate many resources for each letter unit, such as unused supplies, pictures from magazines, worksheets, patterns for art projects, and so on, storage of these items can present a challenge. One way to organize this collection is to have a box for each letter of the alphabet. Cover each box with colored adhesive paper and glue the letter of the alphabet on the front of each box. The boxes may be attractively displayed on top of your highest bookshelf or another convenient and out-of-the-way place. When needed, take down the box appropriate for the week and sift through all of the treasures inside!

Evaluating the Results

In this age of accountability, consider your evaluation techniques thoughtfully and choose an approach that meets not only your district's criteria for your class, but also your personal needs for the individual assessment and mastery of the presented material. You may wish to briefly evaluate the children at the conclusion of each letter you are studying to measure each child's understanding. Some general screening objectives are listed below. You will be presenting many other skills as well and may wish to consider using a yearly comprehensive evaluation, such as the *Brigance Diagnostic Inventory of Early Development*.

❖ Identifies the upper case letter in print.

❖ Identifies the lower case letter in print.

❖ Writes the upper case letter using the correct strokes.

❖ Writes the lower case letter using the correct strokes.

❖ Identifies words that begin with the letter sound.

Aa

Acorns

❖ Encourage the children to collect acorns to bring to school. On a sheet of heavy paper, make a very large A with a heavy glue line. Invite the children to arrange the acorns along the glue line to make an "Acorn A."

❖ Give each child an acorn. Show the children how to draw a simple picture of an acorn. Help the children describe the acorn using all of their senses, except taste, and invite them to add more details to their pictures if they wish.

❖ Teach the children to sing "I'm a Nut" from *Wee Sing Silly Songs*. Invite the children to pretend to be acorns. Begin by having the children lie on the floor. Join the children on the floor and say, "Pretend you are beginning to grow. (Bring your arms up slowly and then gradually bring your body up off the floor.) Now you are a mighty oak tree. (Stand up tall, arms out.) Here comes a little breeze. (Sway back and forth.) Uh oh, here comes a terrible storm! (Make exaggerated swaying motions.) The storm stops and your drooping branches begin to sparkle as the sun comes out. (Stand up tall and straight.)"

❖ Explain that an acorn is a seed and, if planted, may grow into a mighty oak tree. Help the children plant some acorns and see what happens.

❖ Show the children an acorn squash. Put an acorn and the acorn squash side-by-side. Discuss how the acorn and acorn squash are alike and how they are different. Ask the children how they think an acorn squash got its name. Help the children see that an acorn squash is shaped like an acorn. Use the squash to make "A-Okay Acorn Squash."

A-Okay Acorn Squash

acorn squash	Cut an acorn squash in half lengthwise.
butter	Scoop out the pulp and seeds with a
brown sugar	spoon. Put the squash face down in a
cinnamon or	baking pan and pour in about 1/2 inch of
nutmeg (optional)	water. Bake for 25 minutes at 375°. The
	squash is done when the flesh is soft.
	Pour the water out and turn the squash
	over. Put a little butter and brown sugar
	over the squash. Add cinnamon or
	nutmeg, if desired. Then put the squash
	back into the oven until the butter has
	melted.

Acrobatics

❖ Invite the children to perform acrobatic feats. Arrange to take the class to the gym. Put down a gymnastic mat and encourage the children to do somersaults, head stands, back bends, bridges (lie on your back and push up to a bridge), rocking horses (lie on your stomach, grab your feet with your hands, and rock back and forth), log rolls (lie on your back with your arms over your head and legs straight down and roll over and over), and balls or egg rolls (sit down, bring your knees up to your chest, wrap your arms around your knees and roll around like a ball). Challenge the children to lie on their stomachs and try to touch their toes to their heads.

❖ Sponsor a "Gymnastics Meet." Invite parents as guests. Encourage the children to perform a variety of acrobatic feats.

Action

❖ Collect action picture cards, such as the cards contained in Peabody language kits. Help the children identify the action or actions illustrated in each picture.

❖ Play "Name the Action." Whisper an action (swimming, hammering, dancing, and so on) to one child. Encourage that child to pantomime the whispered word for the other children to guess. Whisper a new action word to the first child who guesses correctly.

❖ Help the children think of an action for each letter of the alphabet. Then read *A-B-C-ing: An Action Alphabet* by Janet Beller (see the unit book review). Invite the children to pantomime each action as you read.

Address

❖ Encourage each child to memorize his or her address. Draw and cut out a large construction paper house to place on a bulletin board. Then, as the children memorize their addresses, invite each child to pin his or her name and address on the house shape.

❖ Invite the children to sing their addresses to the tune of "Rain, Rain, Go Away." For example, "My name is Elsie Jenkins. This is where I live. 3541 Oak Grove, Middlebury, Texas, USA." (See "My Name and Address" from *Wee Sing Children's Songs and Fingerplays*.)

❖ Provide opportunities for the children to practice writing their addresses from memory.

Age

❖ Encourage each child to learn his or her age. Help the children practice answering the question "How old are you?" both orally and by showing the appropriate number of fingers.

❖ Help each child learn to write his or her age.

❖ Invite those children with siblings to share what it feels like to be the youngest or oldest child in the family. Invite the children to complete the sentence, "I know how to _____ because I am _____ years old."

Airplane

❖ Read *Paper Airplane* by Fulvio Testa (see the unit book review). Make simple paper airplanes. Choose several simple designs to fold step-by-step in front of the class. Invite the children to follow each step. Ask parent volunteers or older students to help. Then sponsor a flying contest. Award inexpensive prizes for the airplanes that are flown the farthest, highest, and so on. (Check the airlines to see if they might donate "junior wings" as prizes.)

❖ If possible, plan a class field trip to an airport to watch the airplanes land and take off. Try to arrange for the children to tour the airport and look inside an airplane.

❖ Discuss why we have airplanes. Help the children compare air travel with other forms of transportation. Then make a class list of some of the advantages and disadvantages of air travel.

❖ Read aloud *Curious George at the Airport* by Margret Rey and Allan J. Shalleck, *Airplanes* and *Airport,* both by Byron Barton, and *The Little Airplane* by Lois Lenski (see the unit book review). Invite the children to pretend to be airplanes. Take the children outside or to a gym. Show the children how they might put their arms out for wings and zoom high and low and all around the school yard or gym.

Alike

❖ Play the "Alike Game." You will need a set of letters and alphabet flash cards. Arrange the alphabet cards along the chalkboard ledge. Hold up a letter and ask for a volunteer to point to the matching card. Try this with teams as well. More advanced children may be challenged to match upper case letters with lower case letters.

❖ Help the children explore the words *alike* and *not alike.* Show the children two shapes, numbers, colors, or letters and ask the children if the items are alike. To encourage higher-order thinking skills, ask the children to name at least one common attribute for each pair of items, whether the items are alike or not. For example, a square and a circle are not alike, but they are both shapes, are drawn with lines, and are closed figures.

❖ Make a set of "Alike" and "Not Alike" index cards. On each card, write two letters of the alphabet. On some cards, write two letters that are alike. On others, write letters that are not alike. Help the children sort the cards into "Alike" and "Not Alike" stacks.

Alphabet

❖ Encourage the children to trace, copy, or write the alphabet. Arrange the class into small cooperative learning groups. Give each child a cupful of alphabet cereal and a paper plate. Suggest that children spread their cereal out on the paper plates so they may easily see the letters. Have each child read the letters on his or her plate. Then instruct each group to slowly recite the alphabet in unison. Invite the children to eat their cereal letters as the letters are said aloud.

❖ Teach the children to sing the "ABCs" from *Wee Sing Children's Songs and Fingerplays*. This song is sung to the tune of "Twinkle, Twinkle Little Star."

❖ Read aloud to the children *A B See!* by Tana Hoban, *Ed Emberley's ABC* by Ed Emberley, *Albert B. Cub and Zebra: An Alphabet Storybook* by Anne Rockwell, *Dr. Seuss's ABC*, by Dr. Seuss, *The ABC Bunny* by Wanda Gag, *The Great Big Alphabet Book with Lots of Words* by Richard Hefter and Martin S. Moskof, and *The Alphabet Book* by Philip D. Eastman (see the unit book review). Serve alphabet soup as a special treat. Encourage the children to identify as many letters as possible as they eat each spoonful.

❖ Play "Alphabet Bingo." There are several inexpensive commercial games available for purchase or you may make your own. Children may match upper case letters to upper case letters, lower case letters to lower case letters, upper case letters to lower case letters, or any other combination. The first child to cover all the letters on his or her card yells "Bingo!" and wins the game.

Aluminum

❖ Cut aluminum foil into long strips. Have the children use scissors to snip the strips into small squares. On a sheet of construction paper, make a large letter A with a heavy glue line. Invite the children to place the aluminum squares along the glue line to make an "Aluminum A." Point out that aluminum foil is used both to wrap and cook food. Encourage the children to share with the class the ways that aluminum foil is used in their homes.

❖ Explain that aluminum cans are often collected and then used again, which is called *recycling*. Discuss why we recycle aluminum. If you have a recycling center nearby, invite the children to bring empty aluminum cans to school for one week. Then take the cans to the recycling center.

Angel

❖ Cut an isosceles triangle, two rectangles, and a circle from construction paper for each child. Or have the children trace around patterns and cut their own shapes. Show the children how to arrange the shapes to make an angel. Have the children glue the angels on to a half sheet of construction paper. Help the children label their pictures.

❖ Teach the children to sing "Angel Band" from *Wee Sing for Christmas*. Substitute a day of the week for the phrase "Christmas morning" if you don't want this to be a Christmas song.

❖ Invite children to bring angel pictures or ornaments to school. Help the children discuss how various angels are alike and how they are different. Show the children how to draw a simple picture of an angel. Then encourage the children to draw a picture of their favorite angel. Read *The Angel Who Forgot* by Elisa Bartone or *The Star of Melvin* by Nathan Zimelman (see the unit book review).

Animals

❖ Mount pictures of animals on tagboard. Encourage the children to sort the pictures into farm, pet, and zoo categories. Encourage discussion! You might add other familiar pictures and invite the children to sort the picture cards into simpler categories, such as "Animal" and "Not Animal."

❖ Make an animal train along one wall in your classroom. Begin by taping one animal picture to the wall. Help the children describe the animal and name a few of its distinguishing characteristics. Then guide the children to select a picture of another animal that shares something in common with the first animal—both animals are hairy, both animals swim (run, fly), both animals have webbed feet, both animals have beaks or feathers, and so on. Tape the new animal to the wall, describe that animal and name its distinguishing characteristics, and then help the children find another animal picture that connects in some way to the second animal. Continue to build the animal train until the wall is filled or until you run out of pictures!

❖ Play "Who am I?" Give the children clues about an animal and invite them to guess which animal you are describing. Give one clue at a time until the animal is guessed. Ask the children to identify the best clue for each animal. Examples of some possible clues and the correct answers are provided below.

I am very big. I have a trunk. (elephant)
I live on a farm. I lay eggs. I say "Cluck, cluck." (chicken)
I have big floppy ears. I like to hop. I eat carrots. (rabbit)

❖ Ask parent volunteers to provide animal crackers for the class. Help the children identify each animal they eat.

❖ Help the children learn the animal sounds for a variety of animals—ducks say "quack," pigs say "oink," cats say "meow," and so on. Call out animal names and invite the children to make the appropriate sounds. Reverse roles as well—you make the sounds and the children name the animals.

❖ Read *Wild Animals and Their Babies* by Jan Pfloog and *The Aminal* by Lorna Balian (see the unit book review). Tape the letters of the alphabet around the room. Invite the children to cut out pictures from magazines of animals you read about. Then help the children tape each animal picture under the letter of its beginning sound.

❖ Teach the children "Animal Poem" from *Wee Sing Children's Songs and Fingerplays*. This poem describes animals and the ways they move. Invite small groups of children to pantomime their favorite animal movement for the rest of the class.

❖ If a zoo, circus, county fair, or pet store is nearby, plan a field trip. One day before the scheduled trip, ask the children to predict which animals they might see. Write each animal they name on chart paper. When you return from the trip, help the children make another list of the animals they actually saw. Compare the two lists.

Ants

❖ If possible, set up an ant farm in the classroom for the children to enjoy and observe. Ant farm kits are available at most hobby and toy stores. The farms come in different sizes, too. There are even ant communities that have several different areas attached by tubing. If you don't want to purchase an ant farm, borrow one from another teacher.

❖ Show the children how to draw a simple picture of an ant. Arrange for the children to examine an ant under a microscope. Or invite the children to examine an ant with a magnifying glass. Help the children describe the ant using as many of their senses as possible. Then invite children to add more details to their ant pictures.

❖ Read *Ants Are Fun* by Mildred Myrick and *The Antcyclopedia* by Joel Rothman (see the unit book review). Teach the children to sing "The Ants Go Marching" from *Wee Sing Silly Songs*.

Apple

❖ Teach the children the fingerplay "In the Apple Tree" from *Finger Plays* by Liz Cromwell and Dixie Hibner (Partner Press, 1976).

❖ Show the children an apple. Help the children describe the apple using all of their senses, except taste. Then cut the apple into bite-size pieces and invite the children to eat a piece and describe how the apple tastes. Explain that apples are a fruit. Help the children name other fruits, such as oranges, pears, grapes, lemons, peaches, bananas, and limes. Make "Absolutely Amazing Apple Salad."

Absolutely Amazing Apple Salad

3 apples	Peel (or try not peeling!), core, and cut apples into small chunks. Peel and grate the carrots or make long, thin strips with a vegtable peeler. Chop the celery into small pieces. Mix the carrots, celery, and apples together with a fork. Add the other ingredients and mix until well coated with mayonnaise (or yogurt).
6-8 large carrots	
2 small packages raisins	
4 stalks celery	
5 Tbsp mayonnaise (or 3/4 cup lowfat yogurt)	
2 tsp relish (optional)	
1 cup chopped walnuts (optional)	

❖ Give each child an apple. Show them how to draw a simple picture of an apple. Invite each child to take a bite out of their apples and then show them how to draw another picture of the apple with a bite missing.

❖ Hang an apple on a string for each child in your classroom. Challenge the children to try to take a bite from their apples with their hands behind their backs.

❖ Explain that apples grow from seeds. Cut an apple in half and point out the various parts. Invite the children to count the seeds. Encourage the children to draw pictures of the cross section of the apple. Read *Apple Tree! Apple Tree!* by Mary Blocksma and *Apples, How They Grow* by Bruce McMillan (see the unit book review).

❖   Make "Awesome Applesauce."

Awesome Applesauce

6 apples	Wash, pare, cut, core, and chop up the apples. (You may leave skin on for added flavor and texture.) Put the apples, sugar, water, and cinnamon into a covered saucepan. Cook for about 30 minutes. For extra zest, add the cranberries while you are cooking the apples.
2/3 cup sugar (or 4 Tbsp honey)	
1 Tbsp cinnamon	
1 cup water	
1 1/2 cups cranberries (optional)	

❖   Help the children make a book. Use red construction paper shaped like an apple. Suggest that children cut out pictures from magazines of items that begin with the letter A, as well as examples of upper case and lower case A's to glue in the book.

❖   Draw a large tree on a bulletin board covered with white butcher paper. Cut a sponge into round pieces and attach a clothespin to the back of each piece. Give each child a clothespin sponge to dip into red tempera paint and then dab on the tree to look like apples.

❖   Bring in different types of apples, such as green Granny Smith and Red Delicious apples. Invite the children to sample each kind of apple. Survey the class to see which apples the children like best. Graph the results.

❖   Make apple prints. Cut several apples in half crossways and point out the star inside the apple. Help the children use a brush and tempera paint to paint the inside surface of the apple red. Spread a large sheet of white butcher paper on the floor. Draw a large A on the paper and invite the children to take turns printing the apple pattern along the outline of the A. Tape the finished apple print on a bulletin board.

Avocado

❖ Bring several avocados to school. Cut the avocados open to remove the pits. Help the children plant the avocado pits. Stick three toothpicks into the sides of each avocado pit, evenly spaced. Fill a small glass with water. Set the avocado pits with the toothpicks on the glass so that the pointed end of the avocado pit is in the water. Then watch the root of the avocados grow in the water. Replant in loose soil, being careful not to injure the roots.

❖ Make "Astonishing Avocados," better known as *guacamole*. Invite the children to sample the sauce. Then read *Avocado Baby* by John Burningham (see the unit book review).

Astonishing Avocados (Guacamole)

1 avocado	Cut the avocado in half. Remove the pit and the skin. Blanch the tomato (put it in boiling water for a minute or two) and peel. Mash the tomato and avocado together. Add the onions, lemon juice, and salt. Chill or serve immediately with corn chips.
1 tomato	
1/4 cup chopped onion	
1 tsp lemon juice	
dash salt	
corn chips	

Food for Thought

Introducing children to a variety of foods is a wonderful way of reinforcing language concepts. The following foods all begin with the letter A and may be introduced at any time during this unit.

alfalfa sprouts, almonds, alphabet cereal, alphabet soup, ambrosia, American cheese, angel food cake, animal crackers, appetizers, apple butter, apple juice, apples, applesauce, apricot nectar, apricot preserves, apricots, artichokes, asparagus, aspic, avocados

Book Review

Children enjoy hearing good books read aloud. The books listed here are favorites of children and may be used to reinforce the letter A.

Balian, Lorna. *The Aminal,* Abingdon, 1985.
Barton, Byron. *Airplanes,* Harper & Row, 1982.
Barton, Byron. *Airport,* Harper & Row, 1982.
Bartone, Elisa. *The Angel Who Forgot,* Green Tiger Press, 1986.
Beller, Janet. *A-B-C-ing: An Action Alphabet,* Crown, 1984.
Blocksma, Mary. *Apple Tree! Apple Tree!,* Childrens Press, 1983.
Boynton, Sandra. *A Is for Angry: An Animal and Adjective Alphabet,* Workman Publishing, 1983.
Bunting, Eve. *Happy Birthday, Dear Duck,* Ticknor & Fields, 1988.
Burningham, John. *Avocado Baby,* Harper & Row, 1982.
Eastman, Philip D. *The Alphabet Book,* Random House, 1974.

Emberley, Ed. *Ed Emberley's ABC,* Little, Brown and Company, 1978.

Flack, Marjorie. *Angus and the Ducks,* Doubleday, 1989.

Gag, Wanda. *The ABC Bunny,* Putnam Publishing Group, 1978.

Hefter, Richard and Moskof, Martin S. *The Great Big Alphabet Book with Lots of Words,* Putnam Publishing Group, 1974.

Higham, Jon A. *Aardvark's Picnic,* Little, Brown and Company, 1987.

Hoban, Tana. *A B See!,* Greenwillow Books, 1982.

Lenski, Lois. *The Little Airplane,* MacKay, 1980.

Mayer, Mercer. *There's an Alligator Under My Bed,* Dial Books, 1987.

McMillan, Bruce. *Apples, How They Grow,* Houghton Mifflin, 1979.

Most, Bernard. *There's an Ant in Anthony,* William Morrow and Company, 1980.

Myrick, Mildred. *Ants Are Fun,* Harper & Row, 1968.

Pfloog, Jan. *Wild Animals and Their Babies,* Western Publishing, 1987.

Rey, Margret and Shalleck, Allan J. *Curious George at the Airport,* Houghton Mifflin, 1987.

Rockwell, Anne. *Albert B. Cub and Zebra: An Alphabet Storybook,* Harper & Row, 1987.

Rothman, Joel. *The Antcyclopedia,* Publication Development Company, 1988.

Scarry, Richard. *About Animals,* Western Publishing, 1976.

Sendak, Maurice. *Alligators All Around,* Harper & Row, 1962.

Seuss, Dr. *Dr. Seuss's ABC,* Beginner Books, 1960.

Testa, Fulvio. *Paper Airplane,* North-South Books, 1988.

Viorst, Judith. *Alexander and the Terrible, Horrible, No Good, Very Bad Day,* Macmillan, 1972.

Zimelman, Nathan. *The Star of Melvin,* Macmillan, 1987.

Bb

Baby

❖ Ask parents to send some baby and new mother magazines and catalogs to school. Invite the children to look through the magazines and catalogs and cut out pictures of baby items—highchairs, baby food, cribs, baby toys, bottles, diapers, playpens, pacifiers, and so on. Discuss how each baby item is used and then help the children glue the pictures on a large sheet of construction paper.

❖ Teach the children to sing "Rock-a-Bye Baby" from *Wee Sing Nursery Rhymes and Lullabies.* Invite the children to share other lullabies they know as well.

❖ Encourage each child to bring a baby picture of himself or herself to school. Display the pictures on a bulletin board. Invite the children to guess who the babies are. Ask other classroom teachers, the principal, the music teacher, and so on to furnish their baby pictures as well.

❖ Read *The Baby's Catalogue* and *Peek-a-Boo!,* both by Janet and Allan Ahlberg, and *Hush Little Baby: A Folk Lullaby* by Aliki (see the unit book review). Encourage the children in your classroom who have baby brothers or sisters to share something special about "their" babies.

❖ Invite children to share favorite stories they were told when they were very small.

Balance

❖ Challenge the children to try walking with a book balanced on their heads.

❖ Make arrangements with the physical education teacher for the children to work on the balance beam. Have parent volunteers or student helpers act as spotters for the children as they practice on the balance beam. Make sure there is only one child on the balance beam at a time. Help the children practice walking forward and backward, with both hands held or one hand held, heel-to-toe, sideways leading with the left side, and sideways leading with the right side. Suggest that children try to stand on the balance beam and then turn all the way around.

❖ Ask the children to stand with one foot lifted up off the ground. Then have them close their eyes. Discuss what happens!

❖ Tape a long strip of wide tape down the middle of a hallway floor, in the gymnasium, or outside. Challenge the children to walk along the tape line. See who can walk the farthest without stepping off the tape.

Ball

❖ Provide opportunities for the children to practice bouncing playground or tennis balls. Have children bounce balls using both hands and then using only one hand. Invite pairs of children to bounce and catch and then throw and catch different size balls. Challenge the children to bounce balls to ball-bouncing rhymes, such as "One, Two, Three O'Leary" and "Categories" from *Wee Sing and Play*.

❖ Help the children make a large class collage of pictures of baseball and basketball players. Invite the children to look through sports magazines, such as *Sports Illustrated,* to find appropriate pictures.

❖ Sponsor a basketball-shooting contest. Look for a lowered basket or have the children throw the ball or beanbags into a trash can instead.

❖ Discuss the various types of balls. Make a list of the balls the children name. Suggest that children bring to school several different types of balls for display. Show the children how to draw a simple picture of a ball. Then invite the children to draw pictures of their favorite balls.

❖ Read *Curious George Plays Baseball* by Margaret Rey and Allan J. Shalleck (see the unit book review). If possible, arrange for the children to practice batting using a large plastic bat and ball.

❖ Teach the children to sing "Take Me Out to the Ball Game." Point out that this tune is a favorite among dedicated baseball fans and is often sung during the 7th-inning stretch of a baseball game.

❖ Ask the physical education instructor to come visit your classroom and teach the children a simple game with balls, such as a modified version of kick ball or volleyball using a beach ball.

❖ Arrange a student-faculty baseball or basketball game at your school. Or ask a high-school coach to bring the baseball or basketball team over in uniform to your school to play an exhibition game for the children. After the game, invite the coach and players to meet the children and give them a few pointers.

Balloons

❖ Give each child in your classroom a balloon. Have the children practice blowing up the balloons. Help each child tie his or her balloon and then play "Balloon Keep It Up." See how long the children can keep their balloons up in the air without letting them touch the ground.

❖ Show the children how to draw a simple picture of a balloon. Then invite children to draw three big balloons on large sheets of painting paper. Suggest that the children paint each balloon a different color.

❖ Read *Benjamin's Balloon* by Janet Quinn-Harkin (see the unit book review). Blow up and tie a balloon for each child. After the children have played with the balloons, challenge the children to sit on their balloons and pop them! Declare the first child to pop his or her balloon the winner!

❖ Play "Balleyball"—a variation of volleyball. In this game, teams of children hit a balloon across a net or a string tied across the classroom.

Banana

❖ Take a survey to find out how many children in your classroom like bananas. Graph the results. Then make several different banana dishes for the children to sample, such as "Banana-Nut Spread," "Berry Bananas," and "Bravo Banana Pudding." Take the same survey again and graph the results. Compare the two graphs.

Banana-Nut Spread

3 ripe bananas
6 Tbsp peanut butter
graham crackers

Mash the bananas in a small bowl, add the peanut butter, and mix. Spread on graham crackers or use as a dip for bear-shaped crackers. Makes 6 servings.

Berry Bananas

ripe bananas
fresh strawberries or blueberries (or both)
yogurt or milk (optional)
brown sugar (optional)

Slice the bananas. Wash and clean the berries. Layer the banana slices and berries in a dish. If desired, add yogurt or milk and sprinkle with brown sugar.

Bravo Banana Pudding

instant vanilla pudding or banana pudding
milk, according to pudding directions
jar with a tight lid
1 small cup or bowl per child
vanilla wafers
bananas
Cool Whip (optional)

Mix the pudding and milk in a jar and shake. Put a vanilla wafer in the bottom of each child's cup. Add sliced bananas (the children may slice their own with a plastic picnic knife) and then some pudding. Invite each child to make his or her own serving in a small cup. Add a tablespoon of Cool Whip to the top, if desired.

❖ Show the children a banana. Point out that a banana is a fruit. Encourage the children to name other fruits. Help the children describe the banana using all of their senses. Ask the children to identify the characteristics of a banana that make it different from other fruits. Show the children how to draw a simple picture of a banana. Then invite the children to add more details to their pictures.

Bathroom

❖ Invite the children to bring their favorite bathtub toy to school. Provide a large water-filled tub for the children to float their toys in or cut a large pond-shaped sheet of blue butcher paper to place on the floor. Read *The Beast in the Bathtub* by Kathleen Stevens (see the unit book review).

❖ Help the children make a list of the items found in a bathroom, such as toilet paper, a sink, towels, soap, makeup, medicine, a toilet, toothpaste, a toothbrush, a cup, a scale, a bathtub, and a shower curtain. Encourage the children to find pictures of these items in old magazines, cut out the pictures, and then use the pictures to make a collage.

Beads

❖ Provide opportunities for the children to string beads. Begin by having the children string the beads in any order. More advanced children may be challenged to string beads in specific patterns. Start with one attribute, such as size, color, or shape, alternating the beads in a creative pattern. Add to the complexity of the patterns as the children are ready. Use commercial pattern cards, or make sets of your own, that show patterns of varying degrees of difficulty. Invite the children to string beads to match the patterns on the cards.

❖ Encourage the children to sort beads according to attributes of size, shape, or color.

❖ Have the children draw a large letter B with glue on a sheet of construction paper. Then invite the children to arrange beads along the glue line to make a "Beady B."

Beans

❖ Ask each child to bring one small bag of dried beans of any kind to school. Mix all the beans together in one large container. Have the children sort the beans, putting like beans together. Teach the children the names of the different types of beans, too.

❖ Point out that beans are a vegetable. Ask the children to name as many different types of beans as they can, such as kidney beans, lima beans, chili beans, butter beans, string beans, black beans, northern beans, pinto beans, navy beans, and wax beans. Then make "Bean Salad."

Bean Salad

1-lb can green beans	Open and drain the cans of beans. Cut the bell pepper into small pieces, discarding seeds and pulp. Mix the beans and bell pepper in a large bowl. Add the sugar to the dressing (if desired), pour over the bean mixture, and mix. Cover the bowl and refrigerate overnight, or at least 4 hours. If desired, serve the salad with brown bread and butter.
8-1/2 oz can wax beans	
8-oz can dark red kidney beans	
1 medium bell pepper	
3/4 cup Italian dressing	
2 tsp sugar (optional)	

❖ Have each child make a large letter B with a heavy glue line on a sheet of construction paper. Then invite the children to arrange a variety of beans along the glue line to make a "Beany B."

❖ Invite the children to taste raw beans. Cook some green beans as well so the children can compare the taste between raw and cooked beans.

❖ Give each child one sectioned half of an egg carton and a large handful of dried beans. Post a number between one and ten (depending on the maturity of the children) somewhere in the classroom. Ask the children to count that many beans into each section of their egg cartons. Change the number each day.

Bear

❖ Sponsor a "Bear Day." Invite each child to bring to school a favorite stuffed bear, animal, or doll. Plan to have a "Bear Picnic." Go outside and enjoy the sun or, on a cold day, hold the picnic inside! Help the children make bear-shaped invitations to take home to their teddy bears. Plan a "Bear Menu"—honey and peanut butter sandwiches, berries, carrot sticks, Berry Blue Kool-Aid, and bear-shaped cookies. Help the children make a "Welcome Bears" sign to hang in the classroom as well. Invite the children to sit on blankets.

❖ Have each child draw a large letter B with a pencil on a piece of blue, black, or brown construction paper. Give each child a small cupful of little bear-shaped cookies. Have the children arrange the little bears along the drawn B to make a "Beary B."

❖ Teach the children to sing "The Bear Went Over the Mountain" from *Wee Sing Silly Songs*. Read *The B Book* by Stan and Janice Berenstain (see the unit book review).

❖ Serve bear cookies modeled after the Berenstain Bears as a special treat (if these cookies are available in your area). The cookies come in boxes similar to animal crackers and have a picture of one of the Berenstain Bears on each cookie.

❖ Read *Country Bear's Good Neighbor* by Larry D. Brimner (see the unit book review). Focus the children's attention on the lovely pictures. The book also contains a recipe for "Country Bear's Good Neighbor Cake," which makes a delicious treat. The cake must be cooked in the oven and has an apple-cinnamon flavor.

❖ Teach the children the poem and motions to "Teddy Bear" from *Wee Sing Children's Songs and Fingerplays* or *Wee Sing and Play*.

❖ Cut circles of various sizes from brown construction paper. Help the children arrange the circles on sheets of construction paper to make little bears. Suggest that children make a blue bow tie from construction paper and glue on two buttons for eyes. Display the finished pictures on a bulletin board with the title "The Bear Facts."

❖ Purchase wrapping paper that features bears. Cut out the bears from the wrapping paper. Draw and cut out a large letter B from construction paper and invite the children to glue the wrapping paper bears on the B to make a "Bear Paper B."

Beautiful

❖ Make "Beautiful B Banners." Cut large triangles from blue, brown, or black construction paper. Encourage the children to use paint, glitter, paper scraps, and other available materials to make a big B on the banner. Have the children cut out pictures from magazines of items that begin with the letter B to glue to the other side of the banners. Tape or staple the triangular banners to newspaper sticks. Newspaper sticks may be made by rolling a sheet of newspaper tightly, starting at one corner and rolling diagonally. A small piece of tape can be used to keep the newspaper tight.

❖ Help the children make a list of beautiful items, such as a rainbow, a ring, or a sunset. Invite each child to draw a picture of the item that he or she thinks is most beautiful.

Bedroom

❖ Show the children how to draw a simple picture of a bed. Have the children color the bedspread blue. Encourage the children to draw pictures of their own beds as well.

❖ Invite the children to cut out pictures from magazines of bedroom items, such as beds, blankets, lamps, nightstands, alarm clocks, curtains, dressers, and pillows. Use the pictures to make a collage.

❖ Ask the children if they ever take naps. Point out that naps can be special times. Ask the children where their favorite napping place is. Then read *The Napping House* by Audrey Wood (see the unit book review).

Big

❖ Read *Big and Little, Up and Down* by Ethel S. Berkowitz, *Ton and Pon: Big and Little* by Kazuo Iwamura, and

Sesame Street Big Bird and Little Bird's Book of Big and Little by Emily Kingsley (see the unit book review). Help the children recall the big items mentioned in each book.

❖ Encourage the children to name as many big items as possible. Write each item they name on chart paper. Then ask the children to look through magazines for pictures of the items on the list—elephants, refrigerators, houses, trucks, trees, giants, and so on. Invite the children to cut out the pictures and glue them on half sheets of construction paper. Ask the children to label each picture, too. Assemble all of the children's papers to make a "BIG Book."

Bird

❖ Make bird feeders. Mix birdseed and peanut butter together. Then invite the children to use a popsicle stick or tongue depressor to scrape the mixture onto wide-spaced pine cones. This is best done over a sheet of waxed paper. You might also string together pieces of bread, orange slices, cranberries, and popcorn. If you wish, send home a list with the children of foods that birds like to eat and invite each child to bring one of these foods to school. Then make the bird feeders from whatever foods the children bring. Hang the food outside for the birds. If possible, hang the feeders on a tree that can be seen from your classroom so the children may watch the birds eating.

❖ Have each child make a large letter B with glue on a sheet of blue construction paper. Invite the children to sprinkle birdseed along the glue line. Wait a few minutes and then help the children shake the excess birdseed from the paper to reveal a "Birdseed B."

❖ Read aloud *The Blue Bird* by Maurice Maeterlinck (see the unit book review). Invite the children to make a bird from construction paper. Give each child two different circle patterns to cut out of colored paper. Have the children glue the two circles on a half sheet of construction paper. Explain that the smaller circle is the head and the larger circle is the body. Cut several 1" x 6" strips of construction paper. Invite the children to select four strips to make a tail for their birds. Then show the children how to make a diamond-shaped beak. Cut a small piece of paper in a diamond shape, fold it in half, and glue one side on the bird's head. Eyes may be drawn with a marker or made from scraps of paper.

❖ Teach the children to sing "Baby Bird" from *Wee Sing Children's Songs and Fingerplays* and "Blue Birds" from *Wee Sing and Play*.

Birthday

❖ Sponsor a class birthday party. Make a birthday cake. Put candles on the cake, too. Invite the children to sing "Happy Birthday" to everyone before they blow out the candles. For an extra surprise, use the candles that do not blow out! (Have a glass of water close by in which to dip the burning candles when you are finished.) Invite the children to wear ready-made birthday hats or design your own. Corrugated bulletin-board border paper cut to each child's head size and stapled make quick-and-easy birthday hats. Encourage each child to cut out two pictures from magazines of items that begin with the letter B to glue on their hats as well.

❖ Encourage each child to learn his or her birth date. Make a large birthday cake from construction paper. Have each child draw, color, and cut out a candle from construction paper. As the children learn their birth dates, invite them to write their names on the candles and glue their candles to the cake.

❖ Read *The Secret Birthday Message* by Eric Carle and *It's Your Birthday* by Gena Neilson (see the unit book review). Encourage each child to share with the class something special he or she has done to celebrate a birthday.

Blocks

❖ Invite children to use 1-inch colored blocks, wooden building blocks, or building bricks to make a letter B. Challenge the children to make as many different B's as possible.

❖ Have the children build block towers with 1-inch colored blocks or building blocks. Sponsor a contest to see which child or team of children stacks the most blocks or makes the highest towers.

❖ Build a simple structure with blocks. Then challenge the children to reconstruct your block model using blocks of their own. For more advanced children, build a structure and have the children study the structure for a few minutes. Cover the structure and challenge the children to build the model from memory. Start with the models provided below.

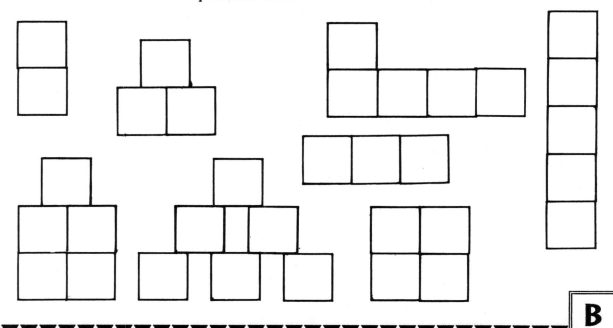

❖ Set up a "Building Center" with any building blocks available to you. Encourage the children to play with the blocks and build a variety of structures. Invite children to bring structures to school that they may have built at home as well.

Blow

❖ Invite the children to blow bubbles. Make your own bubble solution by mixing 2/3 cup liquid dish-washing detergent with one gallon of water. Allow the solution to sit for at least one day before using. Give each child a straw and a cup half-filled with the soapy solution. Cut the straw at an angle at one end. Dip the angled end into the soap and blow through the other end. Encourage the children to try using other items to make bubbles, too, such as pipe cleaners, plastic berry baskets, six-pack soft drink holders, egg poacher trays, funnels, or metal canning jar lids. Suggest using a wooden spool, dipping one end in the soap and blowing through the other. Or try a styrofoam cup with a hole punched in the middle of the bottom. Hold a straw firmly in the hole, put the top rim in the bubble solution, and then blow through the straw.

❖ Make "blow" paintings. Put large dabs of watered-down tempera paint on sheets of paper. Invite the children to blow the paint around the paper with a straw. Interesting abstract designs can be created when complementary colors such as red/yellow/orange, blue/green/yellow, or red/blue/purple are used. For a different effect, let the first color dry before adding another color.

❖ Sponsor a bubble-gum blowing contest. Give each child a piece of sugarless bubble gum. At your signal, invite the children to unwrap the bubble gum, chew it, and then try to be the first one to blow a bubble. See who can blow the biggest bubble as well.

❖ Teach the children the choosing rhyme "Bubble Gum" from *Wee Sing and Play*.

Blue

❖ Have the children use scissors to snip strips of blue construction paper into small squares. Ask the children to use glue to draw a large letter B on a piece of construction paper. Then invite the children to arrange the blue pieces along the glue line to make a "Blue B."

❖ Invite the children to eat fresh blueberries or make blueberry muffins. Then read *Blueberries for Sal* by Robert McCloskey (see the unit book review).

❖ Sponsor a "Blue Day." Encourage the children to wear something blue on a specific day. Make B's from blue construction paper for anyone who forgets. Invite the children to help make Berry Blue sugar-free Kool-Aid to serve as a special treat. Read *New Blue Shoes* by Eve Rice (see the unit book review).

Boat

❖ Teach the children to sing "Row Row Row Your Boat" from *Wee Sing Around the Campfire*.

❖ Read *Who Sank the Boat?* by Pamela Allen, *Boat Book* by Gail Gibbons, and *Boats* by Byron Barton (see the unit book review). Give each child a large white sheet of construction paper. Suggest that the children use watercolors or tempera paint to paint a dark blue bottom for the ocean and a light blue top for the sky. Have the children draw and cut out a boat to glue on the background. Show the children how to make a hull, mast, and sail for the boat from white construction paper. Have the children decorate the sail with B's.

Body

❖ Play "Simon Says." Give directions using parts of the body. For example, you might say, "Simon says put your elbows on your knees," "Simon says wiggle your wrist," "Simon says put your hands on your hips," and then "Put your ankles together." (Gotcha!)

❖ Teach the children to sing "Head and Shoulders" from *Wee Sing Children's Songs and Fingerplays.*

❖ Help the children learn to identify more difficult parts of the body, such as the chest, knees, heels, elbows, ankles, jaw, shoulders, hips, waist, and wrist. Provide opportunities for the children to practice naming the body parts. Reverse the directions. Name the body parts and invite the children to point to the parts you name.

❖ Teach the children to sing "Hokey Pokey" from *Wee Sing and Play.* Substitute other body parts besides the traditional ones.

❖ Look in catalogs for pictures of people. The pictures should include the entire body. Mount the pictures on pieces of tagboard. Cut each picture into simple puzzle pieces and put the pieces in an envelope. Make a puzzle for each child. Distribute the envelopes to the children. Challenge the children to open their envelopes, empty the puzzle pieces out on their desks, and put the puzzles together correctly. When the children finish a puzzle, have them put the pieces back in the envelope, sign their name on the envelope, and pass the puzzle to another child. Continue until all the children have worked all of the puzzles.

❖ Teach the children to sing "If You're Happy and You Know It" from *Wee Sing Children's Songs and Fingerplays*. Substitute body parts, such as "If you're happy and you know it beat your chest (bend your knees, click your heels, wiggle your hips, or shake your wrist)."

❖ Challenge the children to discover how many parts of their bodies bend—knees, elbows, fingers, neck, and waist. Then do bending exercises. Count "B-1, B-2, B-3," and so on.

Books

❖ Set up a "Book Center." Display several books that have B's in the title, such as *The B Book* by Janice and Stan Berenstain and *The Butter Battle Book* by Dr. Seuss, for the children to browse through during independent time (see the unit book review).

❖ Sponsor a "Book Day." Invite each child to bring a favorite book from home to share with the class. Read several of the books aloud. Point out the B words in the titles.

❖ Discuss why we have books. Take the children to your school library (and the public library, if possible). Ask the librarian to share a story with the class that reinforces the letter B.

Bottom and Top

❖ Play "Simon Says" using directions, such as "Touch the top of your head," "Touch the bottom of your foot," and "Touch the top of your desk."

❖ All week, encourage the children to draw a green line across the top of their papers and a red line across the bottom. Suggest that children draw the lines on every paper before they begin each assignment.

❖ Give each child a sheet of paper. Help the children draw blue, black, and brown lines from the top to the bottom of the paper. This is an activity children can do on the back of every ditto.

Boys

❖ Write all the boys' names in the class on the chalkboard. Encourage the children to copy the names or have them copy the first letter of each name as you write. Have the children circle all the upper case B's with a blue crayon and all the lower case b's with a brown crayon.

❖ Write each boy's name on a flash card. Provide opportunities for the children to practice reading each flash card until they recognize all the boys' names.

❖ Have the children cut out pictures from magazines of boys to glue on a sheet of newsprint. Label the finished collage "B Is for Boys." Read *The Very Little Boy* by Phyllis Krasilovsky (see the unit book review).

Bread

❖ Read *What Was It Before It Was Bread?* by Jane B. Moncure, *From Grain to Bread* by Ali Mitgutsch, and *A Visit to the Bakery* by Sandra Zeigler (see the unit book review). If possible, make arrangements for the class to visit a bakery. Help the children make a list of questions to ask the baker.

❖ Bring in different breads or ask each child to bring from home three to four slices of pumpernickel, rye, wheat, or other kinds of bread. Invite the children to taste each bread and vote on their favorite. Discuss how the breads are different and how they are alike in taste, color, size, smell, and so on. Place a few slices of bread in a dark, damp place until the bread molds. Ask the children to discuss how spoiled bread is different from a fresh piece of bread.

❖ Teach the children the tongue twister "Betty Botter" from *Wee Sing Nursery Rhymes and Lullabies*. Invite the children to repeat each line after you. Start slowly and say the words faster as the children are ready. Ask the children to identify all the B words in each line as well.

❖ Make "Banana Bread." Help the children make butter to serve with the bread, too. Invite the children to make a list of other foods that begin with the letter B.

Banana Bread

3 large ripe bananas (about 1 1/2 cups)	Mash the bananas in a bowl with a fork. Mix the other ingredients together in another bowl. Fold in the bananas. Bake in a greased pan for 1 hour at 350°.
1/2 cup wheat germ	
1 tsp baking soda	
1/2 tsp salt	
2 cups flour	
1/2 cup melted butter	
2 eggs	
1 cup apple juice concentrate	
1/2 cup sugar	
2 tsp vanilla	
3/4 cup vegetable oil	
1 cup chopped nuts (optional)	

Butter

1 pint whipping cream	Pour the cream into a container. Shake untill butter forms. Drain any excess liquid and add salt to taste. Serve on biscuits, brown bread, banana bread, bagels, or buns.
salt	
plastic container, jar with a tight lid, or baby food jar for each child	

❖ Invite a parent, grandparent, or another interested person to come visit your classroom and demonstrate making biscuits. Use the homemade butter to spread on the biscuits when ready.

Breakfast

❖ Cut out pictures from magazines of breakfast foods, such as milk, eggs, toast, fresh fruit, fruit juices, cereal, and bacon. Discuss which foods are good for breakfast. Make sample breakfast menus by helping the children glue food pictures on paper plates. Write "B Is for Breakfast" on each plate.

❖ Encourage each child to discuss what he or she would like to eat for breakfast. Help the class decide what foods should be eaten to make a healthy breakfast. Discuss why breakfast should be eaten. Read *Breakfast Time, Ernest and Celestine* by Gabrielle Vincent (see the unit book review).

❖ Plan and prepare a well-balanced breakfast. Invite the children to help cook the breakfast and enjoy!

Bridge

❖ Invite the children to play and sing "London Bridge" from *Wee Sing and Play*. Show the children a picture of a real bridge. Discuss why we have bridges. Encourage the children to use blocks to build a bridge.

❖ Teach the children how to lie on their backs with their hands over their heads and push up to make a bridge. Have other children crawl under the "bridges."

Brown

❖ Put small dabs of red, yellow, and blue or orange and black fingerpaint on fingerpaint paper. Invite the children to mix the colors together with their fingers to make a brown color. Then have the children use one finger to write B's in the paint. Encourage each child to save his or her best B. Display the dried pictures on a large bulletin board. Point out the different shades of brown.

❖ Make brown rice or brown bread. Encourage the children to describe the food as they eat it. Then ask the children if brown rice or brown bread is a good name for the food. Help the children recall other foods that are brown, such as baked beans, bacon, chocolate-chip cookies, nuts, brown sugar, cinnamon, chocolate ice cream, fudge, root beer, colas, and tea.

❖ Have each child make a letter B with glue on a sheet of dark brown construction paper. Cut brown paper bags into strips. Invite the children to snip the strips into small squares and arrange the squares along the glue line to make a "Brown Paper Bag B."

❖ Cut out a large B from brown construction paper. Invite each child to cut out B's from old magazines to glue on the brown construction paper B.

❖ Make "Brown Cows." Point out how this drink got its name—"brown" is for the color of root beer and "cow" is for the milk in the ice cream.

Brown Cows

	Put one scoop of chocolate ice cream in a glass of root beer.
root beer chocolate ice cream	

❖ Stick an adhesive letter B on the shirt of each child whose name begins with the letter B. The letters may be purchased from most office supply or art stores.

Bulletin Board

❖ Make a bulletin board with layers of different colored borders (you might want to use only brown, black, and blue). More advanced children might help you design and cut the borders. In the center of the board, write "B Is for Bulletin-Board Borders."

Bumblebee

❖ Teach the children the simple fingerplay "Bumblebee" from *Wee Sing Children's Songs and Fingerplays*.

❖ Show the children how to draw a simple picture of a beehive and a bee. Explain that a bee is an insect with three body parts. Help the children name other insects, such as a mosquito, fly, flea, roach, beetle, tick, and grasshopper.

❖ Teach the children to sing "Baby Bumblebee" from *Wee Sing Silly Songs*. Ask your school librarian for a film about bumblebees. Children may find the life cycle of the queen, drone, and worker bees fascinating. Invite the children to taste some honey.

Bunny

❖ Teach the children to sing "Little Bunny Foo Foo" from *Wee Sing Silly Songs*. Children really love this little song! Then invite the children to add features to a letter B to make a simple picture of a bunny.

❖ Read aloud *The Runaway Bunny* by Margaret Wise Brown, *Bunches and Bunches of Bunnies* by Louise Mathews, and *The ABC Bunny* by Wanda Gag (see the unit book review). If possible, arrange for someone who has a live bunny to bring the bunny to school for the children to observe for a day.

❖ Help the children make "Bunny Babies."

Bunny Babies

1 boiled egg	Put a lettuce leaf on a small plate. Cut the egg in half lengthwise. Put one half of the egg on the lettuce, yolk-side down, to form the bunny's face. Cut the other half lengthwise and use as ears. Add raisins for eyes and the celery or carrot sticks for whiskers. Makes 1 salad.
lettuce	
2 raisins	
celery or carrots cut in thin strips	

Bus

❖ Invite a bus driver to come visit your classroom and talk to the children about bus rules. If possible, arrange a class trip on a city or school bus. Read *School Bus* by Donald Crews, *Big Paul's School Bus* by Paul Nichols, and *The Very Bumpy Bus Ride* by Michaela Muntean (see the unit book review).

Butterfly

❖ Fold a piece of white construction paper in half and cut out a butterfly shape. Give each child a butterfly shape. Invite the children to drop small amounts of colored tempera paint on one butterfly wing. Then have them refold the paper in half and press all along the wing. The children may then reopen the butterflies to reveal a lovely design. If you wish, cut a butterfly body from black construction paper for each child to glue on their butterflies after the paint has dried. Mount the butterflies on yellow construction-paper circles.

❖ Encourage the children to recall items that older brothers and sisters have outgrown and have either discarded or passed on to the children. Point out that as we get older, our needs and interests change. Then read *The Very Hungry Caterpillar* by Eric Carle and *From Egg to Butterfly* by Marlene Reidel (see the unit book review).

❖ Encourage the children to catch butterflies to bring to school. Suggest that the children put the butterflies in a jar with holes punched in the top and a leaf or two. Show the children how to draw a simple picture of a butterfly. Invite the children to add more detail to their pictures by examining the butterflies in the jars. Encourage children to color the butterflies, too. Keep the butterflies for one day and then release them.

Buttons

❖ If you have a large supply of buttons, give each child a handful. Off-color buttons may often be purchased cheaply at fabric stores. Have the children make a large letter B with a heavy glue line on construction paper. Invite the children to arrange the buttons along the glue line to make a "Button B." You may wish to save the buttons and do the same activity without glue.

❖ Encourage the children to sort buttons according to one attribute—size, shape, or color. Then invite each child to select his or her favorite button and draw a picture of it.

Ask the children to share their pictures with the rest of the class and tell why they chose that particular button.

Food for Thought

Introducing children to a variety of foods is a wonderful way of reinforcing language concepts. The following foods all begin with the letter B and may be introduced at any time during this unit.

bacon, bacon bits, bagels, baked beans, banana bread, bananas, barbecue, barley, beans, bean sprouts, bear-shaped cookies, beef, beef sticks, beets, bell peppers, berries, beverages, birthday cake, biscuits, black beans, blackberries, black-eyed peas, bleu cheese, blintzes, blueberries, blueberry muffins, blueberry pancakes, bologna on bread, Boston-baked beans, boysenberries, bran, bran cereals, bran muffins, Brazil nuts, bread and butter, bread pudding, bread sticks, broccoli, broth, bouillon, brown bread, brown-ies, brown rice, brown sugar, Brunswick stew, Brussels sprouts, butter beans, buns, buttermilk, butter-scotch pudding, three-bean salad

Book Review

Children enjoy hearing good books read aloud. The books listed here are favorites of children and may be used to reinforce the letter B.

Ahlberg, Janet and Ahlberg, Allan. *Peek-a-Boo!*, Viking Press, 1981.

Ahlberg, Janet and Ahlberg, Allan. *The Baby's Catalogue*, Little, Brown and Company, 1983.

Aliki. *Hush Little Baby: A Folk Lullaby*, Prentice Hall, 1968.

Allen, Pamela. *Who Sank the Boat?*, Putnam Publishing Group, 1983.

Asch, Frank. *I Can Blink*, Crown, 1986.

Barton, Byron. *Boats*, Harper & Row, 1986.

Berenstain, Stan and Berenstain, Janice. *The B Book*, Random House, 1971.

Berkowitz, Ethel S. *Big and Little, Up and Down*, Harper & Row, 1950.

Brimner, Larry D. *Country Bear's Good Neighbor*, Orchard Books, 1988.

Brown, Margaret Wise. *Big Red Barn*, Harper & Row, 1989.

Brown, Margaret Wise. *The Runaway Bunny*, Harper & Row, 1972.

Carle, Eric. *The Secret Birthday Message*, Harper & Row, 1986.

Carle, Eric. *The Very Hungry Caterpillar*, Putnam Publishing Group, 1989.

Crews, Donald. *School Bus*, Greenwillow Books, 1984.

Dabcovich, Lydia. *Sleepy Bear*, E. P. Dutton, 1982.

Flack, Marjorie. *Ask Mr. Bear*, Macmillan, 1986.

Freeman, Don. *Beady Bear*, Penguin Books, 1977.

Gag, Wanda. *The ABC Bunny*, Putnam Publishing Group, 1978.

Galdone, Paul. *The Three Bears*, Ticknor & Fields, 1985.

Gibbons, Gail. *Boat Book*, Holiday House, 1983.

Gibbons, Gail. *Happy Birthday!*, Holiday House, 1986.

Graham, Margaret B. *Benjy and the Barking Bird*, Harper & Row, 1971.

Ivimey, John W. *The Complete Story of the Three Blind Mice*, Ticknor & Fields, 1987.

Iwamura, Kazuo. *Ton and Pon: Big and Little*, Bradbury Press, 1984.

Kingsley, Emily. *Sesame Street Big Bird and Little Bird's Book of Big and Little*, Western Publishing, 1982.

Krasilovsky, Phyllis. *The Very Little Boy*, Doubleday, 1953.

Maeterlinck, Maurice. *The Blue Bird*, Philosophical Publishing, 1985.

Mathews, Louise. *Bunches and Bunches of Bunnies,* Scholastic Press, 1980.

Mayer, Mercer. *Bubble Bubble,* Macmillan, 1980.

McCloskey, Robert. *Blueberries for Sal,* Penguin Books, 1976.

McLeod, Emilie W. *The Bear's Bicycle,* Little, Brown and Company, 1975.

Mitgutsch, Ali. *From Grain to Bread,* Carolrhoda Books, 1981.

Moncure, Jane B. *What Was It Before It Was Bread?,* Child's World, 1985.

Muntean, Michaela. *The Very Bumpy Bus Ride,* Parents Magazine Press, 1982.

Murphy, Jill. *What Next Baby Bear!,* Dial Books, 1986.

Neilson, Gena. *It's Your Birthday,* Lauri, Inc., 1986.

Nichols, Paul. *Big Paul's School Bus,* Prentice Hall, 1981.

Quinn-Harkin, Janet. *Benjamin's Balloon,* Parents Magazine Press, 1979.

Reidel, Marlene. *From Egg to Butterfly,* Carolrhoda Books, 1981.

Rey, Margret and Shalleck, Allan J. *Curious George Plays Baseball,* Houghton Mifflin, 1986.

Rice, Eve. *New Blue Shoes,* Penguin Books, 1979.

Seuss, Dr. *The Butter Battle Book,* Random House, 1984.

Stevens, Kathleen. *The Beast in the Bathtub,* Harper & Row, 1987.

Vincent, Gabrielle. *Breakfast Time, Ernest and Celestine,* Greenwillow Books, 1985.

Wood, Audrey. *The Napping House,* Harcourt Brace Jovanovich, 1984.

Zeigler, Sandra. *A Visit to the Bakery,* Childrens Press, 1987.

Zolotow, Charlotte. *Big Brother,* Harper & Row, 1960.

B

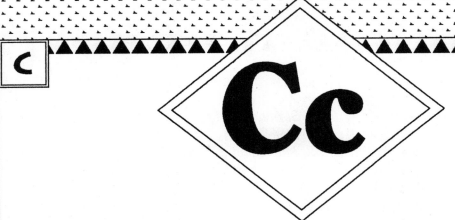

Cactus

❖ Read *The One-Hundred-Year-Old Cactus* by Anita Holmes (see the unit book review). Show the children a cactus plant. The Christmas cactus is especially nice and blooms around December. Help the children compare the cactus with other plants. Point out that since a cactus needs less water than other plants, it can live and grow in hot, dry areas.

Calendar

❖ Remind the children that calendars help us keep track of the days, weeks, and months of the year. Make a class calendar for each month. Review the day of the week and the date each day. Invite the children to practice saying the days of the week from memory. Add the date on the calendar as well. At the end of the month, encourage the children to copy your master calendar to make individual calendars of their own for the coming month.

❖ In December, collect old calendars of different types. Hold up each calendar for the children to see and ask, "Is this a calendar? How do you know?"

Candle

❖ Provide art supplies for children to make a pretend candle. Use toilet-paper tubes for the candle. Help the children paint the tubes with tempera paint. Show the children how to stuff red, orange, and yellow tissue paper in the top of the tubes for the flame and then glue a strip of construction paper around the base for the candle holders. Help the children glue the toilet-paper tubes to small paper plates.

Candy

❖ Make "Cream Cheese Candy."

Cream Cheese Candy

powdered sugar
1 oz softened cream cheese
1/8 tsp flavoring (mint, maple, or raspberry)
2–3 drops food coloring

Mix cream cheese, flavoring, and food coloring with fork. Form marble-sized balls. Roll in powdered sugar. Chill. Makes 1 serving.

❖ Discuss why cake, candy, cupcakes, and cookies should not be eaten often. These foods cause tooth decay, can make you sick if you eat too much, may cause headaches, have lots of calories and very few vitamins, and usually spoil appetites. Help the children make a list of some foods that are healthier snacks, such as fruit, cheese, and milk.

❖ Invite the children to make a candy cane. Give each child one white pipe cleaner and one red pipe cleaner. Show the children how to twist the pipe cleaners together to make a striped stem. Then have them bend the stem into a candy cane shape.

Cards

❖ Invite the children to sort a deck of playing cards into like cards—aces together, 2's together, 3's together, and so on. Remove the jokers and face cards and help the children first sort the cards according to suits. Then help them sequence the cards in each suit from one (ace) to ten.

❖ Teach the children card games, such as "War," "Uno," and "Old Maid." Adapt the games, if necessary. For example, you might have children use only cards under five for "War" and just use some of the cards in "Uno."

❖ Save and collect old Christmas cards. Use the cards to make a Christmas card alphabet book. Help the children find a card to represent each letter of the alphabet (a-angel; b-bow, bell, baby; c-candy cane, candle, cookie; d-doll, drum; e-elf, evergreen; f-fruitcake, fireplace; g-gift, garland; h-holly; i-ice; j-jingle bells; k-Kris Kringle; l-lights, list; m-Mary, Mrs. Claus, mailbox, mistletoe; n-Noel; o-ornament; p-poinsettia, popcorn garland; q-quiet as a mouse; r-Rudolph, reindeer, ribbon; s-Santa, stocking, star; t-toys, tree; u-universe; v-Vixen the reindeer; w-wreath, white Christmas, wise men; x-short abbreviation for Christmas; y-you; and z-zzzz sleeping sounds as you wait for Santa).

Carrot

❖ Bring several carrots to school. Explain to the children that carrots are a vegetable. Help the children name other vegetables, too. Clean and cook some of the carrots. Make "Crispy Carrot Coins" with the raw carrots. Then invite the children to taste both the raw and cooked carrots. Ask the children to discuss how raw and cooked carrots are alike and how they are different. Survey the children to find out whether most children in the class prefer eating carrots raw or cooked. Graph the results of your survey.

Crispy Carrot Coins

carrots
peanut butter (or Ranch dressing)
toothpicks (optional)

Slice carrots into coins. Put each carrot piece on a toothpick, if desired, and dip into peanut butter or dressing.

❖ Give each child a carrot. Show the children how to draw a simple picture of a carrot. Then help the children describe real carrots using all of their senses. Ask the children to draw and color a picture of their real carrots. Cut the real carrots into 2- or 3-inch pieces. Have the children use a pencil to lightly draw a big letter C on a sheet of construction paper. Then show the children how they may use the carrot pieces like a rubber stamp. Invite each child to dip their carrots into orange tempera paint and make prints along the pencil line to make a "Carrot C."

❖ Read *The Carrot Seed* by Ruth Kraus (see the unit book review). Grow a carrot. Select a carrot that still has green leaves and stems attached. Cut the carrot about two inches from the top. Cut off all the wilted leaves and trim the stems back to one inch. Place the carrot top in a shallow bowl with the cut end down. Place pebbles around the carrot and then fill the bowl half full of water. Set the bowl in a sunny window. New sprouts will appear in about a week. Once the carrot has sprouted, plant it in some soil and enjoy watching it grow!

Cars

❖ Invite children to cut out pictures of cars from old magazines. Use the pictures to make a collage.

❖ Discuss why we have cars. Help the children make a list of other vehicles that help people travel from one place to another, such as vans, boats, airplanes, bicycles, motorcycles, trucks, jeeps, station wagons, buses, and trains. Survey the children to see how many children have used each method of transportation. Graph the results.

❖ Invite the children to bring toy cars from home to share with the class. Help the children arrange the cars in the shape of a large letter C. Read *Cars* by Anne Rockwell (see the unit book review).

❖ Children love to make car noises. Invite the children to follow behind you along an imaginary road and pretend to be cars. Go fast and "zoom," go slowly, stop quickly and "eek" as the brakes are applied, stop and turn, go around lots of curves, "putt-putt-putt" with engine trouble, and so on. Assign different children to take turns role-playing the lead car.

Cassette

❖ If you have a cassette recorder in your classroom, this is a good time to teach the children to use it properly. Cut a large C from tagboard and hang it over your cassette recorder. Invite the children to sign their names on the C when they have demonstrated individually that they can turn the machine on and off, put a tape in, take a tape out, and adjust the volume.

❖ Tape record yourself, the entire class, or individual students saying the ABC's, counting, and singing songs and fingerplays. Replay the tape for the class and ask the children to guess the identity of each voice they hear.

❖ Play a variety of cassette music during rest and quiet times. Suggest that children bring tapes of their favorite music from home as well.

❖ Check out simple read-a-long books and cassettes for the children to enjoy in a listening center. Choose cassettes that reinforce C words. You might make a tape of yourself reading a story as well.

Cat

❖ Have each child draw a simple cat shape on a large piece of paper. Invite the children to paint their cats black and then cut out the cats when the paint is dry. Suggest that children add eyes and whiskers to their cats. Paint a fence on bulletin-board paper and place the cats along the fence with the title "We Are the Cat's Meow."

❖ Read *Cat in the Hat* by Dr. Seuss, *Have You Seen My Cat?* by Eric Carle, *Cats! Cats! Cats!* by Bernard Wiseman, *Millions of Cats* by Wanda Gag, and *Calico Cat Looks at Colors* by Donald Charles (see the unit book review). Show the children how to draw a simple picture of a cat with a curly tail. Invite children to draw pictures of their favorite storybook cats, too.

❖ Help the children make "Paper-Doll Cats." Fold black paper accordion-style. Then show the children how to draw a simple cat shape on the top fold. Point out that the pattern must touch both sides of the folded paper. Help the children carefully cut out the pattern and then pull the cat design apart to reveal "Paper-Doll Cats."

❖ Play "Copycat." Stand in front of the class and demonstrate a movement, such as shaking your arms, standing on one foot, making a funny face, and so on. Challenge the children to copy what you do. After you have acted out four or five movements, invite the children to take turns being the leader.

❖ Place a piece of carbon paper between two sheets of typing paper. Staple the sheets together. One sheet may be cut into fourths and used for four students. Encourage the children to draw a simple cat and practice making C's. Then have the children pull up the carbon to reveal the copy underneath.

Catalog

❖ Have an assortment of catalogs available. Ask each child to browse through the catalogs and cut out five favorite items. Have the children glue the pictures on a sheet of construction paper with the title "C Is for Catalogs."

❖ Invite each child to tear a page from a catalog. Show the children how to cut the page into strips and the strips into small squares. Have the children use glue to make a letter C on a piece of construction paper. Then invite the children to arrange the catalog pieces along the glue line to make a "Catalog C."

Class

❖ Invite the children to look into mirrors and draw self-portraits. Display the finished portraits on a bulletin board with the title "C Is for Class."

❖ Write the names of all the children in the class on the chalkboard. Help the children read the names and then copy each name on their own papers. (You may wish to give less experienced children individual copies of the names or have these children write only the first letter of each name.) Ask the children to use a crayon to circle all of the C's in each name.

❖ Make flash cards of the children's names. Use the cards to help the children learn to recognize their classmates' names.

Clay

❖ Encourage the children to play with clay. Make "Clever Clay." This clay is very similar to commercial playdough. Invite the children to pound and squeeze the clay, pull it apart, make flat round cakes, create rolled ropes and balls, and so on.

Clever Clay

2 cups flour 1 cup salt 2 cups water 2 Tbsp vegetable oil 4 tsp cream of tartar food coloring	Mix together all of the ingredients in a bowl. Pour the mixture in a pan and cook on medium heat. The clay is done when it pulls away from the sides of the pot without sticking. For clay that is simpler to make but doesn't last as long, use a box of Bisquick and add water to achieve the desired consistency. Add flour as necessary to prevent sticking. This clay may be saved in the refrigerator for several weeks.

❖ Collect a variety of cookie cutters. Invite the children to use the cookie cutters to make clay shapes. Look for large seasonal cookie cutters and alphabet cookie cutters, too.

Clean

❖ Emphasize putting toys away when they are no longer being played with and the importance of keeping individual spaces neat and clean. Give out "Best Cleaner" buttons all week to children who keep their spaces clean. Give buttons to the children who follow directions for clean-up as well.

❖ Set up a "Cleaning Center." Include a small broom, mop, dustpan, sponge, apron, feather duster, a play or real vacuum cleaner, and so on. Demonstrate the proper use of each cleaning utensil and then encourage the children to practice using these items.

Clock

❖ Make paper clocks. Show the children how to draw a clock face on a paper plate. (More advanced children may be able to write the numbers on the clock face themselves.) Help the children attach construction-paper hands with a brad to the paper plates. Identify the big hand and little hand. If the children are ready, use the clocks to tell the time to the hour.

❖ Discuss why we have clocks. Then teach the children to sing "'Round the Clock" from *Wee Sing Children's Songs and Fingerplays*. This song is sung to the tune of "Twinkle, Twinkle Little Star" and explains the function of a clock. "'Round the Clock" may also be used to help children identify times for getting up, going to bed, eating meals, and so on.

Cloth

❖ Explain that cotton grows on plants. Cotton is made into thread, the thread is woven into cloth, and the cloth is sewn into clothing. Read *From Cotton to Pants* by Ali Mitgutsch (see the unit book review). Cut cotton cloth into strips (off-colors are often on sale at fabric stores, or ask someone who sews to save you some scraps). Invite the children to feel the cloth and decide whether warm or cold weather clothing might be made from cotton.

❖ Have each child make a letter C with glue on a sheet of construction paper. Then invite the children to arrange cotton balls along the glue line to make a "Cotton C."

❖ Invite children to feel corduroy material and decide if corduroy would be used to make warm or cold weather clothing. Read *Corduroy* by Don Freeman (see the unit book review). Discuss why the bear might have been named Corduroy.

❖ Cut strips of corduroy and cotton cloth into small squares. Glue each fabric piece on a tagboard card. Help the children sort the fabric cards into the two material types, first by using their sense of sight and then by using only their sense of touch.

❖ Discuss why we wear coats. Encourage the children to cut out pictures from magazines of different types and colors of coats. Suggest that children make a closet for the coats by folding a piece of construction paper the long way. Children may glue a small construction-paper circle on the closet for a doorknob and write "My Coat Closet." Invite the children to glue the pictures of coats inside.

Clothing

❖ Invite children to cut out pictures of clothing from magazines. Have the children glue their pictures on a sheet of construction paper to make a collage. Read *Clothes* by Peter Curry and *New Clothes for Alex* by Mary Dickinson (see the unit book review). Teach the children to sing "What Are You Wearing?" from *Wee Sing Children's Songs and Fingerplays*.

❖ Help the children brainstorm a list of words that might be used to describe different days (hot, cold, rainy, and so on).

Give each child a sheet of construction paper divided into thirds. Ask the children to select a word from the class list to write in one section or draw a picture to represent different types of days. Then encourage the children to cut out magazine pictures of clothing that illustrate what they would wear for each type of day. Suggest that children glue the pictures on the appropriate sections of their papers.

❖ Make flash cards with magazine pictures of clothing. Find a picture of gloves, mittens, a coat, a jacket, a raincoat, an umbrella, boots, high heels, tennis shoes, a hat, a shirt, a dress, a suit, a tie, a belt, jeans, shorts, a swimsuit, a skirt, and so on. Challenge the children to sort the cards into categories.

❖ Play "Touch Clothes." Begin by having the children stand in an open space. Instruct the children to touch a shoe that one of their classmates is wearing. More than one child may touch the same shoe. Then quickly give other instructions, such as "Touch a sweater," "Touch a pair of long pants," "Touch a pair of short pants," or "Touch a necklace."

❖ Discuss how clothespins are used. Help the children clip clothespins all around the top of a large coffee can. Write a number on each clothespin and challenge more advanced children to clip the clothespins around the top of the coffee can in sequential order. Invite the children to take the clothespins off in order, too. Store the clothespins inside the can.

❖ Play "Drop the Clothespin." Set a coffee can on the floor close to the back of a chair. Have each child count out ten clothespins. Invite the children to take turns kneeling on the chair and with their arms resting on the back of the chair, drop the clothespins into the can.

Clouds

❖ Read *Hi, Clouds* by Carol Greene (see the unit book review). Invite children to use tempera paint to make large gray or white clouds on blue construction paper. To give the clouds some texture, suggest that the children glue cotton on some of them.

❖ Show the children how to fold a sheet of blue construction paper in half. Then have them open the folded papers. Drop a large dab of white tempera paint along the inside fold. Instruct the children to refold the papers and smooth them with their hands. Have the children open their papers once again to reveal a cloud. Encourage the children to look for other pictures in the cloud shapes.

❖ Read *It Looked Like Spilt Milk* by Charles G. Shaw on a nice cloudy day (see the unit book review). If possible, take the class outside and invite the children to lie down on blankets on the ground and look at the clouds as you read. Encourage the children to look for people and objects in the cloud shapes.

Clover

❖ If clover is in season, invite the children to pick some to bring to school. Cut out a large letter C from a coral sheet of construction paper. Have the children glue the clovers on the C.

Clown

❖ Paint clown faces on all interested children. Clown makeup is readily available around Halloween. If you wait until after Halloween, you may often buy makeup at a discount. Zinc-based sticks, marketed as a sun protector, come in colors and work nicely as well. Or make your own makeup by adding a small amount of tempera paint to some cold cream (don't add food coloring because it will stain). Take pictures of your cute "clowns." Cold cream can be used to remove the makeup as well.

❖ Help the children make a clown face. Give each child a paper plate, a sheet of colored construction paper, and an inflated and tied balloon (use both round and long balloons). Invite the children to use crayons, construction paper, and any other materials you can provide to make a clown face on the paper plates. Punch a small hole in each child's paper plate for the nose. Then show the children how to pull the knot of the balloon through the hole and tape the knot to the back of the paper plate.

❖ Show the children how to draw a simple picture of a clown. Then read *The Clown-Arounds* by Joanna Cole and *C Is for Clown* by Stan and Janice Berenstain (see the unit book review). Invite the children to draw their favorite clowns.

Coal

❖ Make coal or charcoal crystals. Divide the class into small cooperative learning groups. Give each group eight pieces of coal or charcoal briquets to put in a tray (microwave entree dishes work well). Help the children mix together 2 tablespoons each of salt, water, and bluing (bluing is available at the grocery store in the laundry section) to pour over the coal or charcoal. Suggest that children add drops of food coloring wherever they want color, too. Then have children coat each charcoal piece with a few drops of ammonia. The next morning, if the children do not see crystals beginning to form, repeat the procedure.

❖ Invite the children to draw pictures using coal or charcoal. Point out that coal and charcoal may be messy. Spread lots of newspapers over the work area and encourage the children to wear paint shirts as well. Have the children use the charcoal like a pencil to make C's on a sheet of construction paper.

Coconut

❖ Help the children make "Coconut Compote" for a special treat.

Coconut Compote

1 can pineapple chunks
1 cup raisins
fresh fruits in season (bananas, apples, oranges, pears, peaches, and so on)
shredded coconut

Cut the fruits into bite-size pieces. Combine all the ingredients, except the coconut, in a saucepan over low heat (including the pineapple juice). Heat until slightly bubbly. Serve warm in small bowls with a generous amount of shredded coconut sprinkled over the top.

❖ Demonstrate how to crack a coconut. Make holes in the coconut's eyes (the three little black spots) by hammering a large nail into the eyes and then pulling the nail out. Pour out the liquid and save it. Put the coconut in a 350° oven for about 20 to 30 minutes. This will make the shell easier to remove. Cool the coconut, wrap it in a towel, and use a hammer to break the shell. Pry the shell off with a blunt knife and use a potato peeler to remove the thin brown layer underneath. Cut the coconut into little chunks. Make coconut milk by heating grated coconut in the coconut liquid (or water) just to the point of boiling. Cool and strain. Invite the children to sample the coconut and coconut milk.

Coins

❖ Bring to class an assortment of coins. Invite the children to help count the number of coins at the beginning of each day and then again at the end of the day. Help the children sort the coins into like stacks. Discuss how the coins are alike and how they are different, too. Point out each coin's color and size. Invite the children to feel around the outside edge of each coin, weigh each different coin, and so on.

❖ Give each child a sheet of typing paper and a coin. Have the children place the coin under the typing paper and feel the coin with their fingers. Invite the children to hold the coin in place as they use the side of a crayon to gently rub over the coin to make a rubbing. Encourage the children to make rubbings of pennies, nickels, dimes, and quarters. Then challenge the children to identify each coin by its rubbing.

❖ Give each child a penny, a nickel, a dime, and a quarter. Hold up one coin and ask the children to hold up a matching coin. For more advanced children, say the coin name and ask the children to hold up that coin.

❖ Put one coin inside a cloth bag (or "feely" box, if you have one). Invite the children to reach inside the bag and identify the coin using their sense of touch. Encourage the children to first feel for size. Point out that the difference between the penny and dime may be determined by feeling for the thickness of the outside edges.

❖ If you have a set of coin ink stamps, invite the children to use the rubber stamps to make coin prints all around a large construction paper C. Encourage the children to make prints of all the different coin stamps. Invite the children to color each print as well. Later, ask the children to identify each coin print.

Cold

❖ If possible, choose a cold day to discuss with the children different ways of staying warm—putting on a warm coat, wrapping up in a blanket, wearing a sweater, staying inside, and so on. Ask each child to divide a sheet of paper in half and write "hot" on one side and "cold" on the other. Then invite the children to cut out pictures from magazines of cold and hot environments and clothing to glue under the appropriate column headings.

❖ Glue pictures of hot and cold foods on tagboard cards. Help the children sort the pictures into hot and cold categories.

❖ Write "hot" on one side of the chalkboard and "cold" on the other side. Help the children brainstorm lists of words for each heading. For example,

Hot	Cold
soup	ice
hot chocolate	ice cream
sun	refrigerator
stove	snow

Colors

❖ Read *Colors* by John J. Reiss and *Is It Red? Is It Yellow? Is It Blue?* by Tana Hoban (see the unit book review). Cut a large letter C from white construction paper. Invite the children to use watercolors to paint the C different colors.

❖ Hold up a red object and ask the children to name the color. Help the children name other items in the classroom that are red as well. Repeat the activity using a variety of other colors.

❖ Play "I Spy." Choose one child to be "it." Invite that child to select any item in the classroom, and say, "I spy something red (or whatever color you choose)." The first child to guess the item correctly is invited to be "it" the next time.

❖ Look around the classroom for objects that may be sorted by color, such as colored blocks, buttons, and jar lids. Provide the children with as many sorting-by-color tasks as possible.

- ❖ Make several large letter C's from cardboard. Encourage children to trace around one of the C's to make their own construction-paper letters. Suggest that the children color their C's and then cut out the letters.

- ❖ Help the children review the color words. Write each color word on flash cards and provide opportunities for the children to practice reading the words aloud.

- ❖ Set up a "Coloring Center." On a table, place coloring supplies, such as crayons, coloring books, drawing paper, tracing paper, markers, and colored pencils. Arrange for each child to have an assigned time to visit the "Coloring Center" each day.

- ❖ Help the children make color caterpillars. Give the children construction-paper circles, one for each of the eight basic colors. Tape one circle to a classroom wall. Add eyes and antenna to make the caterpillar's head. Then invite the children to add a colored circle for each of the colors they can identify.

Comics

- ❖ Invite the children to share their favorite comic strips with the class. Display a different comic strip each day on a bulletin board.

- ❖ Save the daily comic strips and the Sunday color comics. Cut the comics into individual strips. Show the children how to cut the strips into separate frames, following the frame markers. Cut out a large construction-paper letter C. Make it large enough to fit the size of a bulletin board. Invite the children to glue five or six of their favorite comic frames on the large C. Encourage the children to read or tell about the comic strips they choose as well.

Computer

❖ Invite a guest speaker to visit your classroom and demonstrate the use of a computer. If possible, encourage the
computer operator to make and print out a picture of a C
word, such as "cake," for the children to color.

❖ If you have access to a computer, use it! Teach the children a computer game. There is software now available
for very young children. Some of the programs are
excellent for teaching the alphabet. The more exposure
the children (and you!) have to the computer, the more
fun it will be for everyone.

Confetti

❖ Explain that small pieces of paper thrown into the air at
parties, celebrations, and parades is called *confetti*.
Confetti is usually available at party supply stores year-
round. Invite the children to make their own confetti by
cutting wrapping paper, magazine pages, or other paper
scraps into very small bits. Then designate one day as a
"Celebrate School Day." Give each child some confetti to
throw at the end of that day. The children will have great
fun, but it will be quite messy! Use this opportunity to
teach the children how to use a broom or vacuum
cleaner as well.

❖ Have the children make a letter C with glue on a sheet of
construction paper. Then invite the children to sprinkle
confetti over the glue. When the glue is dry, have the
children gently shake off the excess confetti to reveal a
"Confetti C."

Cookies

❖ Discuss how crackers are a form of cookie, but most crackers contain less sugar. Give each child several bite-size crackers and small squares of cheese. Have the children make a letter C with a pencil on a sheet of construction paper. Invite the children to arrange the crackers and cheese along the pencil line to make a "Crackers and Cheese C." Encourage the children to eat the crackers and cheese when they are finished.

Corn

❖ Read *Corn Is Maize: The Gift of the Indians* by Aliki (see the unit book review). Then help the children make corn bread as a special treat.

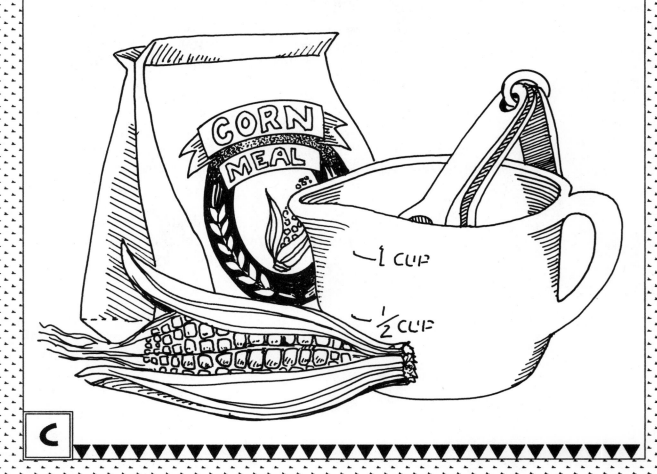

❖ Have the children make a letter C with glue on two pieces of construction paper. Invite the children to sprinkle cornmeal over the glue on one of the sheets and arrange popcorn kernels along the glue line on the other sheet of paper. When the glue is dry, have the children gently shake off the excess cornmeal and popcorn to reveal a "Cornmeal C" and "Popcorn C." Pop any extra popcorn kernels for the children to eat.

❖ If possible, make "Corn-on-the-Cob" for the children to sample. Encourage the children to name other foods that are yellow, such as bananas, squash, lemons, egg yolks, butter, pineapples, eggnog, and pears.

Corn-on-the-Cob

1 ear of corn in the husk per child
butter or margarine
salt and pepper

Invite the children to husk their own ears of corn by pulling off the husk and taking off all of the little silky threads. A vegetable brush will help remove those last small threads. Give each child a piece of aluminum foil. Show them how to rub butter on their corn and add salt and pepper. Then encourage the children to wrap their ears of corn in the foil. Bake about 10 to 15 minutes in a 400° oven.

Counting

❖ Count from one to ten and from one to twenty or thirty every day with the class. Provide opportunities for the children to count individually, with a partner, and in small groups.

❖ Read *Anno's Counting Book* by Mitsumasa Anno, *One Two Three: An Animal Counting Book* by Marc Brown, *Ten Black Dots* by Donald Crews, *One, Two, Three* by Peter Curry, and *One Was Johnny: A Counting Book* by Maurice Sendak (see the unit book review). Encourage the children to count everything all day long at every opportunity. Count the number of boys and girls present, the number of children eating in the cafeteria or bringing their lunches, the number of cups and napkins needed for a snack, and so on. Have the children count their fingers every day, too. When the children can count the fingers on one hand, help them count the fingers on both hands, and so on.

❖ Teach the children to sing "One, Two, Buckle My Shoe," "Rickety, Tickety," and "Ten Little Fingers" from *Wee Sing Children's Songs and Fingerplays*.

Crawl

❖ Sponsor crawling relays. Draw two large letter C's on the floor with chalk or make the letters with tape. Divide the class into two teams. Assign one of the C's to each team. Then invite the team members to crawl along the C in turn. The first team to finish crawling is the winner.

❖ Invite the children to make C shapes with their bodies. For example, show the children how to make a C by cupping their left hand. The children may also lie on the floor on their left side and, with their arms over their heads and their legs straight out in front, curve their backs to make a C. Or, suggest that children stand up straight, put their left arms straight out in front, and then bend the elbows and curve the hands to make a C. Encourage the children to make C shapes with their bodies in other ways as well.

Cream

❖ Invite children to fingerpaint with shaving cream on their desk tops. Encourage the children to wear paint shirts. Have the children smear the shaving cream over their desk tops and then use a single finger to write some C's.

Crooked

❖ Teach the children to sing "There Was a Crooked Man" from *Wee Sing Nursery Rhymes and Lullabies*. Encourage the children to draw some crooked lines, straight lines, curly lines, thick lines, thin lines, and so on.

Cucumber

❖ Show the children some cucumbers. Explain that cucumbers are often used as a salad vegetable. Help the children name other vegetables that are put in salads. Invite the children to make "Cucumber Cuties" and "Crunchy Cool Cucumbers."

Cucumber Cuties

1 large cucumber
soft cream cheese
bread slices or crackers
salt and pepper

Wash and pare the cucumber. Spread cream cheese on crackers or bread that has been cut into small rounds. Thinly slice the cucumber. Place a cucumber slice on each cracker or bread round. Sprinkle with salt and pepper. Serve as open-faced sandwiches.

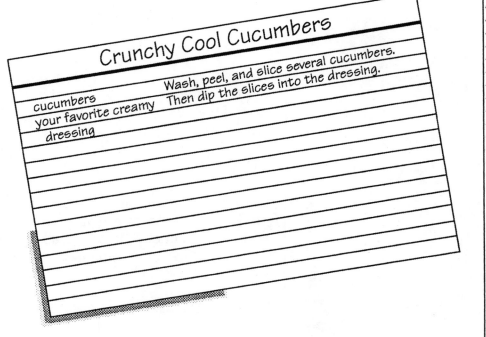

Crunchy Cool Cucumbers

cucumbers
your favorite creamy
dressing

Wash, peel, and slice several cucumbers.
Then dip the slices into the dressing.

❖ Cut a cucumber into several 3-inch pieces. Have the children draw a letter C with a pencil on a piece of construction paper. Then invite the children to dip the cut end of a cucumber piece into tempera paint and make prints along the pencil line to make a "Cucumber C."

Custodians

❖ If possible, arrange for the class to visit the custodian's supply closet. Ask a custodian to talk to the children about his or her job and how each cleaning item is used. Label each item that is discussed. Suggest that the custodian point out how it makes the job easier when the children pick up their own trash and keep their desks clean. When the children return to the classroom, encourage each child to draw a picture of the custodian and dictate sentences about what the custodian does. Write the sentences under the children's pictures. Give the finished pictures to the custodian as a thank-you gift. Or display the pictures somewhere in the school for other children to look at and enjoy.

Cutting

❖ Invite the children to practice free cutting. Start with snipping. Give the children strips of paper. The length doesn't matter, but the width should be 2/3 the length of the scissors blade. Have the children draw a letter C with a pencil on a sheet of construction paper. Then invite the children to arrange the snipped paper along the line to make a mosaic of the letter C.

❖ Show the children how to fringe paper. Give the children strips of paper about 6 to 8 inches wide and about 1 to 2 inches longer than the scissors blade. Instruct the children to make cuts side-by-side all along the strips to make a fringe. Give each a child a cutout of a cowboy coat. Then suggest that they glue the fringed pieces along the sleeves, opening, and coat bottom.

❖ Give the children paper that is 6 to 8 inches long and about 6 inches wide. Instruct the children to cut the paper into strips by making cuts with their scissors from the bottom to the top of the paper. Explain that they may use their holding hand to move the paper as they cut. Invite each child to staple the best cut strips on a bulletin board to form a crooked line. Title the bulletin board "There Was a Crooked Strip."

Food for Thought

Introducing children to a variety of foods is a wonderful way of reinforcing language concepts. The following foods all begin with the letter C and may be introduced at any time during this unit.

cabbage, cake, cantaloupe, carrot juice, carrots, carrot salad, cashews, casserole, catfish, catsup, cauliflower, clamato juice, clams, cobbler, cocoa, coconut, cold cuts, cole slaw, collard greens, consommé, cookies, corn bread, corned beef, corn dogs, corn muffins, corn-on-the-cob, cottage cheese, crab, crab apples, crackers, cranberries, cream, cream cheese, creamed corn, crepes, cucumbers, cupcakes, curry, custard

Book Review

Children enjoy hearing good books read aloud. The books listed here are favorites of children and may be used to reinforce the letter C.

Aliki. *Corn Is Maize: The Gift of the Indians,* Harper & Row, 1976.

Anglund, Joan W. *The Brave Cowboy,* Harcourt Brace Jovanovich, 1976.

Anno, Mitsumasa. *Anno's Counting Book,* Harper & Row, 1977.

Berenstain, Stan and Berenstain, Janice. *C Is for Clown,* Random House, 1972.

Brown, Marc. *One Two Three: An Animal Counting Book,* Little, Brown and Company, 1976.

Carle, Eric. *Have You Seen My Cat?,* Putnam Publishing Group, 1987.

Carle, Eric. *The Very Hungry Caterpillar,* Putnam Publishing Group, 1986.

Charles, Donald. *Calico Cat Looks at Colors,* Childrens Press, 1975.

Cole, Joanna. *The Clown-Arounds,* Parents Magazine Press, 1981.

Crews, Donald. *Ten Black Dots,* Greenwillow Books, 1986.

Curry, Peter. *Clothes,* Price Stern Sloan, 1984.

Curry, Peter. *One, Two, Three,* Price Stern Sloan, 1983.

Dickinson, Mary. *New Clothes for Alex,* Andre Deutsch, 1984.

Freeman, Don. *Corduroy,* Penguin Books, 1968.

Gag, Wanda. *Millions of Cats,* Putnam Publishing Group, 1977.

Giff, Patricia R. *The Candy Corn Contest,* Dell Books, 1984.

Greene, Carol. *Hi, Clouds,* Childrens Press, 1983.

Hoban, Tana. *Is It Red? Is It Yellow? Is It Blue?,* Greenwillow Books, 1978.

Holmes, Anita. *The One-Hundred-Year-Old Cactus,* Macmillan, 1983.

Kraus, Ruth. *The Carrot Seed,* Harper & Row, 1945.

Mitgutsch, Ali. *From Cotton to Pants,* Carolrhoda Books, 1981.

Reiss, John J. *Colors,* Macmillan, 1987.

Rockwell, Anne. *Cars,* E. P. Dutton, 1984.

Sendak, Maurice. *One Was Johnny: A Counting Book,* Harper & Row, 1962.

Seuss, Dr. *Cat in the Hat,* Beginner Books, 1957.

Shaw, Charles G. *It Looked Like Spilt Milk,* Harper & Row, 1988.

Wiseman, Bernard. *Cats! Cats! Cats!,* Parents Magazine Press, 1984.

Dd

Dad

❖ Invite each child to draw a picture of his or her dad or an uncle, brother, stepfather, or some other father figure. Have each child dictate something about his or her dad as you write the sentence or sentences under the picture. Gather all of the pictures together to make a class book. If you have access to a copy machine, reduce the size of the pictures to fit four to eight pictures on one page. Make a title page that says "D Is for Daddy" or "Daddies Are Divine!"

❖ Encourage each child to learn his or her dad's full name. Send home a permission slip with each child before doing this activity. Some parents may prefer that their children learn a stepfather's name, and so on. Respect the parents' wishes.

❖ Sponsor a "Dad's Day" at school. Be sensitive to those children who don't have dads—or have dads who live too far away to visit. Invite all dads to eat lunch at school with their children. After lunch, invite one or more of the dads to read aloud *Just Me and My Dad* by Mercer Mayer and *Just Like Daddy* by Frank Asch (see the unit book review).

D

Daisies

❖ Place some freshly cut daisies in water. Ask the children to predict what will happen to the flowers if you add a few drops of food coloring to the water. Drop food coloring in the water and invite the children to watch the flowers change colors. Explain that flowers and other plants get water through their stems.

❖ Show the children how to draw a simple picture of a daisy. First, ask each child to draw a small circle with a stem. Next, have the children draw a petal on the top of the circle, then a petal on the bottom, a petal on the left side, and finally a petal on the right side. Then invite the children to fill in the remaining spaces with more petals.

❖ Read *Daisy* by Brian Wildsmith (see the unit book review). This book is about a cow named Daisy. Encourage the children to think of girls' and boys' names that begin with the letter D, such as Dale, Daniel, Daphne, Darlene, David, Dawn, Deborah, Dee, Delilah, Delores, Desiree, Desmond, Diane, Dick, Dixie, Dominick, Donald, Donna, Doreen, Dorinda, Doris, Dorothy, Douglas, and so on.

Dance

❖ Sponsor a dance. Play contemporary music for the children to dance or move to as they feel the rhythm of the music.

❖ Play "Follow the Leader" while dancing. Choose one child to be the leader. Play some music and encourage everyone to do what the leader does. When the music stops, invite the leader to choose another child to be the leader.

D

Days

❖ Teach the children to sing "Days of the Week" from *Wee Sing Children's Songs and Fingerplays.* Provide opportunities for the children to say the days of the week in order every day. Name the days as a class and then invite individual children to say the days, too.

❖ Find the day of the week on the class calendar. Discuss how each day is different. For example, Monday is the first day of the school week and Friday is the last day. Tuesday might be music day, Thursday might be art day, and so on. Point out that Saturday and Sunday are weekend days. On these days, children might watch cartoons, visit friends, play games, sleep late, and so on. Encourage each child to share his or her special reasons for remembering each day of the week. The reasons don't matter as long as the children have a way of distinguishing one day of the week from another.

❖ Write the days of the week on flash cards. Use the cards each day. Encourage the children to put the cards in sequential order as well. Provide opportunities for more advanced children to read the flash cards individually in sequential and in random order. Invite children to copy the days of the week as you write them in order on the chalkboard.

Dentist

❖ Discuss why we have dentists. Point out that dentists fix our teeth, fill cavities, and help us learn to take good care of our teeth. Read *The Berenstain Bears Visit the Dentist* by Stan and Janice Berenstain (see the unit book review).

❖ Help the children make a collage of foods that cause rapid tooth decay, such as candy, cake, cookies, colas, and so on. Invite the children to look through magazines to find pictures of these foods. Have the children cut out the pictures and glue them on a piece of white construction paper cut in the shape of a tooth.

❖ Invite a dental assistant or hygienist to visit your classroom and explain proper brushing techniques. Some technical schools encourage school visits as part of their students' training.

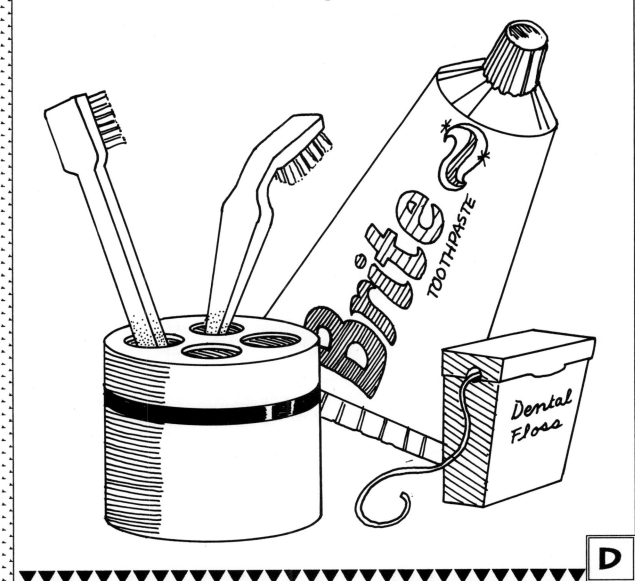

Diamond

❖ Make diamond-shaped booklets. Cut two pieces of construction paper and several sheets of typing paper in a diamond shape and staple the pages together. Give each child a booklet. Suggest that children write "My Diamond Book" on the front. Encourage the children to cut out pictures from magazines of items that begin with the letter D. Invite the children to cut out a variety of upper and lower case D's to put in the booklet, too.

❖ Draw a diamond shape on the chalkboard and help the children copy what you do stroke for stroke on their own papers. Show the children that they may also draw a diamond shape by folding a sheet of paper into fourths, unfolding the paper, and then connecting each midpoint. Give each child a handout of dot-to-dot diamond shapes.

Dictionary

❖ Ask the children if they know what a dictionary is and what it is used for. Have several picture dictionaries available for the children to browse through, such as *The Cat in the Hat Beginner Book Dictionary* by Philip D. Eastman (see the unit book review). Turn to the D section and help the children identify the pictures.

❖ Post a different D word on a bulletin board each day. Read and discuss the meanings of the featured words as a class. Then challenge the children to use the words in conversation sometime during that day.

Different

❖ Help the children explore the word *different*. Show the class groups of three colors, shapes, numbers, or letters. Two of the items should be the same. Ask the children to discuss how the items are alike and then ask them to point out the item that is different. For children who have difficulty, use concrete items, such as two shoes that are alike and one that is different, or two unsharpened pencils that are alike and one that is sharpened.

❖ Make a set of flash cards. On each index card, draw or glue pictures of two items that are the same and one that is different. Label each picture or drawing as well. Use familiar shapes, letters, or numbers. Invite the class to identify the different item on each card as you hold the flash cards up for them to see.

Dime

❖ If you have a dime rubber stamp, use it to make dime prints (heads and tails) all along a letter D cut from light-colored construction paper. Invite the children to look at the dime prints and describe what is on each side.

❖ Make dime rubbings. Give each child a real dime and a fourth of a sheet of typing paper. Have the children place their dimes under the paper and then locate the dimes with their fingers. Instruct the children to hold the dimes in place with one hand while they gently rub a crayon sideways over the dimes with their other hand. Encourage the children to try different colored crayons. Have the children make rubbings of both the front and the back. Discuss the pictures found on both sides.

Dip

❖ Help the children make "Delicious Dippy Dip." Serve with fresh raw carrots, celery, cucumbers, broccoli, and cauliflower. Point out that these vegetables are nutritious because they contain very little fat.

Delicious Dippy Dip

1/4 cup cottage cheese
2 Tbsp grated cheddar cheese
1/4 tsp dill
1/2 tsp Worcestershire sauce
dash salt
chopped celery, bacon bits, parsley, pimiento pieces (optional)

Mix all ingredients together in a bowl. Chill before serving.

Dirt

❖ Read *Dig, Drill, Dump, Fill* by Tana Hoban (see the unit book review). Find a place where children may dig in the dirt safely. Or fill a large container with potting soil. Provide sand shovels and large spoons and invite the children to fill a small cup with dirt. Have the children wash their hands well after digging. Ask the children to make a letter D with glue on a sheet of construction paper. Then invite the children to sprinkle some of the dirt over the glue. When the glue dries, have them shake off the excess dirt to reveal a "Dirty D."

Dishes

❖ Invite children to make a collage with pictures of dishes cut from magazines. Encourage the children to find pictures of plates, cups, saucers, and bowls to glue on a piece of construction paper.

❖ Discuss why we have dishes. If you have dishes in your classroom, or if you have play dishes in your kitchen center, invite the children to wash dishes. A large plastic dishpan works nicely if a sink is not available. Use a drainer for the clean dishes.

❖ If possible, arrange for the children to tour the school kitchen. Ask the cooks to demonstrate how dishes are washed at school. Ask the cooks if the children might help clean up the kitchen.

Doctor

❖ Use a play medical kit to help the children learn about medical supplies. Take everything out of the kit and display the items on a table. Discuss the name of each item and how the doctor uses it. Invite the children to draw a picture of their favorite items. Ask each child to dictate a sentence or two about how the item he or she draws is used. Write the sentence below the child's drawing.

❖ Discuss why we have doctors. Point out that doctors try to make us well, give us medication, and help us when we are sick. Invite the children to share experiences they have had at the doctor's office or in the hospital.

❖ Read *The Berenstain Bears Go to the Doctor* by Stan and Janice Berenstain and *Come to the Doctor, Harry,* by Mary Chalmers (see the unit book review). If there is a hospital nearby, arrange for the class to take a tour of the children's ward.

❖ Discuss what people should do when they are sick. Invite a nurse or doctor to visit the classroom and discuss what the children should do to stay healthy.

Dodge

❖ Teach the class to play "dodge ball." Put the class in the middle of the play area. Ask parent volunteers or other teachers to stand on either side of the children. Have the adults roll or throw a playground ball toward the children and try to hit them below the waist. Encourage the children to dodge the ball. When the children are hit by the ball, they join the adult side and help throw the ball at the remaining children. The last child to remain standing in the center wins.

Dog

❖ Invite the children to make a collage with pictures of different types of dogs cut from magazines. Have the children glue the pictures on construction paper. Encourage the children to select their favorite dog pictures and explain why those dogs appeal to them.

❖ Encourage children with dogs as pets to share their experiences and knowledge. Invite the children to name other types of pets, such as cats, fish, birds, turtles, rabbits, gerbils, guinea pigs, and hamsters as well. Survey the class to see which kind of animal is the most popular pet. Graph the results.

❖ Read *A Dog for Danny* by Inez Hogan and *Big Dog, Little Dog: A Bedtime Story* by Philip D. Eastman (see the unit book review). Make "Dy-no-mite Doggies" for a special treat.

Dy-no-mite Doggies

1 banana per child	Invite the children to assemble the ingredients in any way they wish or they
carrot slices	may follow your directions. Use
marshmallows	toothpicks to attach the various
raisins	ingredients to the bananas. Help the children remove the toothpicks before eating.

Donkey

❖ Teach the children to sing "Sweetly Sings the Donkey" from *Wee Sing Around the Campfire*.

❖ Play "Pin the Tail on the Donkey." To make your own game, draw a picture of a donkey on the chalkboard. Have each child cut out a donkey tail. Stick a piece of folded tape to the back of each tail. Blindfold one child at a time. Gently turn the children around once, and then see if they can "pin" their tails on the donkey.

Doodles

❖ Tape a large sheet of white paper to the chalkboard. Provide a variety of colored markers. Then invite the children to use the markers to fill the paper with doodles. Suggest that the children make:

straight doodles
curly doodles
crooked doodles
zigzag doodles
scribble doodles

❖ Make "Disappearing Delicious Doodles" and watch them disappear!

Disappearing Delicious Doodles

1 cup semisweet chocolate chips or unsweetened carob chips

1/4 cup peanut butter

15-oz can chow mein noodles

1/2 cup apple juice concentrate

1 tsp vanilla

Mix and stir together all ingredients, except the noodles, in a pan over low heat. When the chocolate is melted, add the noodles and stir carefully to coat the noodles with chocolate. Drop by spoonfuls onto wax paper. Harden the doodles in the refrigerator. Then watch them disappear!

Door

❖ Invite the children to decorate the classroom door with pictures of items that begin with the letter D. Encourage children to cut out pictures from magazines and to draw their own pictures, too.

❖ Show the children how to draw a simple picture of a door.

Dots

❖ Use dots to make a letter D. Read *Dots, Spots, Speckles, and Stripes* by Tana Hoban and *Ten Black Dots* by Donald Crews (see the unit book review).

❖ Select cloth with a polka-dot pattern. Cut the cloth into strips. Then invite the children to cut the strips into small squares. Have the children make a letter D with glue on a sheet of construction paper and then arrange the polka-dot squares along the glue line to make a "Polka-Dotted D."

❖ Suggest that the children draw large and small dots on a large sheet of white construction paper. Then invite children to use tempera paint or water colors to paint the dots different colors.

❖ Draw a large letter D with a pencil on a sheet of construction paper. Give each child a sheet of gummed circles. (Use 3/4-inch circles in a variety of colors.) Invite the children to peel the dots off of the sheets and stick the circles along the pencil line to make a "Dotted D."

❖ Provide dot-to-dot worksheets for the children to complete. Consider the developmental level of the children. More advanced children may be able to do number and alphabet dot-to-dots, while other children may be challenged by a few large dots to connect.

❖ Bring in dice for the children to play with in the classroom. Invite the children to throw one die and count the dots to determine the appropriate number. Ask more advanced children to count the dots on two dice. Foam dice are especially good for this activity, but any dice will do. Teach a simple game to small groups using dice.

❖ Teach the children to play any of the many variations of "Dominoes" in small groups. Games may be bought commercially, or make your own set of dominoes by using tagboard rectangles with letters of the alphabet written on each end. Encourage the children to match upper case letters to upper case letters or upper case letters to lower case letters.

Drawing

❖ Set up a "Drawing Center." Hang a banner over the "Drawing Center" that says "D Is for Drawing." Provide pencils, markers, crayons, colored pencils, and drawing paper. Then assign each child some time in the "Drawing Center" each day to draw pictures of items that begin with the letter D. Display the finished drawings on a bulletin board or wall.

❖ Encourage the children to draw simple designs. Draw the following designs on the chalkboard, one stroke at a time, and invite the children to copy the designs. Encourage the children to draw designs of their own creation as well.

Dressing

❖ This week is a good time to reinforce dressing skills, especially the more difficult ones. Send notes to parents explaining the skills that need extra reinforcement at home.

> Puts on a coat.
> Puts on a shirt.
> Unzips a separating front zipper.
> Unsnaps back and front snaps.
> Buttons small front buttons.
> Puts on "pull-up" garments (pants).
> Inserts a belt into pant loops.
> Buckles a belt or shoes.
> Laces shoes.
> Knows which shoe goes on which foot.
> Puts on "pull over" garments (sweater).
> Unzips back (non-separating) zipper.
> Zips front separating zipper.
> Zips front (non-separating) zipper.

❖ Use lacing boards to help the children practice snapping, zipping, and buttoning. You may also fasten old clothes to a board, such as the front of an old blouse. Remember that the board gives the child a different perspective. You might have large clothes available for the children to slip on and off over their regular clothes to practice many of these skills as well.

❖ Set up a "Dress-Up Center." Provide hats, shoes, scarves, sunglasses, and jewelry. Look through your own closet for items. Send a letter home to parents as well. Explain how important pretending and practicing dressing skills are for young children and ask parents to contribute any items. Put a full length, nonbreakable mirror in the "Dress-Up Center," too.

Drum

❖ Show the children how to draw a simple drum. Ask the music teacher to show the class different types of drums. Encourage the children to listen to the sound that each drum makes. If you have a drum in your classroom, invite the children to take turns beating the drum to music.

❖ Read *Hand, Hand, Fingers, Thumb* by Al Perkins and *The Little Drummer Boy* by Ezra Jack Keats (see the unit book review). Help the children make drums. Collect several oatmeal or cornmeal boxes, and coffee or solid shortening tins with lids. Or ask the children to bring in their own boxes or tins to decorate. Have the children paint the cardboard containers. Cover the metal cans with adhesive paper and suggest that children use colored tape to make designs. Have the children use pencils, chopsticks, wooden spoons, sticks from rhythm instruments, or their hands for drumsticks. Invite the children to play their drums in time to music.

Duck

❖ Read *Make Way for Ducklings* by Robert McCloskey (see the unit book review). Invite the children to draw a simple picture of a duck. Help the children make up a name for their ducks, such as "Ducky Douglas."

❖ Play "Duck Duck Goose." Invite the children to sit in a circle. Choose one child to be "it." That child walks around the outside of the circle and says "duck" as he or she gently touches each child's head. When "it" comes to a child that he or she wishes to choose, he or she says "goose." The "goose" must then chase "it" around the circle. If "it" returns to the empty space without being tagged, the "goose" is the next child to be "it." A tagged child sits in the "mush pot" (the space in the center of the circle) until another child is caught and takes his or her place.

❖ Teach the children to sing "Six Little Ducks" from *Wee Sing Nursery Rhymes and Lullabies.* Give each child six small duck-shaped crackers to eat as they sing the song.

❖ If possible, arrange to take the children to a nearby pond where ducks are found. Take bread or crackers for the children to feed the ducks.

Food for Thought

Introducing children to a variety of foods is a wonderful way of reinforcing language concepts. The following foods all begin with the letter D and may be introduced at any time during this unit.

date-nut bread, dates, deviled crab, deviled eggs, dill pickles, dip, dressing, dried fruit, dumplings

Book Review

Children enjoy hearing good books read aloud. The books listed here are favorites of children and may be used to reinforce the letter D.

Aliki. *Digging Up Dinosaurs,* Harper & Row, 1981.
Asch, Frank. *Just Like Daddy,* Prentice Hall, 1981.
Berenstain, Stan and Berenstain, Janice. *The Berenstain Bears Go to the Doctor,* Random House, 1987.
Berenstain, Stan and Berenstain, Janice. *The Berenstain Bears Visit the Dentist,* Random House, 1981.

Chalmers, Mary. *Come to the Doctor, Harry,* Harper & Row, 1981.

Crews, Donald. *Ten Black Dots,* Greenwillow Books, 1986.

Eastman, Philip D. *Big Dog, Little Dog: A Bedtime Story,* Random House, 1973.

Eastman, Philip D. *The Cat in the Hat Beginner Book Dictionary,* Random House, 1984.

Freeman, Don. *Dandelion,* Penguin Books, 1977.

Hoban, Tana. *Dig, Drill, Dump, Fill,* Greenwillow Books, 1975.

Hoban, Tana. *Dots, Spots, Speckles, and Stripes,* Greenwillow Books, 1987.

Hoff, Syd. *Danny and the Dinosaur,* Harper & Row, 1978.

Hogan, Inez. *A Dog for Danny,* Garrard, 1973.

Keats, Ezra Jack. *The Little Drummer Boy,* Macmillan, 1987.

McCloskey, Robert. *Make Way for Ducklings,* Penguin Books, 1976

McLenighan, Valjean. *One Whole Doughnut...One Doughnut Hole,* Childrens Press, 1982.

Mayer, Mercer. *Just Me and My Dad,* Western Publishing, 1977.

Most, Bernard. *Whatever Happened to the Dinosaurs?,* Harcourt Brace Jovanovich, 1984.

Perkins, Al. *Hand, Hand, Fingers, Thumb,* Random House, 1969.

Wildsmith, Brian. *Daisy,* Pantheon, 1984.

Zallinger, Peter. *Dinosaurs,* Random House, 1977.

Ee

Echo

❖ Teach the children to sing "Billy Grogan's Goat" and "Oh, You Can't Get to Heaven" from *Wee Sing Silly Songs*. Both songs use an echo. Then read *Happy Birthday Moon* by Frank Asch (see the unit book review).

❖ Play "Echo Game." Invite children to echo dictated sentences. Start by dictating three- or four-word sentences and increase the length of the sentences as appropriate. After each sentence has been echoed, ask the children to name the words that begin with the letter E. You may use the following sentences or make up sentences of your own.

> I like eggs.
> Come play with Ellen.
> An eagle flew eleven miles.
> The elephant fell down eight times.
> Ed saw an elk and an eagle.
> I want a red pencil and an eraser.
> Show me your basket and Easter eggs.
> Can I have eggnog to drink today?
> Where are my extra eggs and eleven egg cartons?
> Let's go fly a kite after we do our exercises.

❖ Clap a sequence, such as "clap—clap—rest—clap" or "clap—rest—clap—clap." Challenge the children to clap the same rhythm back to you. Clap longer and more complicated rhythms for the children to echo.

Eggs

❖ Serve scrambled eggs to the children for breakfast one day this week. Invite the children to use an eggbeater to whip the eggs.

❖ Sponsor an "Eggs-travaganza Event." Invite parents or another class as guests. Make "Eggs-cellent Egg Salad" to serve on English muffins, "Easy Egg Drop Soup," "Eggs-citing Eggs (Deviled Eggs)," and "Eggplant Pizza." Serve "Eggs-ceptional Eggnog" to drink.

Eggs-cellent Egg Salad

6 eggs
2 Tbsp sweet relish
2 tsp mustard
3 Tbsp mayonnaise
salt
pepper
bacon bits (optional)
1 grated carrot
(optional)

Boil and shell the eggs. Chop the eggs and then add all ingredients. Mix well and chill before serving.

Easy Egg Drop Soup

2 cans (or 3 cups) chicken broth
2 eggs
dash salt
2 tsp soy sauce
(optional)

Heat the broth until boiling. Whip the eggs in a separate bowl along with the salt. Pour the egg mixture slowly into the boiling broth. The hot broth will cook the eggs into strings. When all of the egg is cooked, the soup is ready to eat. Add soy sauce to taste.

Eggs-citing Eggs (Deviled Eggs)

6 eggs
2 Tbsp sweet relish
2 tsp mustard
3 Tbsp mayonnaise
salt
pepper
bacon bits (optional)

Boil and shell the eggs. Cut the eggs in half lengthwise. Put the yolks in a bowl and arrange the white halves on a plate. Add the other ingredients to the yolks and mash them all together with a fork until well blended. Fill the white halves with the yolk mixture. Makes 12 deviled eggs.

Eggplant Pizza

3 eggplant
3–4 tomatoes
1/2 lb cheese, sliced thin, preferably mozzarella
5 Tbsp margarine
salt and pepper

Wash the eggplant in cold water and then slice into 1-inch thick rounds. Butter the rounds and arrange them on a cookie sheet. Broil for 3–5 minutes or until soft (test with a fork) and a bit brown. Turn the rounds over and butter. Add a tomato slice, a cheese slice, salt, and pepper to each eggplant round. Broil for a few minutes more until the cheese is melted and bubbly.

Eggs-ceptional Eggnog

3 eggs
3 Tbsp sugar or
3 tsp honey
3 cups cold milk
3/4 tsp vanilla
3 cups cracked ice
nutmeg (optional)

Beat the eggs well. Then blend in the milk, sugar (or honey), and vanilla. Add ice and stir. Sprinkle with nutmeg, if desired. Serve chilled.

❖ Set up an "Egg Center." Collect colored plastic eggs, such as the eggs used to package pantyhose. Separate the plastic eggs and have the children practice matching the two halves and putting the eggs back together again. Show the children how to make letters, numbers, and shapes by arranging the egg halves, open side down, on a table.

❖ Hide little prizes in plastic eggs. Put the eggs in a large bucket or basket. Provide opportunities every day for the children to earn points or tokens. At the end of each day, invite the child or children with the most points to select an egg as a prize.

❖ Boil eggs, peel them, and then invite the children to taste. Vote to see whether the children prefer the white or the yolk. Put the eggshells in a paper bag and crush them. Have the children make a letter E with glue on a sheet of construction paper. Then invite the children to sprinkle some of the crushed eggshells on the glue. When the glue is dry, have the children shake off the extra eggshells to reveal an "Eggshell E."

❖ Show the children how to draw a simple picture of an egg. Suggest that children use glitter, crayons, scraps of fabric and yarn, and other materials to decorate their eggs.

❖ Dye and decorate eleven boiled eggs. Make an egg dye by mixing one teaspoon of vinegar with one-half cup boiling water and then adding about twenty drops of food coloring. Have the children use a wax candle to draw a letter E on each egg. Help the children dip the hard boiled eggs into the dye until the desired shade is obtained. The E will magically appear. After the color has dried, it will not rub off. Rubbing the colored eggs with vegetable oil will make them shine. (The eggs may also be colored by dipping clothespin sponges into tempera paint and dabbing the paint onto the eggs.)

❖ Save the shells from boiled eggs. Color the eggshells by putting them in a bowl with one teaspoon vinegar, one-half cup boiling water, and a few drops of food coloring. Give each child a large rectangular piece of white construction paper. Show the children how to use scissors to cut off and round the corners of the paper to make an oval egg shape. Invite the children to paint the white egg shape with glue and then sprinkle the colored eggshells over the glue to make a "Colored Egg."

❖ Explain that birds, chickens, geese, ducks, snakes, snails, spiders, fish, frogs, and turtles all lay eggs. Point out that fertilized eggs hatch into babies. Eggs can differ in size, color, and texture. Bird eggs have a hard shell. Fish, frog, and salamander eggs are coated with a jelly-like substance, and turtle and snake eggs are leathery. Read *Eggs on Your Nose* by Ann McGovern, *Horton Hatches the Egg* by Dr. Seuss, *The Most Wonderful Egg in the World* by Helme Heine, and *The Egg Tree* by Katherine Milhous (see the unit book review).

❖ Show the children how to draw a simple picture of a chick embryo in an egg. Encourage the children to color their pictures as well.

❖ Make or buy Chinese or Vietnamese egg rolls for the children to taste.

Eight

❖ Cut out a large letter E from light-colored construction paper. Show the children how to make the number 8 by making an S and then connecting the bottom point to the top point. Less experienced children may make an 8 by drawing two circles. Invite the children to practice making 8's on their own papers and then invite them to make their very best 8's on the large letter E to make an "Eight E."

❖ Ask each child to bring an empty egg carton to school. On a table, put out an assortment of eight different items, such as buttons, beads, corn, bottle caps, dried peas, pennies, popcorn kernels, and lima beans. Invite the children to count eight of each item to put into each section of their egg cartons.

❖ Give each child eight 1-inch colored cubes. Have the children count the cubes and arrange them on their desktops to make a letter E.

Elephant

❖ Show the children a picture of an elephant. Point out how big the elephant is. Explain that elephants live in the wild, but we can also see elephants in a zoo. Encourage the children to name other zoo animals, such as the zebra, monkey, tiger, lion, gorilla, giraffe, hippopotamus, and rhinoceros. Review with the children any flash cards that you might have of zoo animals as well. If possible, arrange to take the children on a field trip to a nearby zoo.

❖ Invite the children to practice walking like an elephant. Have the children bend over and swing their arms straight down with palms together to make a trunk. Remind the children to walk very slowly!

❖ Have the children study a picture of an elephant very carefully. Focus the children's attention on the elephant's foot. Help the children describe the foot. Then show children how to draw a picture of an elephant's foot. More advanced children might draw the entire elephant.

❖ Read *But No Elephants* by Jerry Smath (see the unit book review). Then teach the children the repeating rhyme "Elephants" from *Sally Go Round the Sun* by Edith Fowke. Begin with one child walking in a circle and at the end of the rhyme, invite that child to choose "another little elephant." That child stands behind the first child and puts his or her hands on the first child's shoulders. Then the two of them walk around in a circle while all of the children repeat the rhyme. At the end of the rhyme, the last child chosen selects "another little elephant." Continue until all of the children have been chosen.

Envelope

❖ Help the children make envelopes. On the front of the envelope, have the children write their names and addresses. Less experienced children may practice making E's on their envelopes. Make a mailbox for all of the envelopes. Invite a different child each day to "deliver" the mail. Ask each child to stand as he or she receives an envelope and recite his or her complete name and address.

❖ Set up an "Envelope Center" for more advanced children. Provide envelopes, a card for each child with his or her name and address written on it, and an assortment of pens and pencils. Invite the children to practice writing their names and addresses on the envelopes.

Eraser

❖ Play the "Eraser Game." Write five to ten words in two columns on the chalkboard. Include the children's names, color words, number words, and days of the week. For less experienced children, write upper and lower case letters of the alphabet. Divide the class into two teams. Ask each team member in turn to point to and read one of the words from their team's column. The children may erase each word they read correctly. If a child misses a word, he or she loses a turn. The first team to erase all the words in their column wins.

Exercise

❖ Do exercises with the class for 10 to 15 minutes each day. Count by E's. For example, E-1, E-2, E-3, E-4, and so on.

Eyes

❖ Discuss the color that eyes can be, such as blue, green, hazel or brown. Invite each child to look in a mirror and decide the color of his or her eyes. Survey the class and record the results on a graph.

❖ Encourage the children to cut out pictures from magazines of eyes. Suggest that children find pictures of animal eyes, too! Invite the children to glue their eye pictures on a bulletin board covered with white paper. Title the bulletin board "The Eyes Have It!" or "E Is for Eyes."

❖ Read *Arthur's Eyes* by Marc Brown and *The Eye Book* by Theodore Le Sieg (see the unit book review). Invite the children to make different faces in a mirror. Have the children focus on how their eyes change with each new expression. Then encourage the children to draw pictures of happy eyes, sad eyes, surprised eyes, and so on.

Food for Thought

Introducing children to a variety of foods is a wonderful way of reinforcing language concepts. The following foods all begin with the letter E and may be introduced at any time during this unit.

egg drop soup, egg foo yung, eggnog, eggplant, egg roll, eggs, enchilada, English muffin, English peas

Book Review

Children enjoy hearing good books read aloud. The books listed here are favorites of children and may be used to reinforce the letter E.

Asch, Frank. *Happy Birthday Moon,* Simon & Schuster, 1988.
Brown, Marc. *Arthur's Eyes*, Little, Brown and Company, 1981.

Fowke, Edith. *Sally Go Round the Sun: Three Hundred Children's Songs, Rhymes and Games,* Doubleday, 1969.

Galdone, Paul. *The Elves and the Shoemaker,* Ticknor & Fields, 1984.

Heine, Helme. *The Most Wonderful Egg in the World,* Macmillan, 1987.

Le Sieg, Theodore. *The Eye Book,* Random House, 1986.

McGovern, Ann. *Eggs on Your Nose,* Macmillan, 1987.

Milhous, Katherine. *The Egg Tree,* Macmillan, 1981.

Seuss, Dr. *Horton Hatches the Egg,* Random House, 1940.

Smath, Jerry. *But No Elephants,* Parents Magazine Press, 1979.

Face

❖ Invite the children to make and eat "Friendly Faces."

Friendly Faces

1 pineapple ring per child	Place a pineapple ring in the bottom of a serving dish. Add a scoop of cottage cheese on top. Use raisins to make facial features and banana slices for ears. Add grated carrot or cheese for hair, if desired.
1 scoop small-curd cottage cheese per child	
raisins	
banana slices	
grated carrot or grated cheese (optional)	

❖ Sponsor a "Funny Face" contest to see who can make the funniest face in the class. Take pictures!

❖ Encourage the children to draw a funny face, a face with a frown, a face with freckles, and so on. Help the children sort the pictures into like categories. Then use the faces to make a bulletin-board display. Each day, feature a different category. Title the bulletin board "I Feel Sad

(Happy, Mad, and so on) When...." Invite each child who has a drawing on the bulletin board that day to complete the sentence. Write each child's sentence on a strip of paper and staple it next to the child's drawing.

❖ Make scary faces. Bring in a flashlight. Turn off the lights and darken the classroom. Then invite each child to shine the flashlight under his or her chin and make a scary face. Vote on the scariest face. Read *It Didn't Frighten Me* by Janet L. Goss and Jerome C. Harste (see the unit book review).

❖ Use tempera paint and a small paintbrush to paint freckles on each child's face. The freckles will wash off with water.

❖ Teach the children to sing "The Hokey Pokey" from *Wee Sing and Play*. Substitute the face, fingers, and feet for the featured parts of the body.

❖ Discuss the parts of the face, such as eyes, eyelashes, eyebrows, nose, mouth, teeth, lips, chin, cheeks, and forehead. Ask the children to point to the appropriate parts of the face as you say each part aloud. Then point to a part of the face and ask the children to say the name.

❖ Give each child a small box or box top with flour sprinkled along the bottom. Invite the children to draw faces in the flour with their index fingers. Children may gently shake their boxes to erase their pictures and start over. Encourage the children to practice making the letter F in the flour, too.

Family

❖ Discuss families and family roles. Point out that each family is different. For example, in some families the mother may go to work and cook the meals, but in another family the father might be responsible for these tasks. Stress the idea that each family member is important and has responsibilities. Encourage the children to share information about their own families.

❖ Read *Families* by Meredith Tax (see the unit book review). Encourage each child to draw a picture of his or her family. Write the names of the family members shown on each child's drawing as well. Make a frame for each child's family portrait by cutting out the middle of a sheet of construction paper and gluing the portrait to the back.

❖ Read *Someday with My Father* by Helen E. Buckley, *The Little Father* by Gelett Burgess, and *A Father Like That* by Charlotte Zolotow (see the unit book review). Ask the children to invite their fathers, uncles, brothers, step-fathers, or other father figures to come visit your class-room and share information about their jobs at work and at home.

Farm

❖ Read *On the Farm* by Richard Scarry and *Animals on the Farm* by Feodor Rojankovsky (see the unit book review). Teach the children to sing "Old McDonald Had a Farm" from *Wee Sing Children's Songs and Fingerplays*. Invite the children to practice making the farm animal sounds. Make a set of flash cards of farm animals, such as sheep, cows, pigs, horses, dogs, cats, chickens, roosters, goats, and ducks. Hold each card up and ask the children to name the animal. If you have a large selection of animal cards, help the children sort the cards into the following categories: "Farm Animals" and "Zoo Animals" or "Farm Animals" and "Not Farm Animals."

❖ Discuss the different types of farms. Some farms special-ize in certain foods. There are wheat farms, orange farms,

FEATHERS

and strawberry farms, for example. Other farms have cows for milking and are called dairy farms. There are egg farms and farms that raise pigs and other livestock for meat. Discuss the types of farms in your area. If possible, arrange for your class to take a field trip to a nearby farm. If you live in a large city, discuss why there aren't any farms nearby.

❖ Ask the children why we have farmers. Point out that farmers raise livestock, grow the foods we eat, and so on. Teach the children to sing and act out "Farmer in the Dell" from *Wee Sing and Play*.

Feather

❖ Help the class make a list of animals that have feathers, such as geese, swans, turkeys, birds, ducks, and chickens. Encourage the children to think of ways feathers can be used. For example, point out that feathers are often used as hat decorations or to fill pillows.

❖ Draw and cut out a large turkey from construction paper to place on a bulletin board. Give the children paper turkey feathers as tokens for good work or good behavior. Invite the children to staple the feathers they receive to the turkey shape. Encourage the children to work together as a class to cover the turkey with feathers.

Feet

❖ Make a "Fancy Footpath." Choose a sunny, warm day and do this activity outside. Cut off a long sheet of bulletin-board paper, brown butcher paper, or freezer-wrap paper. Fill two large styrofoam meat trays with tempera paint, one color in each tray. Put a practice sheet beside each paint tray. Roll out the long sheet of paper for a foot path and place it next to the practice sheet. Set a tray of clean water at the end of the footpath. Invite the children to remove their shoes and socks, step in one or both paint trays, step onto the practice sheet, and then walk along the footpath. At the end of the footpath, have the children step directly into the tray of clean water. Or, if an outside water faucet is nearby, use a water hose to wash the children's feet. Display the finished "Fancy Footpath" along a classroom wall or in a hallway outside your classroom.

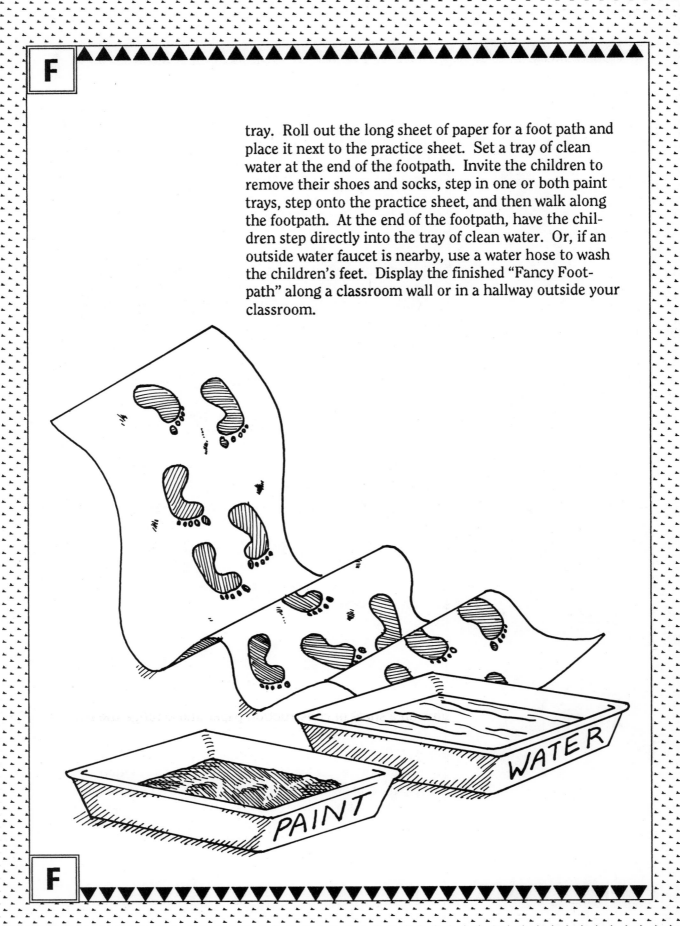

❖ Read *The Foot Book* by Dr. Seuss (see the unit book review). Trace around each child's feet on construction paper. Cut out each set of footprints. Tape the footprints along a classroom wall. Title the wall display "Put Your Best Foot Forward." Encourage the children to identify their own footprints.

❖ Encourage the children to name as many ways as possible to move their feet, such as walking, running, sliding, hopping on one foot, jumping on two feet, galloping, and skipping. Invite the children to practice each movement. Then play "Follow the Leader." Encourage each child to take a turn being the leader. Suggest that the children use as many different foot movements as possible. Remind the children to move forward, backward, and sideways, too.

❖ If you have a soft football, invite interested children to try drop-kicking the football or kicking a stationary football on a tee. Invite the children to look through sports magazines to find pictures of football players. Have the children cut out the pictures and use them to make a football players collage. If you live near a high school, college, or university, invite members of the football team to come visit your classroom and share football information with the class.

Felt

❖ Ask a person who does a lot of arts and crafts to save scraps of felt for your classroom. Give each child a felt square cut into strips. Suggest that the children make a letter F with glue on a sheet of construction paper and arrange the felt pieces along the glue line to make a "Felt F."

❖ Place a different number each day on your flannelboard and invite the children to put the correct number of felt pieces next to the number. Have the children sequence alphabet letters and numbers on the flannelboard, too.

Finger

❖ Cut out a large letter F from light-colored construction paper. Invite the children to lightly pat their index fingers in tempera paint and then make fingerprints on the large F. Show the children that three or four fingerprints together look like a flower.

❖ Discuss what to do when you cut your finger. Wash the cut in running water, dry it off, and then put a bandage on it. Help the children make first-aid posters summarizing the class discussion.

❖ Point out some of the nicknames people have made up for the different fingers. For example, the thumb is sometimes called "thumbkin," the index finger is referred to as "pointer," the middle finger is "tall man," the fourth finger is "ring man," and the little finger is often called "pinky." Encourage the children to predict how each finger might have gotten its nickname. Then teach the children to sing "The Finger Band," "Ten Little Fingers," and "Where Is Thumbkin?" from *Wee Sing Children's Songs and Fingerplays*.

❖ Read *Hand, Hand, Fingers, Thumb* by Al Perkins (see the unit book review). Show the children fingernail files, a fingernail brush, and emery boards. Demonstrate the proper way to clean fingernails. Invite the children to practice cleaning their nails.

❖ Invite the children to fingerpaint. Use an electric mixer to whip two cups of Ivory Snow with 1/2 cup water until creamy. For variety, add a drop of food coloring and sand, salt, or coffee grounds. Encourage the children to smear the mixture all over fingerpaint paper and then use their index fingers to practice making letter F's.

❖ Play the "Finger Game." Call out a number from one to five and ask the children to hold up their hand and show that many fingers. For less experienced children, show the appropriate number of fingers with your hand as a model as you call out the numbers. Invite the children to take turns calling the numbers. Use both hands and the numbers from one to ten for more advanced children.

❖ Show the children several small rubber or plastic finger puppets. Encourage the children to bring finger puppets from home as well. Help the children name each puppet with a word that begins with the letter F, such as Fay, Felix, Flora, Florence, Flower, Floyd, Frances, Frank, Fred, Fritz, and so on. Then provide opportunities for the children to play with the finger puppets.

Fire

❖ Review the school fire-drill rules with the class. Show the children the school fire equipment, such as the fire bell, fire alarm, and fire extinguisher. Discuss how each piece of equipment is used as well.

❖ Discuss the technique of "stop, drop, and roll" for extinguishing clothing fires. Spread mats on the floor and tape inflated balloons to each child's clothing to represent fire. Encourage the children to roll on the mats until the balloons burst and the "fire" is out.

❖ Read *Fire! Fire!* by Gail Gibbons, *Curious George at the Fire Station* by Margret Rey, *The Little Fireman* by Margaret Wise Brown, and *Fire Engines* by Anne Rockwell (see the unit book review). Discuss why we have firefighters. Help the children make a list of questions that they might like to ask a firefighter. Write to a fire station, or arrange for the children to visit one, in order to get answers to their questions.

❖ Discuss what to do in case of a fire. Point out that children should get out of the burning building and go for help. Children can learn to call the fire department or police. Teach the children how to use the 911 emergency number, if it is available in your area.

Fish

❖ Stuff a fish! Cut out two fish patterns (front and back) about the size of a large sheet of white construction paper for each child. Have children paint and then staple around the outside of each fish. Leave one end open for the children to stuff with shredded newspaper. Then staple the ends shut. Hang the stuffed fish from the ceiling for a colorful display.

❖ Talk about fishing. Make a fishing pole by attaching string to a yardstick. Tie a small magnet to the end of the string. Make some small paper fish and attach a paper clip to each. Put the fish inside a "pond" and invite the children to "go fishing." A hula hoop or a large bucket can be used as a pond.

❖ If possible, take your class fishing. Choose a fishing area that has a dock and recruit several adults to supervise. Take a picnic lunch with foods that begin with the letter F, such as fresh fruit, frankfurters, fish-shaped crackers, and fruit juice. Read *Fish Is Fish* and *Swimmy,* both by Leo Lionni (see the unit book review).

❖ Arrange to keep some real goldfish or tropical fish in the classroom for the children to enjoy. You might borrow an aquarium from another classroom or take your class to visit a classroom that has an aquarium.

❖ Have the children make a letter F with a pencil on a sheet of construction paper. Give each child a handful of little fish-shaped crackers. Invite the children to arrange the fish crackers along the pencil line to make a "Fishy F" and then eat the crackers when they are finished.

❖ Teach the children the fingerplay "Five Little Fishes" from *Wee Sing Children's Songs and Fingerplays*.

Five

❖ Read *My Five Book* by Jane B. Moncure (see the unit book review). Teach children to make a number 5 with the instructions "Down, around, and put a cap on it." Encourage the children to practice making 5's. Then give each child an F cut from light-colored construction paper and invite them to make 5's all over the F.

❖ Suggest that children cut out a variety of number 5's from the grocery ad section of the newspaper. Have the children draw a letter F with glue on a sheet of construction paper and then arrange their precut 5's along the glue line to make a "Five's Alive F."

❖ Show the children how to fold a sheet of newsprint into fourths. Have the children write the number 5 in each section. Then encourage the children to count out five fish-shaped crackers to put in each section. Invite the children to eat the snacks when you have checked their sections.

Flag

❖ Show the children examples of several different flags. Point out the symbols on the flags and discuss what each symbol means.

❖ Invite each child to design a flag on a large sheet of white construction paper. Suggest that the children use pencils, markers, crayons, or paint to color their flags. Staple each flag to a dowel stick or a rolled up sheet of newspaper.

❖ Send home a letter requesting parents to send half of a white pillowcase or a piece of white material cut to about that size to school with their child. Explain that the children will tie-dye the material to make a flag. The material need not be hemmed. (Try cutting the material with pinking shears.) Soak all of the material in soapy water to set the dye. Invite the children to select one of the tie-dye patterns provided here. Then tie their material accordingly. Mix dye in a large bucket according to package instructions. Soak the cloth in the dye for approximately twenty minutes. Then rinse the cloth in cool, running water, untie, and hang to dry. Display the flags for all to see.

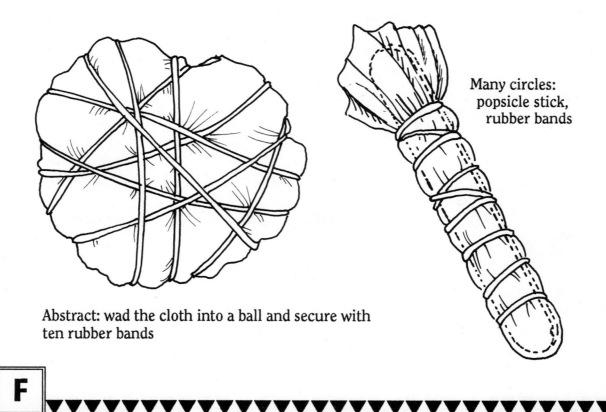

Many circles:
popsicle stick,
rubber bands

Abstract: wad the cloth into a ball and secure with ten rubber bands

Stripes: two rubber bands wrapped tightly at each
place where a stripe is desired

Circle: pull cloth to a
point and wrap with
a rubber band

Circles: twist small sections of cloth and pinch each
section with a clothespin

Flowers

❖ If you have a wallpaper sample book, invite the children to look through the book and find the flowered patterns. Encourage each child to select a favorite page to tear out and cut into strips. Suggest that children exchange some of their strips with friends so that each child has a nice variety. Have the children cut the strips into small squares. Then invite the children to make a letter F with glue on a sheet of construction paper and arrange the flowered wallpaper pieces along the glue line to make a "Flowered F."

❖ Invite the children to cut out pictures of flowers from magazines. Have the children glue their pictures on a piece of construction paper to make a flower collage.

❖ Show the children how to cut a paper plate into a flower shape. Suggest that children paint the circle in the middle yellow and the petals any color. After the flowers have dried, use a black magic marker to trace around the petals.

❖ Make construction-paper flowers. Have the children cut out three circles, each one a different size and color. Show the children how to use scissors to fringe the smallest circle. Invite the children to glue the circles, one on top of the other, starting with the largest circle and ending with the smallest. Bend up the fringed pieces on the smallest circle. Use the flowers to make a "Spring Has Sprung" bulletin board.

❖ Make a paper flower garden on a bulletin board. Invite the children to make a variety of different flowers for the garden. A simple flower may be made by gluing muffin liners to the board. Children need only add a few stems and leaves to complete each flower.

❖ Bring to school any flowers that you might have in your yard. If possible, help the children plant a flower garden at school. Plant flowers individually in milk cartons in your windowsill, in an outside plot, or use a sand or water tray as an indoor flower plot.

Fold

❖ Teach the children to fold washcloths or squares of cloth by matching the corners. Then encourage the children to help with folding the laundry at home.

❖ Provide square sheets of paper for children to practice folding in halves and fourths. Remind the children to match the corners and use their hands to crease the folds. Have the children fold sheets of newsprint into fourths as well. Then have them open the paper and trace over the fold lines with a crayon. Write four upper case and lower case letter sets on the chalkboard and invite the children to copy each set of letters in a different section of their paper. Children may turn their papers over and use the other side as well.

❖ Show small groups of children how to make a fan by folding a sheet of paper accordion style, folding it in half, and then stapling the interior sides together. Suggest that children draw colorful designs on both sides of the paper before folding. Encourage the children to use their fans to cool themselves on a hot day.

Food

❖ Read *The Healthkin Food Train* by Jane B. Moncure and *Foods* by Gloria A. Truitt (see the unit book review). Invite the children to make a collage of their favorite foods. Have the children cut out pictures of their favorite foods from magazines and then glue the pictures to paper plates.

❖ Make "Fantastic French Toast." Encourage the children to name other foods that begin with the letter F, such as figs, fish, flapjacks, fortune cookies, frankfurters, French fries, fruit, and fudge. Invite the children to ask their parents for names of other foods, too.

Fantastic French Toast

sliced bread	Beat the eggs. Add the milk and salt.
1 egg for every 2–3	Soak the bread in the egg mixture and fry
slices of bread	on a heated and greased skillet. Fry until
1/4 tsp oil or butter	both sides are golden brown. Add
(or spray the skillet	toppings, if desired.
with Pam)	
1/2 cup milk	
per egg	
dash salt	
syrup, powdered sugar,	
jelly (optional)	

❖ After lunch each day, help the children identify the foods they ate. Make a list of the foods that begin with the letter F.

❖ Give each child a piece of construction paper and a handful of bran cereal. Have the children draw a large letter F with a pencil on a sheet of construction paper. Then invite the children to arrange the bran flakes along the pencil line to make a "Flaky F." Encourage the children to eat the cereal when they are finished.

Four

❖ Read *My Four Book* by Jane B. Moncure (see the unit book review). Invite the children to practice making number 4's on the chalkboard. Then give each child a precut letter F from light-colored construction paper and encourage them to either write 4's all over the F or cut out a variety of 4's from grocery ads and magazine food ads to glue on the F shape.

❖ Give each child a four-section piece of egg carton. Provide four different items for the children to count, such as fish-shaped crackers, beans, pennies, and popcorn kernels. Invite the children to count four of each item to put in each section of their egg cartons.

❖ Show the children how to fold a sheet of construction paper into four sections. Help them point to each section and count. Give each child ten apple slices. Ask the children to put the correct number of apple slices in each section (one in section 1, two in section 2, and so on). Invite the children to eat the apples after you have checked their work.

❖ Give each child four plastic forks. Ask the children to arrange the forks to make a letter F. Challenge the children to make other letters by arranging three or four forks (A, E, H, I, K, L, M, N, T, V, W, X, Y, and Z).

Friday

❖ Plan a "Fabulous Friday." Encourage each child to bring something from home to share with the class that begins with the letter F, such as a fan, feather, flag, flashlight, flower, or fork.

❖ Help the children locate Friday on a calendar. Then review all of the days of the week. Point out that Friday is the last school day of the week. Encourage the children to recite all of the days of the week.

Friend

❖ Talk about friends. Invite each child to draw a picture of his or her favorite friend. Read *A Friend Is Someone Who Likes You* by Joan W. Anglund, *We Are Best Friends* by Aliki, *Best Friends* by Steven Kellogg, *Friends* by Helme Heine, and *The Berenstain Bears and the Trouble with Friends* by Stan and Janice Berenstain (see the unit book review).

Frog

❖ Teach the children to sing "Little Green Frog" from *Wee Sing Children's Songs and Fingerplays*. Then read *Frog, Where Are You?* by Mercer Mayer and *The Mysterious Tadpole* by Steven Kellogg (see the unit book review).

❖ If possible, catch a frog and bring it to school for the children to observe. An aquarium or goldfish bowl makes a nice holding place. Cover the top with something that has air holes. Release the frog at the end of the day.

❖ Draw pictures of a frog's life. Help the children sequence the pictures. If possible, put tadpoles from a nearby pond in your classroom aquarium. The children may then watch the tadpoles change into frogs.

Fruit

❖ Cut out pictures of different fruits from magazines and glue each picture on a tagboard card. Find pictures of apples, berries, cantaloupes, cherries, coconuts, figs, grapefruits, grapes, lemons, limes, melons, oranges, peaches, pears, pineapples, plums, tangerines, and watermelons. Use the cards as flash cards. Give awards to those children who can correctly name all of the fruits pictured.

❖ Bring real fruit for the children to see and label. Ask each child to bring one fruit from home, such as an apple, banana, nectarine, peach, pear, or tangerine. After the children feel comfortable naming each fruit, put one piece of fruit in a "feely bag." Any type of bag will work, but a cloth bag, such as a pillowcase, is best. Invite children to guess what the fruit is by feeling it through the bag. Discuss why it might be difficult to tell the difference between such fruits as a lemon and lime or a grapefruit and melon. Use the fruits to make "Fabulous Fresh Fruit Salad." Invite the children to sample each fruit as you cut it into bite-size pieces.

Fabulous Fresh Fruit Salad

pineapple tidbits or chunks
various fresh fruits, such as apples, bananas, oranges, pears, peaches, nectarines, tangerines, cherries, grapes, kiwi
canned mandarin oranges (optional)
shredded coconut

Start with the pineapple. Do not drain the juice because it will keep the other fruits from turning brown. Rinse and chop the rest of the fruits. Mix well, coating the fruits with the pineapple juice. Chill or serve. Top with shredded coconut.

❖ Display some fresh and some spoiled or overly ripe fruits. Choose a few pieces of fruit, such as banana slices, to keep on a windowsill. Help the children describe how the fruit looks when it is fresh. Focus the children's attention on the fruit's color, smell, and feel. After the fruit has set for a few days, invite the children to once again describe the fruit. Encourage the children to compare the fresh fruit with the spoiled fruit.

❖ If possible, show the class real figs. Perhaps someone in your class has a fig tree. Explain that figs are eaten by cutting off the top stem and then washing the fig thoroughly. Enjoy the figs with the class.

Furniture

❖ Divide the class into as many groups as you have adult helpers. Assign each group to cut out pictures of furniture for different rooms in a home, such as bathroom, bedroom, kitchen, living room, and den. Have each group glue the pictures they find on a sheet of construction paper to make a collage. Encourage the members of each group to discuss and share the picture collage with the rest of the class.

❖ Cut out pictures of a variety of furniture, such as a bed, dresser or bureau, bookshelf, desk, chair, sofa or couch, and so on. Glue the pictures on tagboard cards and then use them as flash cards to help the children identify the different pieces of furniture. Then help the children sort the cards according to the rooms where each piece of furniture would most likely be found.

❖ Read *From Tree to Table* by Ali Mitgutsch (see the unit book review). Help the children name all the furniture in the classroom that is made from wood.

Food for Thought

Introducing children to a variety of foods is a wonderful way of reinforcing language concepts. The following foods all begin with the letter F and may be introduced at any time during this unit.

figs, fish, fish crackers, flapjacks, flounder fillets, fondue, fortune cookies, frankfurters, French bread, French fries, French toast, fried rice, frosting, fruit, fruit cocktail, fruit roll-ups

Book Review

Children enjoy hearing good books read aloud. The books listed here are favorites of children and may be used to reinforce the letter F.

Adams, Pam. *There Was an Old Lady Who Swallowed a Fly,* Playspaces, 1973.

Aliki. *We Are Best Friends,* Greenwillow Books, 1982.

Anglund, Joan W. *A Friend Is Someone Who Likes You,* Harcourt Brace Jovanovich, 1983.

Arnosky, Jim. *Watching Foxes,* Lothrop, 1984.

Barbaresi, Nina. *A Fox Jumped Up One Winter's Night,* Western Publishing, 1985.

Berenstain, Stan and Berenstain, Janice. *The Berenstain Bears and the Trouble with Friends,* Random House, 1987.

Berenstain, Stan and Berenstain, Janice. *The Berenstain Bears Get in a Fight,* Random House, 1987.

Brown, Margaret Wise. *The Little Fireman,* Harper & Row, 1952.

Buckley, Helen E. *Someday with My Father,* Harper & Row, 1985.

Burgess, Gelett. *The Little Father,* Farrar, Straus and Giroux, 1985.

Ets, Marie H. *In the Forest,* Penguin Books, 1976.

Galdone, Paul. *What's in Fox's Sack?,* Houghton Mifflin, 1982.

Gibbons, Gail. *Fire! Fire!,* Harper & Row, 1987.

Goss, Janet L. and Harste, Jerome C. *It Didn't Frighten Me,* Willowisp Press, 1985.

Heine, Helme. *Friends,* Macmillan, 1986.

Hoban, Russell. *The Little Brute Family,* Avon Books, 1986.

Kellogg, Steven. *Best Friends,* Dial Books, 1986.

Kellogg, Steven. *The Mysterious Tadpole,* Dial Books, 1979.

Lionni, Leo. *Fish Is Fish,* Knopf, 1987.

Lionni, Leo. *Frederick,* Knopf, 1987.

Lionni, Leo. *Swimmy,* Knopf, 1987.

Mayer, Mercer. *Frog, Where Are You?*, Dial Books, 1980.

McGovern, Ann. *Feeling Mad, Sad, Bad, Glad,* Walker and Company, 1978.

Mitgutsch, Ali. *From Tree to Table,* Carolrhoda Books, 1981.

Moncure, Jane B. *My Five Book,* Child's World, 1985.

Moncure, Jane B. *My Four Book,* Child's World, 1985.

Moncure, Jane B. *The Healthkin Food Train,* Child's World, 1982.

Perkins, Al. *Hand, Hand, Fingers, Thumb,* Random House, 1969.

Rey, Margret. *Curious George at the Fire Station,* Houghton Mifflin, 1985.

Rockwell, Anne. *Fire Engines,* E. P. Dutton, 1986.

Rojankovsky, Feodor. *Animals on the Farm,* Knopf, 1967.

Scarry, Richard. *On the Farm,* Western Publishing, 1976.

Seuss, Dr. *The Foot Book,* Random House, 1968.

Tax, Meredith. *Families,* Little, Brown and Company, 1981.

Truitt, Gloria A. *Foods,* Standard Publishers, 1982.

Williams, Garth. *Baby Farm Animals,* Western Publishing, 1983.

Zolotow, Charlotte. *A Father Like That,* Harper & Row, 1971.

Gg

Garbage

❖ Show the children a large garbage bag. Discuss its uses. Then cut the bag into strips. Have each child cut a strip into small squares. Then encourage the children to draw a large letter G with glue on a sheet of construction paper and arrange the garbage bag pieces along the glue line to make a "Garbage Bag G."

❖ Take one large garbage bag outside or give pairs of children several small garbage bags. Encourage the children to fill the bags with papers and trash from the playground and the grounds surrounding the school. Discuss how important it is for everyone to do their part by putting their own trash in a trash can.

Garden

❖ Read *How My Garden Grew* by Anne and Harlow Rockwell and *In My Garden: A Child's Gardening Book* by Helen and Kelly Oechsli (see the unit book review). Help the children plant an outside garden. Plant a few fast-growing vegetables or flowers. Or, if weather or space is a problem, plant a garden inside. A sand or water table makes a nice garden tray.

❖ Invite the children to draw a garden of G's on a bulletin board covered with white construction paper. Help the children draw grass and several stems and leaves. Then invite the children to draw a letter G on top of each stem in an assortment of colors.

Ghost

❖ Make ghost glasses. Help the children cut a strip of black construction paper for a headband. Show the children how to make the ghost lenses from white construction paper. (An adult will need to cut out the inside of each lens.) Staple the lenses to the headband, position the lenses over the child's eyes, and then fasten the headband and lenses around each child's head.

❖ Make "Globby Glue Ghosts." Invite each child to draw a ghost with a pencil or black crayon on a half sheet of notebook paper. Put a sheet of wax paper over each child's ghost drawing. Instruct the children to put glue on the wax paper, following the ghost outline. Encourage the children to use the glue to completely fill in the ghost pattern. In about three days, help the children peel the wax paper off the back of their glue ghosts. Do this carefully so the ghosts will not crack. Invite the children to add two large black eyes with a permanent marker. The glue ghosts will dry a cloudy white and may be hung in a classroom window or from the ceiling.

❖ Read *Grandpa's Ghost Stories* by James Flora and *The Ghost in Dobbs Diner* by Robert Alley (see the unit book review). Encourage the children to share ghost stories with the rest of the class as well. Darken the room and play scary music.

❖ Make "Ghost Treats." Stick a popsicle stick into the bottom of an apple. Cover apples with paper or tissue. Gather the tissue at the base of each apple and tie with green yarn or ribbon. Invite the children to add two green eyes with a magic marker. Make the ghost treats at the beginning of the week and distribute at treat time.

❖ On large sheets of black construction paper, invite each child to draw a simple ghost with white chalk. Have the children paint their ghosts with white tempera paint and then add two black eyes cut from construction paper.

Gift

❖ Invite children to share stories about the best gift they have ever received. Discuss how kindness and love may be considered wonderful gifts. Help the children make a list of kind and loving deeds they might do at home. Then invite the children to fold a sheet of white construction paper in half and draw a picture of a wrapped present on the cover. On the inside, suggest that children draw a picture of a special deed. Encourage the children to take the special gifts home to give to their parents. Read *The Gift* by John Prater (see the unit book review).

❖ Wrap up a small gift for each day of the week. Wrap up items that begin with the letter G, such as gum (sugarless), grapes, gumdrops, and so on. Give a gift each day to the child who earns the most points or tokens.

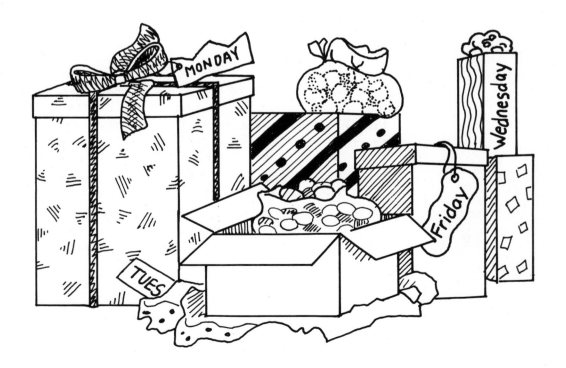

Gingham

❖ *Gingham* will probably be a new word to most children. Explain that gingham is a fabric with checks all the same color. Gather several samples of gingham in different colors and in different-sized checks. (Ask someone who sews to save you gingham scraps.) Invite each child to stand up in turn. Ask the class to decide whether the standing child is wearing gingham. Cut some of the gingham into strips. Ask the children to snip the strips into small squares. Have the children make a letter G with glue on a sheet of construction paper and arrange the gingham pieces along the glue line to make a "Gingham G."

❖ Instruct the children to fold a sheet of green construction paper into fourths. Have the children write a number from one to ten in each section (in sequential or random order). Then have the children count an appropriate number of gingham pieces to place in each section.

Girls

❖ Write several girls' names on the chalkboard. Have the children copy each name on their own papers. Less experienced children might only write the first letter of each name. Or, give the children a typewritten list of all the names. Then instruct the children to circle all the upper case and lower case G's with a green crayon.

❖ Write several girls' names on flash cards. Then encourage the children to use the cards to learn all of the names.

❖ Have the children cut out pictures from magazines of girls to glue on a sheet of newsprint. Label the finished collage "G Is for Girls."

❖ Glue pictures of girls and boys on tagboard cards. Help the children sort the cards into the categories "boys" and "girls." Challenge more advanced children to subdivide the categories into "boys," "men," "girls," and "women."

Globe

❖ Show the children a globe. Help the children locate their state and other places of interest. Point out that the water is blue on the globe, mountains are brown, land is green, and so on. Encourage the class to decide whether the Earth has more land or more water by looking at the globe.

Go

❖ Read *Things That Go* by Anne Rockwell and *Richard Scarry's Cars and Trucks and Things That Go* by Richard Scarry (see the unit book review). Invite the children to make a collage of different modes of transportation, such as bicycles, cars, airplanes, vans, buses, and boats. Encourage the children to cut out pictures of each type of transportation from magazines and glue the pictures on a sheet of green construction paper to make a collage.

❖ Explain to the children that before cars were invented, people used horses to travel from place to place. Encourage the children to practice galloping like a horse—fast and slow. Have the children gallop to music, too.

Gold

❖ Have the children make a letter G with glue on a piece of construction paper. Then invite the children to sprinkle gold glitter over the glue. When the glue dries, have the children gently shake off the excess glitter to reveal a "Golden G." Display the letters on a bulletin board with the title "Go for the Gold!"

❖ Help the children make a list of gold items, such as jewelry, teeth fillings, and so on. Buy some goldfish for your classroom. Put the fish in a goldfish bowl for the children to enjoy. Discuss why these fish are probably called goldfish.

Graham Crackers

❖ Make "Great Grahams," a graham cracker treat.

Great Grahams

peanut butter
graham crackers
miniature marshmallows
raisins

Spread peanut butter on graham crackers. Arrange miniature marshmallows on top in the shape of a G. Broil for a few minutes until the marshmallow tops are golden. Then arrange raisins in the shape of a G on each cracker.

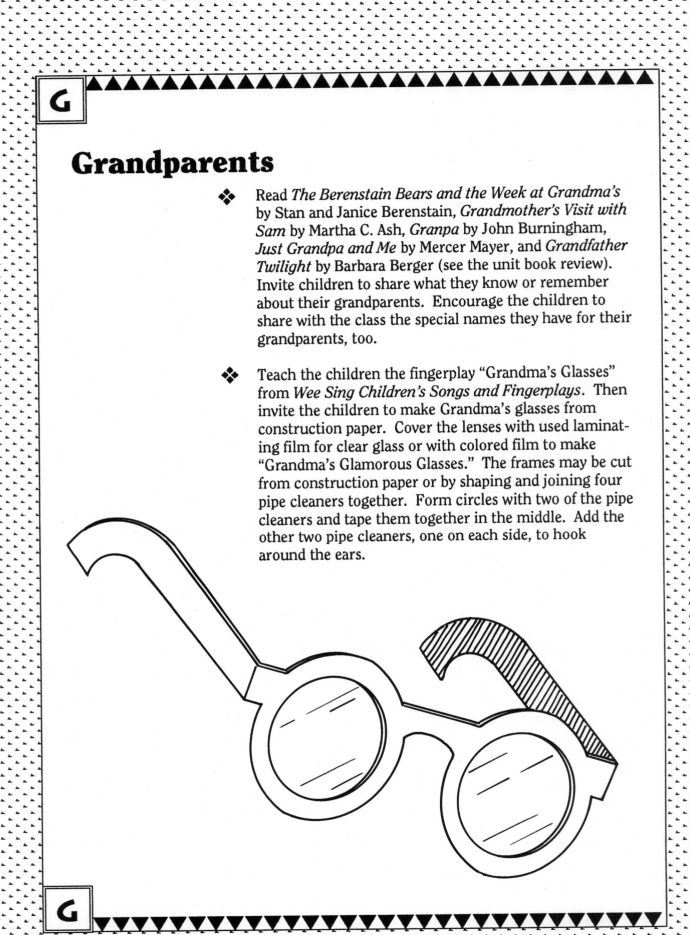

Grandparents

❖ Read *The Berenstain Bears and the Week at Grandma's* by Stan and Janice Berenstain, *Grandmother's Visit with Sam* by Martha C. Ash, *Granpa* by John Burningham, *Just Grandpa and Me* by Mercer Mayer, and *Grandfather Twilight* by Barbara Berger (see the unit book review). Invite children to share what they know or remember about their grandparents. Encourage the children to share with the class the special names they have for their grandparents, too.

❖ Teach the children the fingerplay "Grandma's Glasses" from *Wee Sing Children's Songs and Fingerplays*. Then invite the children to make Grandma's glasses from construction paper. Cover the lenses with used laminating film for clear glass or with colored film to make "Grandma's Glamorous Glasses." The frames may be cut from construction paper or by shaping and joining four pipe cleaners together. Form circles with two of the pipe cleaners and tape them together in the middle. Add the other two pipe cleaners, one on each side, to hook around the ears.

Granola

❖ Make "Glorious Granola." Invite the children to taste each ingredient before you mix all of the ingredients together. When finished, check to see if the children can recall each ingredient.

Glorious Granola

1 cup oatmeal	Mix all of the ingredients together in a bowl. Spread the mixture on a cookie sheet and bake 8–10 minutes at 350°. Cool on paper towels. Break up when cool.
1/3 cup wheat germ	
1/4 cup coconut	
1/4 cup sunflower seeds	
1/4 cup powdered milk	
1 tsp cinnamon	
2 Tbsp honey	
1 Tbsp oil	
1 tsp vanilla	
1/2 cup chopped dates, raisins, chopped nuts, or chopped dried fruit (optional)	
1/4 cup sesame seeds (optional)	

Grape

❖ Make sugarless grape drink as a special treat.

❖ Show the children bunches of red, green, and purple grapes. Help the children describe the grapes using all of their senses, except taste. Then show the children how to draw a simple picture of grapes. Invite the children to taste each type of grape. Ask the children to vote on their favorite kind. Graph the results. Then use the grapes to make "Great Grapes."

Great Grapes

seedless grapes (a combination of red, green, and black)	Rinse the grapes and separate from their stems. Give each child a cone to fill with grapes.
1 ice-cream cone per child	

Grapefruit

❖ Invite the children to help make "Broiled Grapefruit." Encourage the children to taste some of the grapefruit before it is broiled, too. Discuss which grapefruit they like better.

Broiled Grapefruit

grapefruit brown sugar mint sprigs	Cut the grapefruit into slices (about 5–6 slices per grapefruit). Sprinkle with brown sugar and put the slices under the broiler for a few minutes until the sugar bubbles. Decorate with a sprig of mint in the middle of each slice.

❖ Explain that grapefruit is a fruit. Help the children recall other fruits. Encourage the children to compare the taste, size, color, and texture of grapefruit with other familiar fruits. Invite the children to taste white and pink grapefruit. Invite the principal or another teacher to join the children in a taste-testing party. Vote on which kind of grapefruit the children and guests prefer. Serve some grapefruit juice.

Grass

❖ Find a patch of grass that needs to be mowed. Get permission for the children to gently pull up small blades of grass without pulling up the roots. Collect the grass in a paper bag. In the classroom, have the children make a letter G with glue on a sheet of construction paper. Invite the children to sprinkle blades of grass over the glue. After the glue dries, have the children shake off the excess grass to reveal a "Grassy G."

❖ Cut a green sponge into the shape of the letter G. Wet the sponge and then put it in the bottom of a shallow plate. Add a little water to the dish as needed to keep the sponge damp, but not soggy. Invite the children to sprinkle grass seed on the wet sponge and watch grass sprout and grow. Teach the children to sing "The Green Grass Grows All Around" from *Wee Sing Silly Songs*.

❖ Put potting soil or dirt in small butter tubs, one for each child. Invite the children to use markers to draw a face on the tubs. Help the children plant grass seed in the soil according to package directions. The growing green grass becomes green hair.

Gray

❖ Discuss items that are gray. Put large dabs of white and black fingerpaint on fingerpaint paper. Invite the children to mix the colors with their fingers to make gray. When the gray paint is smeared all over the fingerpaint paper, have children use their index fingers to practice making G's.

Green

❖ Read *Green Eggs and Ham* by Dr. Seuss (see the unit book review). Scramble some eggs for the children. Add green food coloring as you scramble the eggs. Serve with small slices of chopped ham. Ask the children to vote on whether they like green eggs and ham. Graph the results.

❖ Make a green collage. Encourage children to cut out pictures of green objects from magazines. Have the children glue their pictures on a bulletin board covered with green paper.

❖ Add green food coloring to a container of glue. Have each child draw a letter G with a pencil on a sheet of construction paper. Then invite the children to follow the outline with the green glue. The glue will dry green.

❖ Put large dabs of blue and yellow fingerpaint on sheets of fingerpaint paper. Ask the children to predict what color these two colors will make when they are mixed together. Then invite the children to use their index fingers to mix the colors and discover green. Add more green and yellow paint to some children's papers to make different shades of green. Encourage the children to smear the fingerpaint all over the paper and then practice making G's. When the pictures are dry, display them together so that children may see the different shades of green. Read *Little Blue and Little Yellow* by Leo Lionni (see the unit book review).

❖ Get some fresh green beans. Cook the green beans and invite the children to taste them. Point out that beans are a vegetable. Help the children compare beans with other green vegetables, such as peas, broccoli, Brussels sprouts, spinach, mustard greens, and asparagus.

Grits

❖ Have the children make a letter G with glue on a piece of construction paper. Then invite the children to sprinkle grits over the glue (quick-cooking grits work best). After the glue is dry, have the children gently shake off the excess grits to reveal a "Gritty G." Next day, when the grits are thoroughly dry, encourage the children to close their eyes and feel the shape and texture of the G.

❖ Cook some quick-cooking grits for the children to taste. Serve with butter or make an instant gravy to put over the grits. Make green grits by adding a few drops of green food coloring to the cooking water.

Groceries

❖ Have the children fold a sheet of paper in half and then open up the paper to reveal two columns. Suggest that they trace over the fold line with a crayon. Ask the children to write "Grocery Store" on one side and "Furniture Store" on the other. Then encourage the children to look through magazines to find pictures of items they might buy at each type of store. Instruct the children to cut out and glue the pictures on the appropriate sides. Or you may precut pictures and have the children sort the pictures to glue under the appropriate headings.

❖ Read *The Supermarket* by Anne and Harlow Rockwell (see the unit book review). Ask the children if they know the name of the grocery store where their families shop. Invite the children to find pictures of groceries to glue on small brown paper bags. Encourage the children to find pictures of packaged foods as they would appear in the grocery store.

❖ If possible, arrange for the class to tour a grocery store. Schedule your trip with the manager so you may take the children during a slow time at the store. Point out the fresh fruits and vegetables in the produce section. Explain also that grocery stores are divided into sections. For example, cereals are grouped together, breads are placed in one section, frozen foods have their own section, and so on. Give each child a card that has a picture of a food item glued on it. Invite the children to work with a partner to find the items on their cards. Have the children write down the aisle number where they found each item.

❖ Set up a "Grocery Center" in the classroom. Encourage the children to bring empty boxes, milk cartons, and other grocery containers from home. Check for cans with sharp corners and tape everything shut. Grocery store setups may be ordered commercially, but you can make your own with shelves, a large refrigerator box with a window cut in it, or an old three-piece puppet theater. Scout around for other items to add, such as a play cash register, play money, paper bags for bagging the groceries, butcher-type aprons for the storekeeper, baskets for shopping, and so on. Look around your own grocery store, too, and ask the manager for any "freebies" that might make your classroom grocery store look more authentic.

Guidance

❖ If you have a guidance counselor in your school, this is a good time to ask him or her to come into your classroom to speak to the children. Ask if your class might schedule a few group guidance lessons on improving self-esteem or some other topic. Arrange for the children to visit the guidance counselor's office as well.

Guitar

❖ Ask the music teacher, or someone who plays the guitar, to show the children a guitar and demonstrate how it is played.

❖ Demonstrate how a guitar and other similar stringed instruments sound. Punch a hole in the center of the bottom of an empty coffee can. Cut a long piece of sturdy string. Tie one end of the string to a paper clip and insert the other end through the hole in the coffee can from the inside of the can out. Set the can upside down on the floor and pull the string up tightly with one hand while holding the can down with your foot. Pluck the string with the other hand. Ask the children to predict whether the sound will become higher or lower as you pull more tightly on the string. Then try it!

Gum

❖ Introduce the children to sugarless chewing gum and bubble gum. Use sugarless gum as a reinforcer for treats. Remind the children where to dispose of their gum when they are finished and how to wrap their gum in a piece of paper so that it will not stick to the sides of a trash can.

❖ Show the children how to draw a simple picture of a gumball machine and a stick of gum.

Food for Thought

Introducing children to a variety of foods is a wonderful way of reinforcing language concepts. The following foods all begin with the letter G and may be introduced at any time during this unit.

garbanzo beans, garlic bread, Gatorade, goulash, graham crackers, granola, grapefruit, grapefruit juice, grape juice, grapes, Greek salad, green beans, greens, green split peas, grits, ground beef, guava, gumbo

Book Review

Children enjoy hearing good books read aloud. The books listed here are favorites of children and may be used to reinforce the letter G.

Alley, Robert. *The Ghost in Dobbs Diner,* Parents Magazine Press, 1981.

Ash, Martha C. *Grandmother's Visit with Sam,* Doris Publications, 1985.

Berenstain, Stan and Berenstain, Janice. *The Berenstain Bears and the Week at Grandma's,* Random House, 1986.

Berger, Barbara. *Grandfather Twilight,* Putnam Publishing Group, 1986.

Bornstein, Ruth. *Little Gorilla,* Ticknor & Fields, 1986.

Burningham, John. *Granpa,* Crown, 1985.

Flora, James. *Grandpa's Ghost Stories,* Macmillan, 1978.

Keats, Ezra Jack. *Goggles!*, Macmillan, 1987.

Krasilovsky, Phyllis. *Very Little Girl*, Doubleday, 1953.

Lionni, Leo. *Little Blue and Little Yellow*, Astor-Honor, 1959.

Mayer, Mercer. *Just Grandpa and Me*, Western Publishing, 1985.

Oechsli, Helen and Oechsli, Kelly. *In My Garden: A Child's Gardening Book*, Macmillan, 1985.

Prater, John. *The Gift*, Penguin Books, 1987.

Rockwell, Anne and Rockwell, Harlow. *How My Garden Grew*, Macmillan, 1982.

Rockwell, Anne and Rockwell, Harlow. *The Supermarket*, Macmillan, 1979.

Rockwell, Anne. *Things That Go*, E. P. Dutton, 1986.

Scarry, Richard. *Richard Scarry's Cars and Trucks and Things That Go*, Western Publishing, 1974.

Seuss, Dr. *Green Eggs and Ham*, Random House, 1987.

Showers, Paul. *Where Does the Garbage Go?*, Harper & Row, 1974.

Hair

❖ Read *Michael's New Haircut* by Karen G. Frandsen (see the unit book review). Discuss how children should take care of their hair to keep it looking nice and clean. Point out that they should wash their hair often, comb and brush it at least daily, have regular haircuts, and eat well-balanced meals.

❖ Label a comb and brush. Show the children how to properly comb and brush one's hair.

❖ Survey the class to see what hair color is most prominent. Discuss colors that hair might be, such as black, gray, blonde, brunette, and auburn.

❖ Invite each child to draw a self-portrait of his or her head showing the face and hair. Provide appropriate colors of yarn for the children to glue on their portraits for hair.

Hammer

❖ Help the children hammer nails into soft wood to make a letter H. Start the nails so they will be correctly placed. Teach the children to sing "Peter Hammers" from *Wee Sing Children's Songs and Fingerplays* (change the words to "Harry Hammers").

Hands

❖ Teach the children to sing "He's Got the Whole World in His Hands" from *Wee Sing Around the Campfire* and the fingerplay "Clap Your Hands" from *Wee Sing Children's Songs and Fingerplays*.

❖ Read *Hold My Hand* by Charlotte Zolotow, *My Hands* by Aliki, and *Hand, Hand, Fingers, Thumb* by Al Perkins (see the unit book review). Help the children make a list of what they can do with their hands, such as wave, clap, brush hair, write, and so on. Help the children learn to play "Drop the Handkerchief" from *Wee Sing and Play*.

❖ Glue copies of a poem about hands on large sheets of construction paper. Give one sheet to each child. Brush tempera paint on the children's palms. (Paint one hand at a time!) Then invite the children to carefully print their handprints on the margins of their poems, one print on each side.

❖ Trace and cut out handprints of each child. Hold up each set of handprints for the class to see and then ask the children to guess whose hands the prints belong to. Then label the handprint pictures with the appropriate child's name. Write all the jobs in the classroom (plant waterer, line leader, paper passer, and so on) on strips of tagboard. Pin the strips on a bulletin board labeled "Helping Hands." Discuss each job with the class. Then, at the beginning of each day, pin a different set of handprints next to each job. The children who have their handprints posted are assigned these jobs for the day.

❖ Teach the children to do "The Hokey Pokey" (from *Wee Sing and Play*) using their hips, hands, hair, heads, and heels.

❖ Discuss the importance of keeping the hands clean, especially before eating. This is a good time to make sure each child is washing his or her hands appropriately.

Happy

❖ Encourage the children to draw a happy face. Then teach the children to sing "If You're Happy" from *Wee Sing Children's Songs and Fingerplays*.

❖ Read *Oh, Were They Ever Happy!* by Peter Spier (see the unit book review). Invite each child to share with the class what makes him or her happy. Write each child's idea on a strip of tagboard. Then help the children sort the strips into categories, such as "toys," "love," "food," and so on.

❖ Look for happy face stickers to use as reinforcers for good work or behavior. You might also use a rubber stamp to print a happy face on the children's papers. Use the rubber stamp to print a happy face on the back of each child's hand as well.

Hat

❖ Read *Old Hat, New Hat* by Stan and Janice Berenstain and *Martin's Hats* by Joan W. Blos (see the unit book review). Sponsor a Hat Day. Invite the children to bring hats from home to wear for the day. Show the children how to draw a picture of a simple hat. Suggest that children draw pictures of their favorite hats.

❖ Make a quick and easy crown hat for each child using a roll of corrugated bulletin-board border. Cut and staple together a piece for each child, depending on his or her head size.

❖ Make a collage of pictures of hats. Have the children cut out pictures from magazines. Then invite the children to glue the pictures on sheets of construction paper. Display the finished collages in the shape of an H on a bulletin board.

❖ Encourage each child to count as far as he or she is able. More advanced children may practice counting to one hundred. Make a "Hundred Hat" for any child who counts to one hundred, or choose another number that all children in your classroom might be able to count to. Make the hats from construction paper.

Hearing

❖ Encourage the children to put their heads down on their desks and close their eyes. Have the children listen quietly for sixty seconds and then recall the sounds they heard. If possible, play environmental recordings or other recordings of sounds for the children to listen to and identify.

❖ Read *Hearing* by Richard L. Allington and Kathleen Krull (see the unit book review). Invite each child to bring something to school that makes a sound. Encourage the children to bring their items in paper sacks to keep them a secret. Ask an adult helper to invite each child to go to another room and tape record his or her object's sound. When all the sounds have been recorded, invite the children to bring their sack of items with them and sit in a circle on the floor with you. Then play the tape. Stop after each sound to encourage the children to guess what the sound might be. Then replay the tape, again stopping after each sound. This time have the child who made the sound stand up, turn his or her back to the children, and take the object out of the bag to make the sound live. If the children still do not know the sound, invite the child to turn around and show the children the secret object!

❖ Read *Bert and Ernie's Harmonica Book* by David Korr (see the unit book review). Bring in a harmonica or a horn for the children to hear. Invite the children to make sounds with the instruments, too.

Heart

❖ Show the children how to make a heart using one of the methods shown here. Invite the children to use the hearts they cut out to make a heart collage. Encourage the children to make the hearts from any color of construction paper.

Fold a sheet of paper in half and slant a tongue depressor on the fold. Trace around the tongue depressor and cut.

Fold a sheet of paper in half with the fold on the left-hand side for a right-handed person. Place your left thumb on the fold and draw around the thumb and cut.

Fold a sheet of paper in half with the fold on the left. Think about making the number 2. Start the 2 on the fold. After going "around" come back to the fold. Cut.

❖ Ask each child to trace around a large heart pattern on white construction paper. Then have the children cut out the hearts. Next, invite each child to smear any color or colors of fingerpaint on a piece of fingerpaint paper and place his or her white heart on the fingerpainting, pressing gently all over. Help the children carefully pick up the white hearts to save the fingerpainted prints. Display the hearts on a bulletin board with the title "You've Gotta Have Heart."

Height

❖ Measure each child's height. Write the heights on cards for the children to take home and share with their families.

Hide

❖ Read *Would You Like to Play Hide-and-Seek in This Book with Lovable, Furry Old Grover?* by Jon Stone (see the unit book review). If possible, take the children outside to play "Hide-and-Seek." Use the choosing rhyme "Hot Potato" from *Wee Sing and Play* to select a child to be "it." Designate a "base," such as a tree. Explain that as "it" covers his or her eyes and counts to ten, the other children are to find a hiding place in the defined area. When "it" finishes counting, he or she says, "Ready or not, here I come" and tries to find and tag one of the hidden children. If the children get to "base" without being tagged, they're safe. The first child tagged is the next "it" and the game starts over. For less experienced children, eliminate the "base." The first hidden child found becomes "it."

❖ Play "What Is Hiding?" Choose four to six items that the children know. Consider using all H items, such as a hammer, hat, heart, hanger, hot rod, or a jar of honey. Arrange the items in a row in front of the children and help the children name each one. Ask the children to close their eyes. Hide one of the items under the table and invite the children to open their eyes and try to guess which item is missing. The child who guesses correctly is invited to come up and hide another item.

Holes

❖ Invite the children to practice using a hole puncher. This is a good task to handle in small groups as most children will not be familiar with a hole puncher. Cut a large letter H from construction or typing paper. Then encourage the children to punch holes in the H.

❖ Place a hole puncher, construction-paper circles about 3 inches in diameter, and a basket in a learning center somewhere in your classroom. Provide opportunities for each child to visit the center and practice punching holes. Suggest that they hold the paper circles over the basket and then punch holes all around the circles (save the punched-out dots for making H's later).

❖ Give each child three construction-paper strips. Make one strip shorter than the other two. Mark dots all the way around the outside edges of the strips. Then encourage the children to punch a hole at each dot. When all the dots have been punched, have the children put their three strips together to form an H. Glue the strips to a sheet of construction paper.

Home

❖ Help the children make a list of activities that are done at home, such as vacuuming, washing dishes, taking a bath, sweeping, talking on the phone, reading a book, washing hands, and eating. Explain that you are going to act out something that is done at home and the children are invited to guess what each pantomime might be. Encourage the first child who guesses correctly to act out a new motion.

❖ Discuss why we have homes. Invite the children to use precut shapes to make a house. For example, a large rectangle might be used for a house or apartment building, a triangle could be used for the roof, two small rectangles put together could be the door, and so on. Ask the children to identify each shape they use and then glue the shapes on a paper-covered bulletin board to make an entire neighborhood. Read *The Little House* by Virginia L. Burton, *I Can Build a House* by Shigeo Watanabe, *The House That Jack Built* by Rodney Peppe, and *Building a House* by Byron Barton (see the unit book review).

❖ Make mobiles. Give the children several different shapes cut from construction paper. Invite the children to use magazines to cut out pictures of people or objects found in homes. Have the children glue the pictures on the construction-paper shapes. Punch a hole in the top of each shape, attach string, and hang the shapes from coat hangers.

❖ If you have a miniature dollhouse in your classroom, take out all of the furniture and help the children identify the pieces. Then encourage children to group the furniture according to the room in which the furniture might be found.

❖ Make a playhouse for the children. Use a large furniture or refrigerator box. Cut out a door and windows. Invite the children to paint the house.

❖ Glue pictures of household items on tagboard cards to use as flash cards. Use magazines to find pictures of a broom, sofa, bed, washing machine, vacuum, iron, dresser, table, chairs, garbage can, and so on.

❖ Send homework home with the children. You might send home a sheet of H's to copy or an assignment where children draw pictures of their houses or apartments.

Hop

❖ Encourage the children to hop across the floor on one foot and then back across the floor on the other. Play music for the children to hop to as well. Then sponsor hopping relays. Serve carrots as treats!

❖ Make a large letter H with tape on the floor, or draw a large letter H with chalk outside on the playground. Then invite each child to hop along the H.

❖ Teach children the "Bunny Hop." If you know the tune, sing the verse. Otherwise, just say the words. Ask the music teacher for a recording. The bunny hop is done by having the children line up behind one another, each child placing both hands on the waist of the child in front. Teach the steps first in a straight line and then after the children learn the steps with the words, form a bunny hop line. Have fun!

❖ Teach the class to play "H-H-Hopscotch." Draw a simple hopscotch pattern in the shape of an H. The size of the squares should be appropriate for the children. Number each of the five squares. The hopscotch pattern and numbers may be made with tape on the floor or drawn with chalk on the playground outside. Give each child a coin, pebble, or bottle cap to throw. This will be called his or her "hoppie." Have each child stand at the starting line and throw the hoppie into square #1. If successful, invite the child to hop on one foot *over* square #1 and into squares #2, #3, #4, and #5 consecutively. Then turn around and hop back into square #4, #3, and #2, bend over to pick up the hoppie in square #1, and then hop *over* square #1 again and out. If this is done successfully, the child repeats the procedure for square #2 and so on, until all five squares are finished. If at any time the child misses the throw, steps on a line, steps out of a box, or puts two feet in a box, he or she loses a turn and returns the hoppie to the last square to be successfully completed. The next child in line is then invited to take a turn and so on until someone finishes all the squares. Have less experienced children hop in each square once without turning around and hopping back. The game may be adapted in any way that will make it easy and fun for the children!

Horse

❖ Read *Once We Had a Horse* by Glen Rounds and *Black Horse* by Marianna Mayer (see the unit book review). Show the children how to draw horses using upper and lower case H's.

❖ If horseshoes are available, teach the children to play a game of horseshoes. Then sponsor a "Horseshoe-Throwing Contest."

Hospital

❖ Read *A Visit to the Sesame Street Hospital* by Deborah Hantzig (see the unit book review). Invite children who have been in the hospital to share their experiences with the rest of the class.

❖ Discuss what to do when a person is hurt. Give each child three first-aid bandages. Show the children how to take the paper off the bandage without touching the gauze part. Have the children use three bandages to make a letter H on a small sheet of construction paper.

Hot

❖ Help the children make a list of hot-weather clothing, such as shorts, swimsuits, T-shirts, and so on. Invite the children to draw a picture of a setting for a hot day. Use yellow construction paper. Then have the children cut out pictures from magazines of people dressed for a hot day and glue the pictures on their drawings.

❖ Play "Hot Potato." Invite the children to sit in a circle on the floor. Play music as the children pass a "hot potato" (bean bag) around the circle from child to child. The child left holding the potato when the music stops leaves the circle. The last child left in the circle wins.

❖ Teach the children the choosing rhyme "Hot Potato" from *Wee Sing and Play*. Suggest that children use this rhyme to determine who is "it" for a game, who is first, or who is line leader, and so on.

Hula Hoop

❖ If available, have several hula hoops in your classroom for the children to enjoy. (You might borrow these from a physical education teacher.) Hold a hula hoop on its side and invite the children to crawl through it. Put a hoop on the floor and encourage the children to jump in and out, around, and so on. Challenge the children to try to roll the hoop on its side. Sponsor a contest to see who can roll the hoop the farthest. Suggest that interested children try twirling the hoop on its side, too.

❖ Teach the children how to twirl a hula hoop around their waists by moving their hips. Challenge the children to try to twirl the hoop around an arm or leg as well.

Hungry

❖ Discuss with the children what they like to eat when they are really hungry. Encourage the children to cut out pictures from magazines of their favorite foods. Have the children glue their pictures on paper plates. Help the children identify all of the food pictures that begin with the letter H. Encourage the children to point out the foods on the school lunch menu each day that begin with the letter H as well, such as hot dogs, hamburgers, ham, and so on.

❖ Sponsor an "H Foodfest." Invite parents as guests. Serve "Hurry-Up Honey Butter on Honey Bread," hot chocolate, "Hot Dog Hot Rods," and "Homemade Heavenly Hash." Encourage the children to help make and serve the food as well.

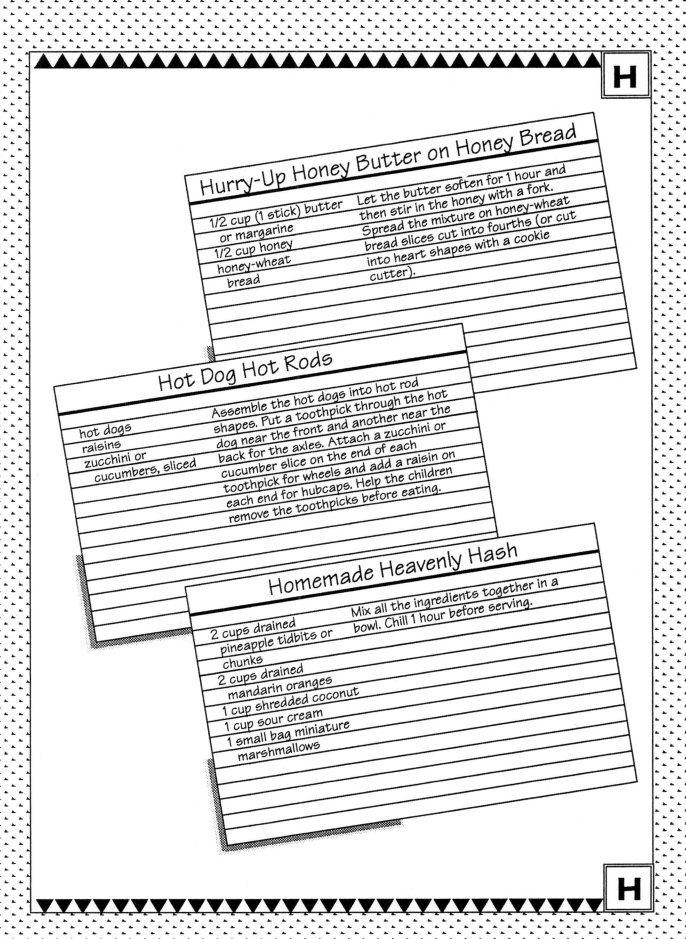

Hurry-Up Honey Butter on Honey Bread

1/2 cup (1 stick) butter
or margarine
1/2 cup honey
honey-wheat
bread

Let the butter soften for 1 hour and
then stir in the honey with a fork.
Spread the mixture on honey-wheat
bread slices cut into fourths (or cut
into heart shapes with a cookie
cutter).

Hot Dog Hot Rods

hot dogs
raisins
zucchini or
cucumbers, sliced

Assemble the hot dogs into hot rod
shapes. Put a toothpick through the hot
dog near the front and another near the
back for the axles. Attach a zucchini or
cucumber slice on the end of each
toothpick for wheels and add a raisin on
each end for hubcaps. Help the children
remove the toothpicks before eating.

Homemade Heavenly Hash

2 cups drained
pineapple tidbits or
chunks
2 cups drained
mandarin oranges
1 cup shredded coconut
1 cup sour cream
1 small bag miniature
marshmallows

Mix all the ingredients together in a
bowl. Chill 1 hour before serving.

Food for Thought

Introducing children to a variety of foods is a wonderful way of reinforcing language concepts. The following foods all begin with the letter H and may be introduced at any time during this unit.

ham, hamburger, hash, hazelnuts, hickory nuts, hoagie, hominy grits, honey, honey bread, honey butter, honeydew melon, hors d'oeuvres, horseradish, hot chocolate, hot dog, hot sauce, hush puppies

Book Review

Children enjoy hearing good books read aloud. The books listed here are favorites of children and may be used to reinforce the letter H.

Aliki. *My Hands,* Harper & Row, 1962.

Allington, Richard L. and Krull, Kathleen. *Hearing,* Raintree Publications, 1985.

Barton, Byron. *Building a House,* Greenwillow Books, 1981.

Berenstain, Stan and Berenstain, Janice. *Old Hat, New Hat,* Random House, 1970.

Blos, Joan W. *Martin's Hats,* William Morrow and Company, 1984.

Burton, Virginia L. *The Little House,* Houghton Mifflin, 1942.

Carle, Eric. *The Very Hungry Caterpillar,* Putnam Publishing Group, 1986.

Frandsen, Karen G. *Michael's New Haircut,* Childrens Press, 1986.

Galdone, Paul. *The Little Red Hen,* Houghton Mifflin, 1985.

Ginsberg, Mirra. *The Sun's Asleep Behind the Hill,* Greenwillow Books, 1982.

Hantzig, Deborah. *A Visit to the Sesame Street Hospital,* Random House, 1985.

Korr, David. *Bert and Ernie's Harmonica Book,* Harper & Row, 1987.

Mayer, Marianna. *Black Horse,* Dial Books, 1984.

Peppe, Rodney. *The House That Jack Built,* Delacorte, 1985.

Perkins, Al. *Hand, Hand, Fingers, Thumb,* Random House, 1969.

Rounds, Glen. *Once We Had a Horse,* Holiday House, 1971.

Spier, Peter. *Oh, Were They Ever Happy!,* Doubleday, 1978.

Stone, Jon. *Would You Like to Play Hide-and-Seek in This Book with Lovable, Furry Old Grover?,* Random House, 1976.

Watanabe, Shigeo. *I Can Build a House,* Putnam Publishing Group, 1985.

Zolotow, Charlotte. *The Hating Book,* Harper & Row, 1969.

Zolotow, Charlotte. *Hold My Hand,* Harper & Row, 1987.

Ii

Ice

❖ Help the children make "Iced Tea." Make lemon ice cubes for the iced tea by freezing a small wedge of lemon in each slot with water in an ice-cube tray. Then invite the children to enjoy drinking the tea as you read *Ice Is...Whee!* by Carol Greene (see the unit book review).

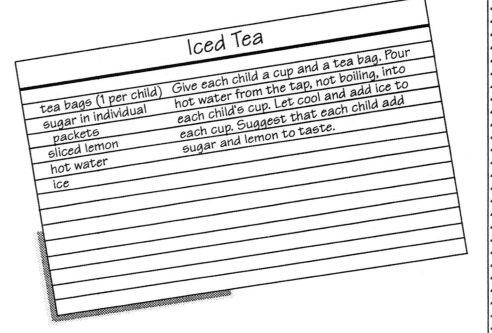

Iced Tea

tea bags (1 per child)	Give each child a cup and a tea bag. Pour
sugar in individual packets	hot water from the tap, not boiling, into each child's cup. Let cool and add ice to
sliced lemon	each cup. Suggest that each child add sugar and lemon to taste.
hot water	
ice	

❖ Sponsor an "Ice-Cream Social." Invite parents as guests. Make "Incredible Ice Cream" and "Instant Ice-Cream Floats." Invite the children and guests to sample various flavors of commercial ice creams as well. Ask the guests and children to vote on their favorite flavors. Graph the results. Read *What Was It Before It Was Ice Cream?* by

Colleen Reece and *From Milk to Ice Cream* by Ali
Mitgutsch (see the unit book review).

Incredible Ice Cream

Mix together all of the ingredients and freeze.

2 eggs
1 cup evaporated milk
1 cup condensed milk
1/2 gal whole milk
2 cups sugar
1 Tbsp vanilla

Instant Ice-Cream Floats

Add one scoop of ice cream to each glass
of ginger ale or cola.

vanilla ice cream
ginger ale or cola

❖ Show the children how to draw a simple picture of an ice-
cream cone. Suggest that they color the ice cream their
favorite flavor.

Incense

❖ Burn a different scent of incense each day. Ask the children to identify each scent. Incense is sold at most card shops in the candle section of the store.

Inch

❖ Measure the height of the children to the nearest inch. Read *Inch by Inch* by Leo Lionni (see the unit book review).

❖ Give each child a ruler. Help the children find the inch marks on their rulers. Call out the numbers one to twelve sequentially and then in random order. Help the children find each number on their rulers.

Initials

❖ Make "Incredible Initials." Write each child's initials on a large sheet of white construction paper. Invite each child to use glue to trace over his or her initials. Then help the children sprinkle glitter over the glue. When the glue is dry, have the children gently shake off the extra glitter. Encourage the children to draw a self-portrait and label the picture "I." Ask the children to dictate a sentence about something they like about themselves or some-thing that they do well. Encourage children to start their sentences with the word *I*. Write the dictated sentences under their self-portraits. Display the self-portraits and the initials together on a bulletin board.

❖ Play "Who am I?" Invite each child to record a clue about himself or herself on a tape recorder. Help each child think of a clue, such as "I ride the bus to school." Have the children end their statements with "Who am I?" Record a clue for yourself, too. When each child has had a turn, play the tape for the class and see if the children can identify each voice they hear.

Insects

❖ Read *An Insect's Body* by Joanna Cole and *Little Bug* by Dick Gackenbach (see the unit book review). Point out that insects have six legs and three body parts—a head, thorax, and abdomen. Help the children name as many insects as possible, such as a mosquito, fly, bumblebee, flea, roach, beetle, wasp, termite, cricket, grasshopper, ant, butterfly, hornet, moth, and dragonfly.

Instruments

❖ Ask the music teacher to show the children various musical instruments and then play a few of them for the class. Display pictures of different instruments on the bulletin board. If possible, arrange for the children to visit an elementary or senior-high band rehearsal or concert.

❖ Invite the children to experiment with a variety of rhythm instruments. Help the children learn the name of each instrument.

Iris

❖ Bring some irises to school for the class to enjoy. Help the children describe the iris using all of their senses, except taste. Then ask the children to compare the iris with other flowers that they know.

Iron

❖ Invite each child to use a crayon to heavily color a large upper case letter I and a large lower case letter i on a piece of paper. Position the colored sheet face down on another sheet of paper and show the children how to run an iron over the top sheet. The design will transfer to the bottom sheet when the crayon melts. Caution the children that an iron is hot and that they should not use an iron without adult supervision.

Ivy

❖ Bring an ivy vine to school for the children to enjoy. Pick several ivy leaves. Invite the children to press the ivy leaves on an ink pad and use the leaves to make ivy prints on construction paper. Suggest that children stamp the ivy prints in the shape of the letter I. Remind the children to be careful because ink will stain.

Food for Thought

Introducing children to a variety of foods is a wonderful way of reinforcing language concepts. The following foods all begin with the letter I and may be introduced at any time during this unit.

ice, ice cream, ice-cream cones, ice-cream sandwiches, iced tea, Italian bread

Book Review

Children enjoy hearing good books read aloud. The books listed here are favorites of children and may be used to reinforce the letter I.

Cole, Joanna. *An Insect's Body,* William Morrow and Company, 1984.

Gackenbach, Dick. *Little Bug,* Houghton Mifflin, 1981.

Greene, Carol. *Ice Is...Whee!,* Childrens Press, 1983.

Lionni, Leo. *Inch by Inch,* Astor-Honor, 1962.

Mitgutsch, Ali. *From Milk to Ice Cream,* Carolrhoda Books, 1981.

Reece, Colleen. *What Was It Before It Was Ice Cream?,* Child's World, 1985.

Jj

Jack and Jill

❖ Help the children make a list of names that begin with the letter J, such as Jack, Jacob, James, Jan, Jane, Janet, Janice, Jason, Jay, Jean, Jenny, Jennifer, Jeremy, Jerome, Jessica, Jill, Jim, Joe, John, Jordan, Joy, Judy, Julie, Juliet, and June. Invite each child in your classroom whose name begins with the letter J to wear a special name tag.

❖ Teach the children to sing "Jimmy Crack Corn" and "John Jacob Jingleheimer Schmidt," from *Wee Sing Children's Songs and Fingerplays* and "Jack and Jill," "Jack Sprat," and "Jack Be Nimble" from *Wee Sing Nursery Rhymes and Lullabies*. Encourage the children to take turns acting out "Jack and Jill."

❖ Show the children a real jack-in-the-box. Then invite children to draw a simple picture of a jack-in-the-box.

Jack-O'-Lantern

❖ Explain to the class that a jack-o'-lantern is a pumpkin with a face cut out of it. Encourage the children to draw many jack-o-lanterns with a variety of different faces, such as scary, funny, mad, and happy. Then help the children make small pretend jack-o'-lanterns out of oranges. Invite the children to use a black permanent marker to draw their favorite jack-o'-lantern faces on the oranges. If you are exploring this letter in October, help the children carve a real jack-o'-lantern as well.

❖ Invite the children to make a jack-o'-lantern by painting the bottoms of two heavy cardboard paper plates with orange tempera paint. When the paint is dry, suggest that children add a face to both plates with construction-paper pieces. Join the two plates with the unpainted sides together. Have the children slip a strip of green construction paper between the plates for a stem and then staple the plates together. Hang the finished jack-o'-lanterns from the classroom ceiling or in the windows.

❖ Teach the children the poem and motions to "Jack-O'-Lantern" from *Wee Sing Children's Songs and Fingerplays.*

Jar

❖ Ask each child to bring to school a plastic jar with a screw-on lid. Set up a "Jar Center." Put the lids in one stack and the jars in another. Challenge the children to match the jars with the lids and then screw the lids on. Encourage the children to practice with the lids. Invite the children to sort the lids by color and size and the jars by size, such as small, medium, and large. At the end of the week, sponsor some relays. Give each team the same number of jars and lids. The members from each team may then take turns matching a lid to a jar, screwing the lid on, and coming back and touching the next child on their team. Each team continues until all jars have lids.

Jeans

❖ Cut up an old pair of blue jeans into 1-inch strips. Have the children cut the strips into small squares. Invite each child to make a letter J with glue on a piece of construction paper and then arrange the jeans pieces along the glue line to make a "Jeans J." Encourage the children to find a picture of a pair of jeans (clothing catalogs are best) to glue on their "Jeans J" as well.

❖ Sponsor a "Jeans Day." Encourage the children to wear jeans, a jeans jacket, jeans overalls, a jeans skirt, and so on. If you have denim jeans or other jeans clothing, wear them as well!

Jell-O

❖ Encourage the children to name as many gelatin flavors as possible. Point out that most gelatin flavors are named for fruits. Vote to see which gelatin flavor is most popular with the children in your class. Then use that flavor to make "Jiggly Jell-O" and "Jell-O Faces."

Jiggly Jell-O

4 cups boiling water

4 envelopes plain gelatin

2 3-oz boxes Jell-O (any flavor)

Add gelatin and Jell-O to boiling water. Stir until dissolved. Pour into a pan and set at room temperature until gelled. Cut the Jell-O into cubes.

Jell-O Faces

1 box Jell-O Pam spray assortment of raisins, grated carrots, grated cheese, colored coconut, and other tidbits	Spray a muffin tin with Pam. Make the Jell-O according to package directions and then pour the Jell-O into the muffin tin. Chill. When firm, unmold the Jell-O. Invite the children to use the tidbits to make facial features.

Jelly

❖ Read *From Fruit to Jam* by Ali Mitgutsch (see the unit book review). Ask the children to name as many fruit-flavored jellies and jams as possible—apple, grape, orange, strawberry, and so on. Invite each child to share with the class the name of his or her favorite flavor of jelly or jam.

❖ Read *The Giant Jam Sandwich* by John V. Lord and Janet Burroway and *Bread and Jam for Frances* by Russell Hoban (see the unit book review). Sponsor a "Giant Jam Session." Split a long loaf of French or Italian bread lengthwise and spread a variety of different jams on one side and peanut butter on the other. Invite the children to help make no-cook "Jiffy Jelly Jam" to spread as well. Put the bread together and then slice into individual portions.

Jiffy Jelly Jam

1 tsp honey 2–3 drops lemon juice 1 cup thawed and drained frozen berries (any kind)	Mash all of the ingredients together with a fork in a small bowl. Then use as a spread.

Jewelry

❖ Get out the clay or playdough and invite the children to make rings, bracelets, and necklaces. Teach the children to make rolled ropes first and then suggest that they press the ends together to make a continuous circle.

❖ Ask parents to send to school any old jewelry that they no longer want. Put the jewelry in your "Dress-Up Center." Label each piece of jewelry, such as necklace, ring, brace-let, watch, and so on.

Jiggle

❖ Invite the children to jiggle to music. Just say the word *jiggle* and play some music. Invite the children to experi-ment with what they think the word means. Encourage the children to name other things that jiggle, such as gelatin, a fat tummy like Santa's, and so on.

Jigsaw

❖ Set up a "Jigsaw Puzzle Center." Put two to six different puzzles of varying degrees of difficulty on the table.

❖ Make "Jigsaw J" puzzles. Cut large letter J's from different colors of construction paper. Glue a white sheet of paper and a colored sheet of paper together before cutting out the J's so the children may easily turn the pieces right side up before starting. Make a puzzle for each child in the class-room. Cut each J into three to five pieces (you can always cut more pieces later if these are too easy). Cut apart each J a little differently. Put the pieces to each puzzle in an envelope. Make extra J's in the same color as the puzzles for children to use as puzzle frames. Glue the matching puzzle frame on the outside of the envelope. Encourage the children to fit the puzzle pieces on the frame, put the pieces back in the envelope, and then trade envelopes with another child. Continue until each child has had an opportunity to independently put together all of the puzzles.

❖ Cut out two large letter J's the size of a bulletin board. Cut apart one J into enough pieces so that each child will have a piece to decorate. Number the pieces to make it easier to put the J back together again and trace over the edges of each piece with a permanent black marker. Give each child a puzzle piece to decorate using crayons, markers, tempera paint, or watercolors. Using the second J as a frame, glue the decorated pieces into place using rubber cement. When all the pieces are reassembled and dry, staple the "Jigsaw J" on a bulletin board.

Jog

❖ Encourage the children to jog. You might try this every morning with the class. Start at a slow easy pace and jog for a short distance.

Juice

❖ Help the children name as many fruits as possible. Discuss whether juice is made from each fruit. List the fruits in two groups on the chalkboard—"fruits that have juices you can buy" and "fruits that normally don't have packaged juices." (Picture cards of fruits are better if you have them.) For example, you can buy the juices from oranges, apples, grapefruits, lemons, limes, grapes, and pineapples. But normally you can't buy the juices from bananas and cantaloupe.

❖ Invite the children to taste-test a variety of fruit juices available on the market, such as orange juice and apple juice (make sure you get fruit juices and not fruit-flavored drinks). You might try making frozen concentrated juices. Make your own juice using the recipe "Jazzy Juice" as well. Ask the children to vote on the juice they like best. Graph the results.

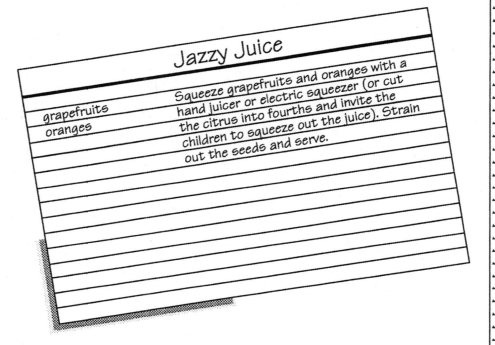

Jazzy Juice

| grapefruits oranges | Squeeze grapefruits and oranges with a hand juicer or electric squeezer (or cut the citrus into fourths and invite the children to squeeze out the juice). Strain out the seeds and serve. |

Jump

❖ Make a large letter J on the floor with tape or draw a letter J with chalk on the sidewalk outside. Have the children make a single-file line at the top of the J. Then invite each child to take a turn jumping with both feet along the J.

Jump

❖ Sponsor a "Jumping Jubilee." Play music for the children to jump to, encourage the children to participate in jumping relays, and teach the children to play "Hi Water, Lo Water." Ask one child to hold one end of a jump rope and have another child hold the other end. Place a mat under the rope in case a child falls. Start with low water (the rope on the floor) and invite the children to jump over the rope. Raise the rope slowly with each new turn. Encourage the children to jump, starting with two feet and landing on two feet. Invite the children to jump over a "Swinging Bridge." Hold one end of the rope and ask a child to hold the other. Gently sway the rope back and forth close to the floor. Encourage the children to jump. Finally, teach the children to "Jump the River." Place two ropes on the floor close together to represent a river. Challenge the children to jump over both ropes. Make the river wider by widening the pieces of rope slowly as the children are ready.

❖ Ask the physical education teacher to instruct the children in the broad jump and then set up a place where it is safe for children to practice.

❖ Teach some jump rope jingles to the children. Encourage the children to recite the jingles as they jump a rope swinging back and forth. Teach "Cinderella," "Two Little Sausages," and "Little Jumping Joan" from *Wee Sing and Play*. Encourage the children to teach the rest of the class jingles that they know as well.

❖ Invite the children to do jumping jacks each morning. Count J-1, J-2, J-3, J-4, and so on.

❖ Teach the children the poem and motions to "Jack Be Nimble." Invite the children to line up and jump over an unlit candle. After all the children have jumped, raise the candle by putting a book under it. Any child knocking the candle over sits out until another child knocks the candle over and takes his or her place.

Junk

❖ Read *The Berenstain Bears and Too Much Junk Food* by Stan and Janice Berenstain (see the unit book review). Encourage the children to suggest some good food snacks, such as fruit, cheese, and raw vegetables.

❖ Invite the children to earn "jolly" dollars—colored slips of construction paper with a J drawn on each one. Use "jolly" dollars all week instead of the usual tokens given for good behavior and work. Ask the children to bring junk to school—anything that is in good shape that the child no longer wants (you may want to limit this so you don't end up with too much). At the end of the week, auction off the junk. The children may use their "jolly" dollars to buy the junk of their choice. Remember, "One person's junk is another person's joy!"

Food for Thought

Introducing children to a variety of foods is a wonderful way of reinforcing language concepts. The following foods all begin with the letter J and may be introduced at any time during this unit.

jam, jambalaya, Jell-O, jelly, jerky, johnnycakes, juice

Book Review

Children enjoy hearing good books read aloud. The books listed here are favorites of children and may be used to reinforce the letter J.

Aliki. *Jack and Jake,* Greenwillow Books, 1986.
Berenstain, Stan and Berenstain, Janice. *The Berenstain Bears and Too Much Junk Food*, Random House, 1985.
Galdone, Paul. *Jack and the Beanstalk,* Ticknor & Fields, 1982.
Hoban, Russell. *Bread and Jam for Frances,* Harper & Row, 1964.
Lord, John V. and Burroway, Janet. *The Giant Jam Sandwich,* Houghton Mifflin, 1987.

Mitgutsch, Ali. *From Fruit to Jam,* Carolrhoda Books, 1981.

Schulman, Janet. *Jack the Bum and the Halloween Handout,* US Committee for Unicef, 1977.

Zolotow, Charlotte. *Janey,* Harper & Row, 1973.

Kk

Kaleidoscope

❖ Bring a kaleidoscope to school for the children to look through. Encourage children who have kaleidoscopes at home to bring them to school to share with the rest of the class.

Key

❖ Help the children make a list of items that may be locked and unlocked with a key. Read *Alfie Gets in First* by Shirley Hughes (see the unit book review).

❖ Collect old keys that are no longer useful. Invite the children to contribute old keys as well. Encourage the children to look at the keys and then guess what each key may have opened. Invite each child to select a favorite key, put the key under a sheet of typing paper, and then find the key with their fingers. Holding the key in place with one hand, have the children rub a crayon over the key to make a rubbing. Some keys make better rubbings than others. Encourage the children to experiment making rubbings with many different keys.

❖ Make a large construction-paper or tagboard key for each child. Write each child's name and address on the tagboard key. Then encourage each child to use the key to practice memorizing his or her address. When the children have memorized their addresses, place the keys on a bulletin board with the title "Keys for Success."

Kick

❖ Encourage the children to practice kicking a rolling playground ball. Then teach them to play "kick ball." Kick ball is played like baseball or softball. There are three bases, a home plate, three outs, two teams, and so on. However, in kick ball, the pitcher rolls a playground ball across home plate and the batter kicks it. It is not really necessary to play positions, but encourage the children to scatter around the infield and outfield. Make the rules as simple as possible.

❖ Invite the children to practice kicking a stationary playground ball. See who can kick the ball the farthest, the highest, and so on. Encourage more advanced children to dropkick a football. Start with a soft football. Invite all children to practice kicking a stationary football on a tee. See who can kick the football the farthest, the highest, and so on.

King

❖ Make a construction-paper pattern for a king's crown. Help the children trace around the pattern on construction paper. Then invite the children to cut out their crowns and decorate them using ribbons, glue, markers, paint, and so on. (Some fast-food restaurants give crowns to children. Ask for a crown for each child or use one for a pattern.) Invite the children to wear their crowns for a day. Read *King for One Day* by Peter Brenner, *King Wacky* by Dick Gackenbach, *The Magic King* by Chuck Hillig, and *King Rollo and the Breakfast* by David McKee (see the unit book review).

❖ Show the children how to draw a simple picture of a king. If available, show the children the video *Wee Sing Presents King Cole's Party: A Merry Musical Celebration.*

Kitchen

❖ Cut out pictures from magazines of kitchen items, such as a stove, microwave, sink, refrigerator, dishes, table and chairs, mixer, telephone, and so on. Glue the pictures on tagboard cards. Use the picture cards as flash cards to help the children learn to identify kitchen items. Encourage the children to help cut out pictures of kitchen items as well. Glue their pictures on a large sheet of construction paper to make a kitchen collage.

❖ Help the children identify any of the equipment and utensils you keep in your classroom for cooking projects. Read *In the Night Kitchen* by Maurice Sendak (see the unit book review).

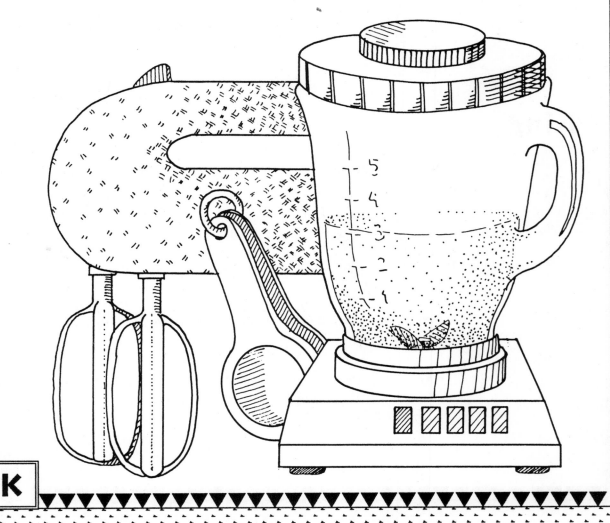

K

❖ Act out something you might do in the kitchen, such as set the table, wash dishes, put away groceries, open cans, break an egg, sweep, eat, stir, put a piece of toast in a toaster, scoop ice cream into a cone, mash potatoes, and so on. Invite the children to guess what you are doing. Encourage the first child who guesses correctly to panto-mime a new action. You may wish to whisper an action in the children's ears.

❖ Set up a play "Kitchen Center." Invite the children to visit the "Kitchen Center" often. Ask questions about the names of the appliances and utensils and what each one is used for. Encourage the children to learn the names of all of the dishes, pots and pans, foods, and so on.

❖ Give each child a handful of kidney beans. Have the children make a large letter K with glue on a piece of construction paper. Then invite the children to arrange the beans along the glue line to make a "Kidney Bean K." Explain that there are many different kinds of beans, such as black beans, chili beans, butter beans, lima beans, green beans, string beans, northern beans, pinto beans, and navy beans. See how many of the beans are familiar to the children.

❖ Give each child a handful of *Special K* cereal. Have the children draw a letter K with a pencil on a sheet of con-struction paper. Then invite children to arrange the cereal along the pencil line to make a "*Special K* K." Encourage the children to eat their K when they are finished. Discuss why *Special K* might be a better choice of breakfast cereal than a cereal that is sugar-coated.

❖ Invite the children to help make "Kool Kiwi Kabobs." Point out why this is a healthy treat.

K

Kool Kiwi Kabobs

kiwi	Peel the kiwi and cut it into thirds. Cut the apples, other fruits, and cheese into small chunks. Invite the children to arrange the fruit and cheese of their choice on skewers or toothpicks. The children may then dip the fruit skewers in orange juice and roll in coconut, if desired. Help the children remove the fruit and cheese from the skewers before eating.
apples	
pears (unpeeled),	
pineapple chunks	
(canned or fresh),	
bananas, melon,	
seedless red or	
green grapes,	
strawberries, and	
other fruits	
cheese	
orange juice (optional)	
shredded coconut	
(optional)	

Kite

❖ Go fly a kite! Help the children make individual kites. Suggest that children paint two diamond-shaped pieces of light-colored construction paper with tempera paint, water colors, crayons, or markers. Staple the two pieces together when they are dry. At each point, staple a ribbon or crepe-paper streamer between the papers. Staple a loop of ribbon or string at the top point to use as a holder. On a nice day, take the children outside to fly their kites.

❖ Read *Curious George Flies a Kite* by Margret Rey and H. A. Rey and *Kites* by Francis H. and Joyce M. Wise (see the unit book review). Make kite sandwiches as a special treat. Cut butter or peanut butter sandwiches in diamond shapes. Serve with sugar-free Kool-Aid.

Food for Thought

Introducing children to a variety of foods is a wonderful way of reinforcing language concepts. The following foods all begin with the letter K and may be introduced at any time during this unit.

kale, ketchup, kidney beans, kiwi, kraut juice, kumquats

Book Review

Children enjoy hearing good books read aloud. The books listed here are favorites of children and may be used to reinforce the letter K.

Brenner, Peter. *King for One Day,* Scroll Press, 1987.

Eugene, Toni. *Koalas and Kangaroos: Strange Animals of Australia,* National Geographic Society, 1981.

Gackenbach, Dick. *King Wacky,* Crown, 1984.

Hillig, Chuck. *The Magic King,* Stillpoint, 1984.

Hughes, Shirley. *Alfie Gets in First,* Lothrop, 1982.

Kanao, Keiko. *Kitten Up a Tree,* Knopf, 1987.

Keats, Ezra Jack. *Kitten for a Day,* Macmillan, 1974.

Kuenn, Nancy. *The Dragon Kite,* Harcourt Brace Jovanovich, 1983.

Mayer, Mercer. *What Do You Do with a Kangaroo?,* Scholastic, 1987.

McKee, David. *King Rollo and the Breakfast,* Creative Education, 1982.

McKee, David. *King Rollo's Playroom,* Creative Education, 1982.

McKee, David. *King Rollo and the Search,* Creative Education, 1982.

McKee, David. *King Rollo's Spring,* Penguin Books, 1989.

McKee, David. *King Rollo's Winter,* Penguin Books, 1989.

Moncure, Jane B. *Kindness,* Childrens Press, 1981.

Oana, Katherine. *Kippy Koala,* University Classics, 1985.

Payne, Emmy. *Katy No-Pocket,* Houghton Mifflin, 1973.

Pfloog, Jan. *Kittens Are Like That,* Random House, 1975.

Rey, Margret and Rey, H. A. *Curious George Flies a Kite,* Houghton Mifflin, 1977.

Sendak, Maurice. *In the Night Kitchen,* Harper & Row, 1985.

Silverstein, Ruth. *Kirby Koala Visits Grandma,* Antioch Publishing Company, 1984.

Wise, Francis H. and Wise, Joyce M. *Kites,* Wise Publishing, 1977.

L1

Lace

❖ Lace may be purchased at fabric stores. Often odd colors or seasonal lace is on sale for as cheaply as a penny a yard! Give each child a strip of lace and invite him or her to cut the lace into little squares. Have the children make a large letter L with glue on a sheet of colored construction paper and arrange the lace pieces along the glue line to make a "Lacy L."

❖ Set up a "Lacing Center." Provide as many lacing cards as possible for the children to practice with. Remind the children to unlace the cards when they are finished.

❖ Use an old tennis shoe to help the children learn to lace a shoe. Check to see that the shoestrings are not frayed and will go easily through the holes. Work with the children individually or in very small groups.

❖ Explain that licorice is sold in long strings called *laces*. Invite the children to try grape, cherry, and original licorice laces. Ask the children to bend their laces to make a letter L. They might try making other alphabet letters with the laces as well.

Ladybug

❖ Have the book *Life of the Ladybug* by Heiderose and Andreas Fischer-Nagel available for the children to browse through (see the unit book review). This book has wonderful photographs of ladybugs. Your librarian may be able to suggest another appropriate book as well. Show the children how to draw a simple picture of a ladybug.

❖ Point out that the ladybug is a useful and harmless insect. The ladybug eats many other insects that are enemies of the farmer. If possible, bring a real ladybug to school for the children to observe for a day.

Lamb

❖ Teach the children to sing "Mary Had a Little Lamb" from *Wee Sing Nursery Rhymes and Lullabies*. Show the children how to draw a simple picture of a lamb. Or give each child a picture of a lamb. Invite the children to glue cotton balls or lamb's wool on the lamb's body. Discuss lamb's wool and how it is used to make clothing. Read *From Sheep to Scarf* by Ali Mitgutsch (see the unit book review).

❖ Point out that a lamb is a baby sheep. If you have a set of farm animal pictures, show the children each card and invite them to name each animal and its baby. Read *Lazy Lions, Lucky Lambs* by Patricia R. Giff and *The Little Lamb* by Judy Dunn (see the unit book review).

Lantern

❖ If possible, bring to school a real lantern, such as the type used in camping. Point out that a lantern is a form of light. Help the children make a lantern. Instruct the children to fold a half sheet of construction paper the long way. Have the children turn their papers so the fold is facing them. Show children how to make cuts along the fold about every 2 inches. Explain to the children that they are to cut from the fold to about 1 inch from the open edge. Caution the children to stop cutting before they reach the open edge. After all the cuts have been made, have the children open their papers, fold the paper the opposite way overlapping the ends, and then staple them together. They may then attach a strip of construction paper to the top for the handle.

Laundromats

❖ Invite the children to share what they know about laundromats. If possible, take the children on a walk to a nearby laundromat and wash a load of clothes. Towels and washcloths are easy for children to learn how to fold. Plan to have a picnic lunch while you wait.

Leaves

❖ Make leaf pictures. You will need an iron, ironing board, wax paper, construction paper, and lots of colorful fall leaves. Choose leaves that are basically flat and without large prominent veins. Invite the children to select three to five of their favorite leaves. Show the children how to position the leaves between two sheets of wax paper. Put a large sheet of construction paper on the ironing board and invite the children, in turn, to put their wax paper and leaves on top. Then place another sheet of construction paper over the top sheet of the wax paper. This will prevent the wax from ruining your iron or the ironing board. Set the iron on a medium-low setting and help the children iron over the top sheet of construction paper until the wax paper underneath gets hot and melts together. Trim the edges of the wax paper and put a colorful construction-paper frame around the leaf pictures. Hang the finished leaf pictures from the classroom ceiling or in a window.

❖ If possible, on a nice fall day, take the children outside to collect leaves. Invite the children to glue their leaves on a large construction-paper L. Dry leaves may be broken into small pieces and glued on a large letter L on another sheet of construction paper. When the glue dries, help the children shake off the excess leaves to reveal a "Leafy L."

❖ Read *Marmalade's Yellow Leaf* by Cindy Wheeler (see the unit book review). Then make leaf rubbings. Find flat leaves with prominent veins. Invite the children to select a favorite leaf. Have them put a sheet of typing paper over the leaf with the underside of the leaf facing up. Encourage the children to hold the paper carefully on the leaf with one hand and rub a crayon over it to make a rubbing. Suggest that children make several overlapping rubbings with orange, red, and brown crayons on yellow construction paper.

❖ Make fall leaves. Cut out several leaf shapes from fall-colored construction paper. Encourage the children to wear paint shirts. Cover a large area with newspaper or an old shower curtain. Give each child two to four paper leaves. Show the children how to wrinkle up each leaf in their fists and then open it up again. (Children love to do this!) Cut a sponge into small pieces and attach a clothespin "handle" to the back of each sponge. Put fall-colored tempera paint in jar lids. Provide two to three sponge pins for each lid of paint. Invite the children to sponge paint their leaves with as many colors as they wish and then dip the leaves quickly in a big pan of water to mix the colors. Place the leaves flat to dry. The children will be surprised at how real these leaves look when they dry. Use the leaves as a bulletin-board border, around a door or window frame, or as part of a lovely fall display.

❖ Teach the children the fingerplay "Leaves" from *Finger Frolics: Fingerplays for Young Children* by Liz Cromwell and Dixie Hibner (see the unit book review).

Left and Right

❖ Teach the children the fingerplay "Right Hand, Left Hand" from *Wee Sing Children's Songs and Fingerplays*.

❖ Put masking tape, a sticker, or a star on the left hand and the left shoe of each child in the classroom. Then give left and right directions to the children, such as "Touch your left ear with your left hand, touch your head with your right hand, point the finger of your left hand, hop on your left foot, shake your right foot," and so on. Use only left directions for children having difficulty.

- ❖ Play "Simon Says" using left and right directions.

- ❖ Encourage the children to write L's down the left side of every paper they use. Reinforce that they are writing on the left side of the paper.

- ❖ Teach the children to sing "Looby Loo" from *Wee Sing Children's Songs and Fingerplays*. Use left and right body parts.

Lemon and Lime

- ❖ Make lemon and lime prints. Cut several lemons and limes in half. Put yellow and green tempera paint in styrofoam meat trays. Have each child draw a large letter L with a crayon on a sheet of construction paper. Then invite children to dip the cut end of a lemon in yellow paint and the lime in green paint and print all along the L line to make a "Lemon and Lime L."

- ❖ Make pretend lemon or lime lollipops. Give each child a square piece of yellow or green construction paper. Show the children how to make the square into a circle by rounding the corners. Glue a popsicle stick or tongue depressor to the back of each circle.

- ❖ Make "Luscious Lemon Limeade." Invite the children to taste the lemons and limes before putting them in the juice. Ask the children if they can tell the difference in the taste between the lemons and limes with their eyes closed. Discuss how lemons and limes are the same and how they are different. Help the children name other fruits that make their own juice, such as oranges, apples, grapefruit, pineapple, and grapes. Make "Lemon Lovelies" to serve with the "Luscious Lemon Limeade."

Luscious Lemon Limeade

lemons and limes	Cut the lemons and limes in half and invite the children to take turns squeezing the juice into their own individual cups. Add water to fill. Give each child a packet of sugar to sweeten the juice. Add ice.
individual packets of sugar	
ice	
water	

Lemon Lovelies

1 cup flour	Mix together the flour, margarine, and powdered sugar in a bowl. Press the dough into an ungreased square pan. Press the dough onto the sides of the pan as well (flour your hands if the dough is sticky). Bake for 20 minutes at 350°. Mix the other ingredients together until light and fluffy. Pour over the crust while it is still hot. Bake an additional 25 minutes at 350°. Cool and serve. Makes about 25 squares.
1/2 cup softened margarine	
1/4 cup powdered sugar	
1 cup granulated sugar	
2 Tbsp lemon juice	
1/2 tsp baking powder	
1/4 tsp salt	
2 eggs	

Library

❖ Arrange for your class to visit the school or public library. Ask the librarian to discuss what he or she does. Then share a book with the children about the letter L. When you return to the classroom, have the children draw pictures of the librarian. Write a sentence under each child's picture as the child dictates what he or she knows about a librarian. Give the pictures to the librarian as a thank-you gift.

❖ Ask the school librarian if you might display some of the children's artwork in the library. If the library has a monthly theme, you might have your class create relevant artwork around that theme. Display some of the children's L classwork, too.

❖ Read *I Like the Library* by Anne Rockwell, *Check It Out! The Book About Libraries* by Gail Gibbons, and *Mr. Noisy Goes to the Library* by Roger Hargreaves (see the unit book review). Ask the librarian to help you work out a system for checking out books. It's a wonderful treat for children to go to the library and learn to select their own reading material.

Line

❖ Encourage the children to follow your directions for drawing lines from the top to the bottom of a sheet of white paper. Invite the children to start on the top left side with any color crayon and draw a line down to the bottom. Then instruct children to select another color to draw more lines from top to bottom as well. Encourage the children to fill their papers with different-colored vertical lines. Invite the children to turn their papers over and make additional lines.

❖ Challenge the children to paint, trace, and draw as many different kinds of lines as possible—vertical and horizontal lines, diagonal lines, vertical lines between writing lines, short lines and long lines, crooked lines and straight lines, curvy lines and curly lines, and so on!

❖ Make a sign, "L Is for Line Leader." Attach a length of yarn to both sides of the sign so it will hang around the line leader's neck. Play "Follow the Leader." Invite the line leader to start the game.

❖ Emphasize walking in a straight line all week. The simplest and most effective way to teach walking in a straight line is through modeling. Frequently praise those children who walk correctly.

Lion

❖ Read *A Lion in the Night* by Pamela Allen and *The Happy Lion* by Louise Fatio (see the unit book review). Make paper lions. Show the children how to fold a sheet of brown or orange construction paper in half lengthwise and then cut a half-oval out of the bottom. This forms the lion's body and legs and enables the lion to stand when the paper is opened. Give the children a square sheet of yellow paper and show them how to make a circle by rounding the corners. Have the children fringe the edge of their circles to make the lion's mane. Children may make the lion's face by rounding a smaller square of brown or orange paper. Facial features may be drawn on with a crayon or marker. Suggest that children make ears from a smaller square of brown or orange paper that has been rounded and then cut in half. Instruct the children to glue the mane on the body first and then glue the face on top. Slip the ears under the face. A scrap of paper may be added for the tail.

Lips

❖ Make a lip pattern for the children to trace on red construction paper. Invite the children to paint the lips with glue and then sprinkle on red glitter. When the glue is dry, help the children gently shake off the excess glitter. The children may then cut out the lips.

❖ Invite the children to put lipstick or makeup sticks on their lips. Then have them make lip prints on contrasting colored paper. Theatrical makeup sticks are available in various colors. White lips may be pressed on dark paper, red lips on white paper, and so on. Have cold cream available for cleaning.

Listening

❖ Take the children on a "Listening Walk." Keep a list of all the sounds the children identify. Encourage the children to add to the list all week.

❖ Set up a "Listening Center." Have several read-a-long books and tapes for the children to listen to and read. Try to find books that reinforce L words.

❖ Review with the children the letters of the alphabet that they have studied so far. Encourage the children to make the sound for each letter. Make this a game that you play every day of the week. You may also reverse the game by making the letter sounds and asking the children to identify the letter names.

❖ Say several words that are unfamiliar to the children and some that the children know well. Ask the children to identify the alphabet letters of the initial consonant sounds.

❖ Invite the children to sit with their backs to you and their eyes closed. Make some familiar sounds, such as sharpening a pencil, clapping your hands, snapping your fingers, writing on the chalkboard, crushing paper, closing a door, running water, throwing paper in the basket, knocking on a door, and whistling. Ask the children to identify each sound they hear.

Little and Large

❖ Read *Big and Little* by Richard Scarry and *Is It Larger? Is It Smaller?* by Tana Hoban (see the unit book review). Explain that the opposite of *large* is *small* and that the opposite of *little* is *big*. Review other opposites by giving the children the first word in a pair of opposites and asking them to give the opposite. For example, you might use the following opposite pairs: long/short, tall/short, slow/fast, go/stop, empty/full, fat/skinny, up/down, in/out, bottom/top, over/under, close/open, above/below, front/back, right/left, on/off, fresh/spoiled, day/night, hot/cold, run/walk, wet/dry, hard/soft, rough/smooth, bad/good, loud/soft, clean/dirty, and first/last.

❖ Draw and cut out sets of large and small objects from construction paper. Glue each large and small picture set on a sheet of construction paper. Then encourage the children to identify the larger picture in each set. Encourage the children to use the words *larger* and *smaller* to describe each set of pictures.

Living Room

❖ Help the children brainstorm a list of items found in a living room, family room, or den. Cut out magazine pictures of furniture and other items found in these rooms as well. For example, you might find a picture of a sofa or couch, end table, coffee table, bookshelf, television, lamp, carpet, pillow, rocking chair, wall pictures, magazine rack, and a plant. Glue the pictures to tagboard to make flash cards to help the children identify these items.

Logs

❖ Invite the children to explore and build a variety of structures with construction logs. Encourage the children to use logs to make a letter L as well. Challenge the children to make a letter L in a variety of ways.

❖ Encourage the children to pretend to be logs. Invite each child to choose a partner and see if they can make an L shape with their bodies. Encourage the children to experiment making an L with their legs or other parts of their bodies, too.

❖ Show the children how to draw a simple picture of a fireplace with logs. Encourage those children who have fireplaces in their homes to share their experiences with logs with the rest of the class.

Long and Short

❖ Cut straws or uncooked spaghetti into long pieces and short pieces. Invite the children to sort the pieces into long and short.

❖ Give each child a sheet of construction paper folded in half and a handful of long and short pieces of straws. Have the children write "long" on one half of the paper and "short" on the other. Ask the children to pick up each straw, decide if it is long or short, and then trace the straw, from top to bottom, on the appropriate sides of their papers. When finished, the children will have one side of long lines and one side of short lines.

Love

❖ Help the children make a love lei to give to someone they care about. You will need 1/2-inch pieces of drinking straws, construction paper, a paper punch, and wire for stringing. Use telephone cable wire. This wire is extremely easy to use for stringing. One piece of cable has many different colored wires. If you don't have telephone wire, try using string or yarn wrapped at one end with masking tape to form a "needle." Encourage each child to draw, color, and cut out several construction-paper flowers or hearts. Punch a hole in the center of each flower or heart. Then show the children how to alternately string pieces of drinking straws and their paper cutouts to make a lei.

❖ Read *Things to Love* by Richard Scarry, *What Is Love?* by Dave Eaton, and *Love* by Jane B. Moncure (see the unit book review). Give each child a large white construction-paper heart. Then encourage the children to draw a picture of someone they love.

Lunch

❖ Read *What a Good Lunch!* by Shigeo Watanabe (see the unit book review). Ask the school dietitian to visit your classroom and discuss which lunch foods are healthy. After the visit, encourage the children to cut out pictures of good lunch foods from magazines. Glue the pictures on paper plates. Ask the lunchroom supervisor if you might display paper-plate collages in the lunchroom.

❖ Help the children identify all the pieces of a place setting, such as a plate, spoon, knife, fork, napkin, and glass. Use large sheets of construction paper as placemats and invite the children to use plastic silverware and paper plates, cups, and napkins to complete the setting. Draw the outline of each piece of the place setting on the construction-paper place mat for the children to match. Then use the place settings at snack time.

❖ Review lunchroom rules with the children. Ask the lunchroom supervisor to spend a few minutes with your class this week reviewing the rules as well. Then provide large sheets of construction paper for the children to make posters illustrating each rule. Display the finished posters in the school lunchroom for other children to see and enjoy.

❖ Have the children make a large letter L with glue on a sheet of construction paper. Then invite the children to arrange lima beans along the glue line to make a "Lima Bean L." Encourage the children to taste a raw lima bean and then cook the leftover beans for the children to sample. Discuss how the raw and cooked beans are the same and how they are different. Help the children name other beans that might be eaten for lunch, such as string beans, baked beans, black beans, wax beans, and kidney beans.

❖ Invite each child to bring his or her lunch to school in a lunch box or lunch bag on a specified day. Then take the children outside for a picnic.

❖ Try "Lotsa Lettuce." Help the children name as many vegetables as possible that might be put in a salad. Then ask each child to contribute one vegetable of his or her choice. You provide the lettuce.

Lotsa Lettuce

lettuce
salad vegetables
(tomatoes, onions,
cucumbers, radishes,
celery, mushrooms,
bell peppers, carrots,
cauliflower, broccoli)
salad dressing of
your choice

Invite the children to help clean the lettuce and break it into small pieces. Put the lettuce pieces in a large salad bowl. Suggest that children help clean and cut the other vegetables as well. Then add each vegetable to the lettuce. Top with salad dressing, if desired.

Food for Thought

Introducing children to a variety of foods is a wonderful way of reinforcing language concepts. The following foods all begin with the letter L and may be introduced at any time during this unit.

lasagne, leeks, leg of lamb, lemons, lemonade, lentils, lettuce, licorice, lima beans, limes, limeade, linguine, liver, liverwurst

Book Review

Children enjoy hearing good books read aloud. The books listed here are favorites of children and may be used to reinforce the letter L.

Allen, Pamela. *A Lion in the Night,* Putnam Publishing Group, 1986.

Berenstain, Stan and Berenstain, Janice. *The Berenstain Bears and the Truth,* Random House, 1983.

Cromwell, Liz and Hibner, Dixie. *Finger Frolics: Fingerplays for Young Children*, Partner Press, 1976.

Dunn, Judy. *The Little Lamb,* Random House, 1978.

Eaton, Dave. *What Is Love?,* Harvest House, 1986.

Elliott, Dan. *Ernie's Little Lie,* Random House, 1983.

Fatio, Louise. *The Happy Lion,* Scholastic, 1986.

Fischer-Nagel, Heiderose and Fischer-Nagel, Andreas. *Life of the Ladybug,* Carolrhoda Books, 1986.

Gibbons, Gail. *Check It Out! The Book About Libraries,* Harcourt Brace Jovanovich, 1985.

Giff, Patricia R. *Lazy Lions, Lucky Lambs,* Delacorte, 1986.

Hargreaves, Roger. *Mr. Noisy Goes to the Library,* Price Stern, 1982.

Hoban, Tana. *Is It Larger? Is It Smaller?,* Greenwillow Books, 1985.

Little, Mary. *ABC for the Library,* Atheneum, 1975.

Mitgutsch, Ali. *From Sheep to Scarf,* Carolrhoda Books, 1981.

Moncure, Jane B. *Honesty,* Child's World, 1981.

Moncure, Jane B. *Love,* Childrens Press, 1981.

Rey, Margret and Shalleck, Allan J. *Curious George at the Laundromat,* Houghton Mifflin, 1987.

Rockwell, Anne. *I Like the Library,* E. P. Dutton, 1977.

Scarry, Richard. *Big and Little,* Western Publishing, 1986.

Scarry, Richard. *Things to Love,* Western Publishing, 1987.

Watanabe, Shigeo. *What a Good Lunch!,* Putnam Publishing Group, 1981.

Wheeler, Cindy. *Marmalade's Yellow Leaf,* Knopf, 1982.

Macaroni

❖ Make macaroni necklaces. Dye macaroni by soaking it in a solution of rubbing alcohol and food coloring. The longer the macaroni soaks, the darker the color. Drain and dry the macaroni on wax paper. Or use tricolored rigatoni, which comes in three colors—white, rust, and green. Invite the children to use telephone cable wire to string the macaroni. If you don't have wire, use yarn or string wrapped with tape at one end to make it easier to go through the eye of the macaroni.

❖ Ask each child to make a letter M with glue on a piece of construction paper. Provide several different types of macaroni (shells, twists, and so on) for the children to arrange along the glue line to make a "Macaroni M." Use the leftover macaroni to make macaroni and cheese.

Machines

❖ Read *Machines at Work* by Byron Barton, *Machines* by Anne Rockwell, and *Mike Mulligan and His Steam Shovel* by Virginia L. Burton (see the unit book review). Encourage the children to cut out pictures of machines from magazines to make a collage. Help the children look for simple and complex machines that have wheels (bicycles), levers (seesaws), wedges and screws (ramps), and tools and gadgets (drills). Other machines might include a dishwasher, washing machine, lawn mower, vacuum cleaner, iron, clock, robot, tractor, dump truck, crane, escalator, typewriter, computer, telephone, car, motorcycle, and so on. Discuss why we have mechanics, too.

❖ Help the children identify machines in the classroom, such as a pencil sharpener, a typewriter, a computer, a stove, and so on.

Mad

❖ Invite each child to share with the class a time when he or she was very mad. Ask the children to identify what makes them mad, too. Encourage the children to draw pictures of a very mad face. Then read *I Was So Mad* by Mercer Mayer (see the unit book review).

❖ Encourage the children to think of constructive methods for dealing with anger. Then suggest that they try some of these methods the next time they get angry. Discuss the following list. Talk about why these methods might help. Talk about some behaviors that would be inappropriate as well, such as calling a person names, fighting, cursing, and so on.

> Take five deep breaths very slowly.
> Count to ten or twenty.
> Say the alphabet out loud.
> Punch a pillow.
> Thumb through a book or magazine.
> Do some sit-ups or other physical exercises.
> Take a walk.
> Go outside and yell and stomp your feet.
> Take a hot bath or cold shower.
> Put on your favorite record or tape.

Magazine

❖ Invite each child to choose a colorful page from a magazine, tear out the page, cut it into strips, and then cut the strips into small squares. Have each child make a large letter M with glue on a sheet of construction paper. Then invite children to arrange the magazine pieces along the glue line to make a "Magazine M."

❖ Make "M Mobiles." Give each child a large cardboard M with holes punched at the points and string pulled through the top for hanging. Invite the children to cut out magazine pictures of items that begin with the letter M. Have the children glue the pictures on both sides of pieces of construction paper cut into the basic shapes. Show the children how to string the pictures together by punching holes at the top and bottom of each construction-paper shape with a hole punch. Use paper clips stretched out to an S shape to hook the pictures together. Children may then attach their strings of pictures to the large letter M.

❖ Give each child a sheet printed with the letters of the alphabet. Then challenge them to find and cut out from magazines a matching letter to glue next to each letter on the sheet. (Less experienced children may only match six to eight letters.) Try both sequential order of letters, such as L, M, N, O, and random order, such as F, C, X, M.

Magnet

❖ Read *Mickey's Magnet* by Franklyn M. Branley and Eleanor K. Vaughn (see the unit book review). Set up a "Magnet Center." On a table, set magnets and an assortment of materials, such as paper clips, pencils, pens, markers, rulers, and so on. Encourage the children to sort the items into two groups—"items that a magnet will pick up" and "items that a magnet will not pick up." Also, put out magnifying glasses and an assortment of items for the children to examine, such as a newspaper, salt, soil, pepper or other spices, fingerprints, and coins.

Mail Carriers

❖ Encourage the children to share what they know about mail carriers. Take the children to see your school mail-box. Plan to meet the mail carrier at the box one day just to say "Hello."

❖ Read *The Jolly Postman* by Janet and Allan Ahlberg, *Postal Workers: A to Z* by Jean Johnson, and *The Post Office Book* by Gail Gibbons (see the unit book review). If possible, arrange for the class to visit a post office and find out how a letter gets from one place to another. Before the field trip, have the children draw pictures or write letters to themselves or to a classmate. Take the letters with you to mail when you visit the post office. See how long it takes for the letters to be delivered.

❖ Make mail hats. Give each child a paper bag, about 7 inches at its widest. Cut each bag about 3 inches from the bottom. Invite the children to paint the bottom section of their bags with blue tempera paint. Cut a bill for each child's hat from black construction paper. Staple the bills to the hats when the paint is dry.

❖ Make a mailbox for the classroom or scout around the school or elsewhere for an old discarded mailbox. A mail-box may be weighted by placing the mailbox post in a large can filled with plaster of Paris. Write each child's name and address on an envelope. Keep the envelopes in the mailbox. Each morning, invite one child to role-play a mail carrier and deliver the letters to the right children.

When the children receive their letters, have them either read or recite from memory their names and addresses and then "mail" their letters again for the next day's delivery.

Map

❖ Collect maps for the children to see and examine. Discuss how a map is used. Cut an old map into strips. Then have the children cut the strips into small squares. Invite each child to make a large letter M with glue on a sheet of construction paper and then arrange the map pieces along the glue line to make a "Map M."

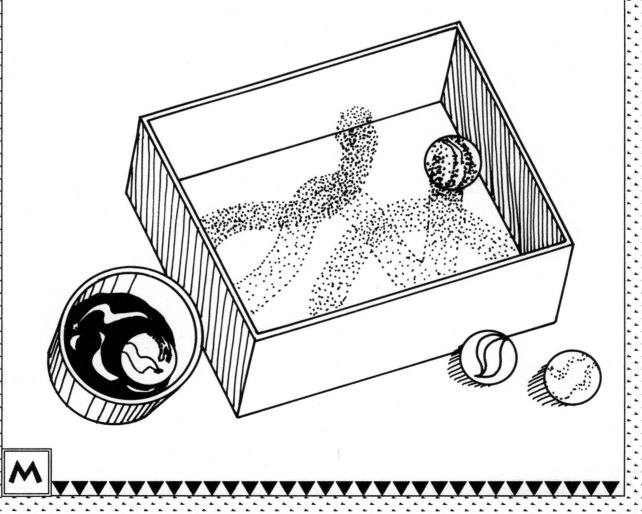

Marbles

❖ Teach the children to play marbles in groups of three or four. Play a simplified version of the game. Draw a circle with a stick in the dirt outside or with a piece of chalk on the floor in the classroom or gym. Put all of the marbles inside the circle and invite each child to select a marble to be his or her "shooter." Taking turns, each child rolls the shooter marble toward the center of the circle and tries to knock the other marbles out. The children get to keep their shooter marbles and any marbles that they knock out of the circle. The children continue to take turns until all the marbles are knocked out of the circle. The child who collects the most marbles wins.

❖ Invite the children to make a marble design, called "Marble Madness." Put a sheet of paper in the bottom of four or five shallow boxes. Put tempera paint in small paper or plastic cups. Put a marble in each cup. Encourage the children to take turns scooping a marble out of the paint cup with a spoon and then dropping the marble in a box. Then show the children how to gently pick up the box and tilt it to roll the marble all over the paper. As the marble rolls, it will leave a path of paint. Suggest that children repeat this process with other marble colors, too.

❖ Make "Marble M's." Make a cardboard letter M pattern for each child to trace around on a sheet of construction paper. Have the children cut out their traced M. Ask each child to put his or her construction-paper M's and a handful of marbles in the bottom of a shallow box. Squirt two large dabs of tempera paint in the bottom of the box (not on the M) and invite the children to gently tilt their boxes back and forth until they have the desired paths across the M. You do not have to take the marbles out each time. Just add two more dabs of paint for the next child.

❖ If possible, get some magnetic marbles for the children to play with. They may be purchased in most toy stores and are lots of fun!

Markers

❖ Point out that markers are easier to use than crayons or a pencil because they flow more easily. Make letter M patterns from heavy cardboard for each child to trace around on a sheet of white construction paper. Suggest that children use magic markers to color their M's.

❖ Set up a "Marker Center." Provide plenty of drawing paper and old markers. Remind the children to press lightly and to put the tops back on the markers when they have finished drawing.

❖ Make medals. Cut out a tagboard circle for each child in your classroom. Write "It's great to be me!" on each circle with a black permanent marker. Invite the children to use the magic markers to decorate their medals. Some children may wish to add ribbon at the bottom of their medals as well. Use real ribbon or help the children cut a ribbon shape from construction paper. Punch two holes in the top of each medal and use string, yarn, or ribbon to hang the medals around the children's necks.

❖ Give each child a marker and sheet of paper. Then encourage the children to copy upper and lower case M's as you write the letters on the chalkboard. Suggest that children keep the palms of their hands raised a little off the paper so the marker will not smear.

Me

❖ Read *Me, Too!* by Mercer Mayer and *Just Me* by Marie H. Ets (see the unit book review). Invite each child to lie down on a sheet of white butcher paper or bulletin-board paper. Trace the outline of each child's body and then have the children draw their clothing, facial expressions, hair, and so on with markers or crayons. Ask older students from another class to come in and help. Cut out the finished drawings and display them along a hallway outside your classroom.

❖ Make "Me Mobiles." Ask the children to remove their shoes and socks. Trace around each child's handprints and footprints on construction paper and then cut the prints out. Give each child a circle. Encourage the children to draw their own facial features on the circles or use scraps of construction paper. Punch a hole at the top of the circle and each handprint and footprint. Tie thread to each child's handprints, footprints, and face drawing and hang all the parts from a coat hanger. Hang the mobiles from the ceiling.

Mittens

❖ Show the children a pair of mittens and a pair of gloves. Invite the children to try the mittens and gloves on, too. Discuss how mittens are like gloves and how they are different. Encourage the children to contribute mittens to hang on a "Mitten Tree" in your classroom. Use a large tree branch or Christmas tree. Invite the children to hang mittens from the tree. At the end of the week, give the mittens to a social organization to distribute to needy children.

❖ Help the children trace around the outline of both hands on a piece of construction paper as if they were wearing mittens. Have each child cut out his or her "mittens," punch a hole near the bottom of each mitten, and tie them together with a piece of yarn. Help the children label the mittens L (left) and R (right). Then encourage the children to hang their mittens around their necks.

❖ Read the nursery rhyme, "Three Little Kittens Who Lost Their Mittens." Then teach the children to sing "Three Little Kittens" from *Wee Sing Nursery Rhymes and Lullabies.*

❖ Discuss when mittens should be worn and why. Then read *Mitten* by Alvin Tresselt and *The Mystery of the Missing Red Mitten* by Steven Kellogg (see the unit book review).

Money

❖ Teach the children how to draw and identify the money symbols for cents and dollars. Then challenge children to look for lots of examples in newspapers, magazines, and other sources. Set aside a bulletin board for the children to fill with the dollars and cents symbols that they find.

❖ If possible, get a money sorter. Some piggy banks take a coin and put it in a stack of like coins. Invite the children to pile pennies in stacks of ten. Challenge some children to roll two stacks of fifty pennies to make a dollar.

Monkey

❖ Read *Monkey* by Mary Hoffman (see the unit book review). Focus the children's attention on the pictures of the monkey. Ask the children if they have seen a monkey and, if so, where they saw one. Help the children name other zoo animals as well.

❖ Help the children learn the fingerplay "Three Little Monkeys" from *Wee Sing Children's Songs and Fingerplays*. Read any of the *Curious George* Books by Margret and H. A. Rey. You can purchase a stuffed Curious George at most children's bookstores and include it in your Reading Center this week.

Monster

❖ Make monster masks. Put a paper plate in front of each child's face and mark the location of each eye. Then cut out the eyeholes. Invite the children to use markers, paint, and crayons to draw scary faces on the masks. Punch a hole on each side of the plate and string with yarn for tying around the back of the child's head.

❖ Invite the children to share any experiences they may have had with monsters. Emphasize that monsters are not real. Talk about happy monsters, such as the ones on Sesame Street. There are many books about the Sesame Street monsters. Read *Clyde Monster* by Robert L. Crowe, *Take Away Monsters* by Colin Hawkins, and *The Monster and the Tailor* by Paul Galdone (see the unit book review).

Moon

❖ Teach the children the simple nursery rhyme "The Moon" from *Wee Sing Nursery Rhymes and Lullabies*. Invite children to draw and then color with wax crayons a picture of the moon and stars. Help the children paint the picture with a thinned black tempera paint to make the sky dark. This process is known as *crayon resist*. The black paint will adhere to the paper, but not where the crayon is colored.

❖ Discuss how the sky is the same and how it is different when it is morning and when the moon is out. Read *Wait Till the Moon Is Full* and *Goodnight, Moon,* both by Margaret Wise Brown (see the unit book review).

Morning

❖ Ask the children to describe how they know when it is morning. Discuss what the children and other members of their family do to get ready for school or work in the morning—get up, get dressed, eat breakfast, go to school, and so on.

❖ Invite the children to draw and then color or paint a picture of a sunrise. Teach the children to sing "Good Morning" from *Wee Sing Children's Songs and Fingerplays*.

❖ If possible, read *One Monday Morning* by Uri Shulevitz on Monday morning (see the unit book review). Point out Monday on a calendar in the classroom. Remind the children that Monday is the first day of the school week. Then help the children recite all the days of the week in order.

Mother

❖ Read *Mothers Can Do Anything* by Joe Lasker and *Are You My Mother?* by Philip D. Eastman (see the unit book review). Have each child draw a picture of his or her mother, aunt, grandmother, or other mother figure. Then encourage the children to dictate something to you that they especially like about their mothers. Write their sentence or sentences under their pictures. Invite the children to take their pictures home to give to their mothers.

❖ Encourage each child to learn his or her mother's full name (check with their mothers first).

❖ Help the children plant marigolds in small empty milk containers. When the plants bloom, suggest that children take the flowers home to their mothers.

Mountain

❖ Show the children how to draw a simple picture of a mountain. Then teach the children to sing "She'll Be Comin' Round the Mountain" from *Wee Sing Children's Songs and Fingerplays* and "The Bear Went Over the Mountain" from *Wee Sing Silly Songs*.

Mouse

❖ Make a set of mouse cards. On several index cards make a simple drawing of a mouse. Leave a different detail out on each card. Show the children each card and ask them to identify the missing part.

❖ Teach the children to figure out simple mazes. It is difficult to find books of mazes that are simple enough for young children who have never done them before, so try making some of your own. An easy mouse maze where the children are instructed to help the mouse find the muffin is illustrated here as an example.

❖ Show the children how to draw a simple picture of a mouse.

❖ Teach the children to sing "Three Blind Mice" from *Wee Sing Around the Campfire*.

Mouth

❖ Encourage the children to discuss what they can do with their mouths, such as smile, eat, talk, and so on. Help the children name all the parts of their mouths—lips, teeth, tongue, and gums.

❖ Have the children cut out pictures of mouths from magazines. Encourage the children to include some animal mouths, too! Make a collage with the mouth pictures.

❖ Gather several foods for each of the four taste groups— bitter, sweet, sour, and salty. Blindfold the children, put small bites of each food in their mouths one food at a time, and see if they can guess what they are eating. Serve "Minute Milk Shakes" as a special treat.

Minute Milk Shakes

3/4 cup milk
1 scoop ice cream
(any flavor)
canned or fresh fruit,
such as bananas or
strawberries (optional)

Mix the milk and ice cream in a bowl. Beat with a spoon or use a mixer or blender. Add fruit, if desired, and serve.

❖ Make bran muffins in muffin tins using liners. Teach the children to sing "The Muffin Man" from *Wee Sing and Play*. Invite children to sing the song as they help you make the muffins.

❖ Have the children make a large letter M with a pencil or crayon on a sheet of construction paper. Then invite the children to arrange sugarless candy mints along the outline of the M to make a "Minty M." Invite the children to eat the M when they are finished!

Mud

❖ Read *Mud Pies* by Judith Grey (see the unit book review). Then invite the children to make mud pies. Use sand pails, buckets, or bowls, and spoons or sand shovels for the children to dig a cupful of dirt (or buy potting soil). Encourage the children to wear paint shirts and spread an old shower curtain over a large table to use as a work space. Or, on a nice day, take the children outside and have them stand around a long table. Add a little water to each child's dirt. The mud should be thick instead of runny. Invite the children to squish the mud through their fingers, make mud "pies," and so on. Have the children put mud on fingerpaint paper, smear the mud all over the paper, and then use their index fingers to practice making the letter M.

Mushroom

❖ Show the children how to draw a simple picture of a mushroom.

❖ Invite the children to taste raw mushrooms. (Caution the children to never eat mushrooms in the wild unless a knowledgeable adult identifies the mushrooms as safe to eat.) Cut up some mushrooms and sauté them in butter. Encourage each child to taste the cooked mushrooms. Then discuss how the cooked mushrooms are the same and how they are different from the raw mushrooms.

❖ Make mushroom prints. Cut raw mushrooms in half the long way. Put tempera paint in a styrofoam meat tray and invite the children to dip the flat half of a mushroom in the paint. The children may then use the mushroom piece to print mushroom shapes on a practice sheet of paper. When children begin to get a good print, invite them to print the mushrooms on a large M cut from construction paper to make a "Mushroom M."

Music

❖ Teach the class to play "Musical Chairs." Instead of the traditional game which eliminates a child each time the music stops, try a more cooperative variation of the game. Play music as usual, starting with one less chair than the number of children you have playing. When the music stops and all of the children must find a seat, encourage one of the children to share his or her seat with the child who is left chairless. Repeat, each time eliminating a chair, and encouraging more and more children to share seats to accommodate everyone. In this game, you eliminate chairs instead of children!

❖ Play lots of music this week for the children's listening pleasure. Try classical music during quiet times.

❖ Ask the physical education teacher to loan your class an exercise record with music especially made for young children. Encourage the children to experiment with different movements, such as walking, running, skipping, hopping, and even bouncing balls.

❖ Ask the music teacher to plan something special with your class this week. Perhaps it can be arranged for the children to see a musical show or concert. Invite an in-school performer to your classroom, teach the class a song about an M word, or even plan a performance by some other school members.

❖ Plan a very simple musical performance with your class, such as a few songs and a dance. Invite another class or parents as guests.

❖ Ask the music teacher to show the class a musical score and then help the children practice drawing whole notes, half notes, and quarter notes. Have him or her explain to your class the different values in the musical notes as well. Cut M's from white construction paper and invite the children to make notes with black crayons.

Food for Thought

Introducing children to a variety of foods is a wonderful way of reinforcing language concepts. The following foods all begin with the letter M and may be introduced at any time during this unit.

macaroni, mangos, margarine, marmalade, matzo, mayonnaise, meatballs, meat loaf, melon, milk, minestrone, molasses, muffins, mushrooms, mustard

Book Review

Children enjoy hearing good books read aloud. The books listed here are favorites of children and may be used to reinforce the letter M.

Ahlberg, Janet and Ahlberg, Allan. *The Jolly Postman,* Little, Brown and Company, 1986.

Asch, Frank. *Milk and Cookies,* Parents Magazine Press, 1982.

Barrett, Judith. *Cloudy with a Chance of Meatballs,* Macmillan, 1985.

Barton, Byron. *Machines at Work,* Harper & Row, 1987.

Berenstain, Stan and Berenstain, Janice. *The Berenstain Bears and the Messy Room,* Random House, 1987.

Branley, Franklyn M. and Vaughn, Eleanor K. *Mickey's Magnet,* Scholastic, 1988.

Brown, Margaret Wise. *Goodnight, Moon,* Harper & Row, 1977.

Brown, Margaret Wise. *Wait Till the Moon Is Full,* Harper & Row, 1948.

Burton, Virginia L. *Mike Mulligan and His Steam Shovel,* Houghton Mifflin, 1977.

Carrick, Donald. *Milk,* Greenwillow Books, 1985.

Crowe, Robert L. *Clyde Monster,* E. P. Dutton, 1976.

Eastman, Philip D. *Are You My Mother?,* Beginner Books, 1960.

Ets, Marie H. *Just Me,* Penguin Books, 1965.

Galdone, Paul. *The Monster and the Tailor,* Ticknor & Fields, 1982.

Gibbons, Gail. *The Post Office Book,* Harper & Row, 1982.

Graham, John. *I Love You, Mouse,* Harcourt Brace Jovanovich, 1976.

Grey, Judith. *Mud Pies,* Troll Associates, 1981.

Hawkins, Colin. *Take Away Monsters,* Putnam Publishing Group, 1984.

Hoffman, Mary. *Monkey,* Random House, 1984.

Johnson, Jean. *Postal Workers: A to Z,* Walker and Company, 1987.

Kellogg, Steven. *The Mystery of the Missing Red Mitten,* Dial Books, 1977.

Lasker, Joe. *Mothers Can Do Anything,* Albert Whitman, 1972.

Mayer, Mercer. *I Was So Mad,* Golden Press, 1983.

Mayer, Mercer. *Me, Too!,* Western Publishing, 1985.

McNaught, Harry. *Muppets in My Neighborhood,* Random House, 1977.

Rockwell, Anne. *Machines,* Macmillan, 1972.

Shulevitz, Uri. *One Monday Morning,* Macmillan, 1986.

Tresselt, Alvin. *Mitten,* Lothrop, 1964.

Wiseman, Bernard. *Morris the Moose,* Harper & Row, 1989.

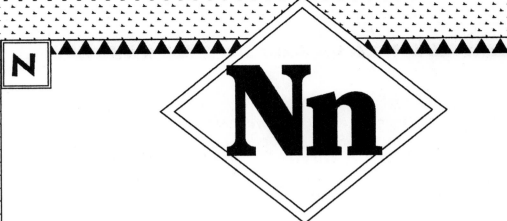

Nachos

❖   Invite the children to help make "Nachos."

Nachos	
round or triangular corn tortilla chips	Arrange the chips in a single layer on a cookie sheet. Top each chip with 1/2 tsp of refried beans and then 1/2 tsp salsa.
1 can refried beans	Add a small amount of cheese (grated or
1 small jar mild salsa or taco sauce	cut into small chunks) to the top of each. Put the cookie sheet in a 425° oven,
6 oz cheddar or Monterey Jack cheese	watching carefully, until cheese melts and bubbles.

Name

❖   Make "Nice Names."

Nice Names

cupcakes
icing of choice
alphabet cereal

Make and ice cupcakes or buy ready-made cupcakes. Spread the alphabet cereal in a single layer on wax paper. Invite each child to choose the letters in his or her first name. Invite the children to arrange the letters on the cupcakes to spell their names.

❖ Invite the children to copy on their own papers the first and last names of all the children in the class as you write the names on the chalkboard. Then help the children use a red crayon to circle all of the upper and lower case N's. Make a prepared master of all the students' names for the less experienced children. Help them circle the N's on the master.

❖ Read *The Boy Who Would Not Say His Name* by Margaret Hillert (see the unit book review). Provide opportunities for the children to answer the question, "What is your name?" Encourage more advanced children to learn their first, middle, and last names.

❖ Make name puzzles to help children who have difficulty sequencing the letters of their name. Cut out several 1-inch squares of colored construction paper. Write each letter of a child's name on a separate square and then glue the letters in sequence on a quarter sheet of construction paper. Write each letter of the child's name again on separate squares and store these squares loosely in a library pocket glued to the back of the name puzzle. Make a name puzzle for each child. Instruct the children to match and line up each loose letter with the prepared name puzzle, saying each letter aloud as they match the letters in order from left to right. Name puzzles may be made for last names once the first names are memorized. (It is important for children to visualize the order of the letters in their names when they are learning to print their names.) Remove the name puzzle models when the children are ready and give them only the individual letter pieces to sequence in order.

❖ Provide opportunities for the children to practice writing their names in answer to the written statement: "Name: _____." Start by teaching the children to write each letter of their names, learning one letter at a time, practicing on newsprint. After the letters have been mastered, move to newsprint folded in half and then into fourths. When the children feel comfortable writing their names on the newsprint divided into fourths, move to large lined paper. After the children have had experiences visualizing the left-to-right letter sequence, help them work on correct letter formation. Invite the children to practice correct letter formation and left-to-right sequencing (you might use dots or have the children trace over your letters at first). Monitor the children closely to make sure they are forming the letters correctly.

❖ Name tags will help children learn their classmates' names. Make name tags for the children to wear while they are working on this letter. Write each child's name on a large rectangular piece of tagboard. Punch holes on both ends of each strip and put yarn through so the children may wear the name tags around their necks. Help the children label their crayon boxes, coat hooks, chairs, work spaces, and other personal items in the classroom to provide practice recognizing their own names and their classmates' names.

❖ Make name mobiles. Draw a circle, square, triangle, and rectangle on heavy paper for each child. Invite the children to cut out the shapes and then punch a hole at the top and bottom. Have the children write "My" on both sides of the circle with a black crayon or marker. Have the children write "name" on both sides of the rectangle, "is" on both sides of the triangle, and the child's own name on both sides of the square (you might have to do the writing for less experienced children). Show the children how to straighten out four paper clips to make an S shape. Then help the children use the paper clips to hook the shapes together. Use yarn to hang each mobile above the child's desk.

❖ Make flash cards of all the children's names. Give a star, rubber stamp on the back of the hand, or some other reward to each child who learns all of the names.

Napkin

❖ Demonstrate how to correctly use a napkin at mealtime. Give an "N Is for Napkin" award to each child who uses a napkin correctly without being told. Make the award by first cutting out a circle from colored construction paper. Write "N Is for Napkin" on the circle. Then unfold a paper napkin, pull the middle portion to a point, and tape the point to the underside of the circle.

❖ Reinforce using a tissue for coughing, sneezing, and blowing the nose. Have tissues available for the children's use in your classroom. Ask each parent to contribute a box of tissues at the beginning of the year (or use a roll of toilet paper inside a tall tissue box dispenser—the tall dispensers fit perfectly over a toilet paper roll).

❖ Give each child a plain white paper napkin. Invite the children to fold the napkins any way they choose. The folding does not need to be symmetrical—the napkin may even be wadded up. Have the children slowly drop food coloring on the napkin (use the drop control vials). Encourage the children to use colors that blend to make another color, such as red and yellow, red and blue, or blue and yellow. Help the children unfold the napkins very carefully. Place the napkins on sheets of construction paper and glue the corners down. Glue a frame over the top (a sheet of construction paper with the center cut out) in a complementary color. These colored napkins make beautiful abstract designs.

Neck

❖ Discuss when a necktie may be worn. Cut out necktie patterns from heavy cardboard. Invite the children to trace a necktie on a piece of white construction paper and then use crayons, markers, watercolors, or tempera paint to make designs. Show some real neckties to the children as models.

Nest

❖ Make "Nice Nutty Noodly Nests."

Nice Nutty Noodly Nests

1 package butterscotch morsels 1 jar salted nuts 1 can Chinese noodles jellybeans, grapes, or cooked peas butter (optional)	Melt the butterscotch morsels in a pan over low heat. Remove from the heat and add the nuts and noodles. Give each child a small piece of wax paper and about 2 tablespoons of mixture. Invite the children to form the mixture into a nest shape. Suggest that children put butter on their hands to keep the mixture from sticking. When the mixture is hard, have the children add jellybeans, grapes, or cooked peas for eggs.

❖ If possible, bring an abandoned bird's nest to class for the children to see. Help the children identify the various materials that birds use to make nests. Show the children how to draw a simple picture of a large nest. On a nice day, take the children on a walk outside to collect items that a bird might use to build a nest. Encourage the children to look for leaves, straw, and small sticks. When you return to the classroom, put glue in a small container and invite the children to use paintbrushes to paint glue all over their nest pictures. Have the children arrange several of the collected items on the glue. The glue dries fast, so encourage the children to work quickly. Suggest that children add some small blue construction-paper circles for eggs, if they wish.

❖ Invite children to play with nesting cups or nesting blocks. Use nesting cups and blocks to reinforce sequencing by size for children still having difficulty.

Net

❖ Display a real net in the classroom. Encourage the children to guess how the net might be used. Explain that nets are used to catch butterflies, to pull big fish out of the water after they have been hooked, to catch minnows for fishing bait, to catch shrimp in salt water, and so on. See how many other uses the class can think of for nets. Purchase some netting at a fabric store to show the children. Discuss when netting might be used on clothing. Point out that netting is used on many dance costumes, formal dresses, hat veils, and wedding dresses. Ask the children to discuss how a net used for catching fish and net fabric are alike and how they are different.

Newspaper

❖ Bring a newspaper to school and point out the various parts to the children. Help the children find the comics, want ads, for-sale ads, weather, movies, and news sections. Cut a section of a newspaper into strips and invite the children to cut the strips into small squares. Have the children make a large letter N with glue on a piece of construction paper and arrange the newspaper pieces along the glue line to make a "Newsy N."

❖ If possible, arrange for the class to visit the local newspaper office. When you return to the classroom, help the children make newspaper hats. Give each child a double folded piece of newspaper. With the folded side at the top, help the children turn the corners in to meet in the center. Show the children how to fold the bottom up on each side and tape to hold. Suggest that children use markers to write N's all along the brim.

❖ Give each child a quarter piece of newspaper. Invite the children to use a red crayon to circle as many N's as they can find on the sheet (especially the N's in the titles and bold print).

Nickel

❖ Make patterns of the letter N from heavy cardboard. Help the children trace around a pattern on light-colored construction paper. Invite the children to cut out their letters and then use a nickel rubber stamp to stamp nickel prints all over their construction paper N's. (Inexpensive head and tail rubber stamps may be purchased commercially.)

❖ Make rubbings of a nickel. Give each child a real nickel and a sheet of typing paper. Instruct the children to position the paper over the nickel and then find the nickel with their fingers. Invite the children to hold the nickel in place with one hand and rub over the nickel with a crayon with their other hand. Encourage the children to make rubbings of the heads and tails and then discuss the prints.

Night

❖ Invite children to paint night pictures on sheets of black construction paper. Show the children how to round the corners of a small, square sheet of yellow construction paper to make a round moon. Provide adhesive stars or have the children tear up small pieces of white construction paper to represent stars.

❖ Help the class make a list of the activities they do after dark, such as sleep, eat supper, put on pajamas, watch TV, take a bath, and so on. Read *The Nighttime Book* by Mauri Kunnas, *At Night* by Anne Rockwell, *Night in the Country* by Cynthia Rylant, *There's a Nightmare in My Closet* by Mercer Mayer, and *Goodnight, Goodnight* by Eve Rice (see the unit book review).

Noise

❖ Invite children to make "a joyful noise" this week. Gather a variety of rhythm instruments. Then play some music and invite the children to play along. Lead a parade throughout the school!

❖ Read *Sounds All Around* by Jane B. Moncure, *My Very First Book of Sounds* by Eric Carle, and *Noisy* by Shirley Hughes (see the unit book review). Ask each child to cut out pictures from magazines of noise makers, such as cars, machines, instruments, and people. Encourage the children to discuss their pictures with the class and then glue their pictures on a bulletin board covered with paper.

❖ Make a balloon "Noise Band." Give some children inflated and tied balloons. Invite these children to make noise by thumping and rubbing the balloons. Give other children inflated and tied balloons that contain a few paper clips or some rice. Invite these children to make "noise" by shaking their balloons. Invite the children who are able to blow up a balloon by themselves to make noise by blowing up a balloon and stretching the neck to make squeaks. Try having the "Noise Band" accompany music, or just say, "Make noise" and "Now stop!"

Noodles

❖ Give each child a letter N cut from construction paper and a handful of uncooked noodles. Put glue in a plastic lid, invite the children to dip their noodles into the glue, and arrange the noodles on the construction-paper N.

❖ Make "Buttered Noodles." Invite the children to taste an uncooked noodle. Then after they taste the cooked noodles, discuss how the uncooked and cooked noodles are alike and how they are different.

Buttered Noodles

1 8-oz box noodles	Boil 3 quarts of water and then add the noodles. Add the oil to the water to prevent sticking. Boil 7 to 10 minutes and then drain in a colander. Melt the butter. Pour over the noodles and coat well.
water	
2 tsp oil	
4 Tbsp butter	
or margarine	

Noon

❖ Explain that noon is the same as 12:00. Demonstrate on a toy clock that both the long hand and the short hand point straight up to the 12 when it is noon. Invite the children to discuss what they might be doing at noon.

❖ Praise the first child each day this week who reminds you when it is exactly noon.

Nose

❖ Discuss the nose and the function of a nose. Encourage the children to name the five senses. Invite the children to cut out pictures of noses from magazines to make a collage. Remind children to select animal noses, too.

❖ Cut a large letter N from white construction paper. Then, if available, invite the children to use scented markers or scented pencils to color the N. Help the children identify each of the scents.

❖ Use scented stickers as reinforcers this week for good work, good behavior, and so on. Encourage the children to close their eyes and try to identify the smell of each sticker.

❖ Read *Arthur's Nose* by Marc Brown and *The Nose Book* by Al Perkins (see the unit book review). Draw a red letter N on each child's nose with lipstick. The lipstick may be removed easily with cold cream.

❖ Gather a variety of foods that might be identified by their smell. Challenge the children to close their eyes and take a sniff as you hold each food under their noses.

Numbers

❖ Play "Number Bingo." There are inexpensive commercial games available, or make your own game. The object of the game is for each player to match the numbers on the playing card with the number cards the "caller" holds up. When a child covers all the numbers on his or her card, he or she yells "Bingo" and wins the game. Most "Number Bingo" games are played with the numbers one to twenty, but may be made for one to ten or one to thirty.

❖ Help the children write numbers in sequence from one to ten. Add more numbers as the children are ready. Give the children having difficulty dot numbers to trace. Then provide fewer and fewer dots with each trial until the children are writing the numbers without assistance.

❖ Invite the children to practice writing numbers on the chalkboard in small groups. Suggest that each group watch as you write a number on the board. "Talk" the number through. For example, say "Down and stop" as you make number one, "Around and over" as you make number two, "Around and around" as you make number three, "Down, over, down" as you make number four, and "Down, around, put a cap on it" as you make number five. Then have the children practice writing that number. Write a large number on the chalkboard for the children to trace over if they are having difficulty making their own numbers. Encourage these children to say the instructional words as they trace over the number until they can write the number without the extra help.

❖ Provide opportunities for the class to recite the numbers from one to ten in unison every day. Add more numbers as the class is ready (you might count during calendar time by having the children count the days as you point to them on the calendar). Invite the children to recite individually and in a variety of groupings, such as all the girls, all the boys, all children wearing red, children who have an N in their first name, and so on.

❖ Write the numbers one to ten on flash cards. Then use the flash cards to help children read the numbers aloud as you flash the cards in sequential order and then in random order. Add more numbers as the class is ready.

❖ Give each child a set of numbered index cards in a personalized envelope. Give each child numbers according to his or her own ability. Each day, set aside a few minutes to invite the children to take out their envelopes and sequence the number cards in order. When children sequence their cards correctly without assistance, add more numbers.

❖ Read *Numbers* by John J. Reiss (see the unit book review). Teach the children to sing "This Old Man" from *Wee Sing Nursery Rhymes and Lullabies* and "One, Two, Buckle My Shoe" from *Wee Sing and Play*.

❖ Give each child a heavy cardboard pattern of the letter N. Have the children trace around the N on light-colored construction paper and then cut it out as well. Suggest that children make nine 9's on the N. Some children may wish to cut out 9's from the grocery section of a newspaper and glue those numbers on the N instead.

❖ Give the children large pieces of newsprint to fold into fourths. Have children trace along the fold line with a crayon. Ask the children to write a number 9 on each folded section and then give each child a handful of noodles and a plastic lid filled with glue. Instruct the children to dip the noodles into the glue and then arrange nine noodles in each section of the newsprint.

Nurse

❖ Invite the school nurse to come visit your classroom and explain to the children what a nurse does.

❖ Discuss why we have nurses. Point out that nurses help to keep us well, take care of sick people, take care of us when we get hurt, help doctors, and so on. Read *I Can Be a Nurse* by June Behrens (see the unit book review).

❖ Invite the children to role-play being a nurse. Encourage them to pantomime taking a patient's temperature, weighing and measuring a person, taking someone's blood pressure, giving a shot, placing a bandage on an arm or leg, and so on.

Nuts

❖ Put out a bag of assorted nuts in the shell, such as walnuts, Brazil nuts, peanuts, pecans, hickory nuts, almonds, pistachios, and so on. Help the children sort the nuts into like stacks. Then crack the nuts and invite the children to eat them. Vote to see which nuts the children like best. Put the nutshells in a paper bag and use a hammer to crush them into little pieces. Have each child make a large letter N with glue on a sheet of construction paper and sprinkle the nut shells along the glue line. When the glue is dry, help the children carefully shake off the excess shells to reveal a "Nutty N."

❖ Teach the children to sing "I'm a Nut" from *Wee Sing Silly Songs*.

❖ Set up a "Nut Center" this week. Set out large nuts, bolts, and washers. Then invite the children to practice sorting and fitting these objects together.

Food for Thought

Introducing children to a variety of foods is a wonderful way of reinforcing language concepts. The following foods all begin with the letter N and may be introduced at any time during this unit.

nachos, navy beans, nectarines, Neapolitan ice cream, noodles, Northern beans, nut bread, nuts

Book Review

Children enjoy hearing good books read aloud. The books listed here are favorites of children and may be used to reinforce the letter N.

Behrens, June. *I Can Be a Nurse,* Childrens Press, 1986.
Brown, Marc. *Arthur's Nose,* Little, Brown and Company, 1986.
Carle, Eric. *My Very First Book of Sounds,* Harper & Row, 1986.
Hillert, Margaret. *The Boy Who Would Not Say His Name,* Modern Curriculum Press, 1989.
Hughes, Shirley. *Noisy,* Lothrop, 1985.
Kunnas, Mauri. *The Nighttime Book,* Crown, 1985.
Mayer, Mercer. *There's a Nightmare in My Closet,* Dial Books, 1986.
Moncure, Jane B. *Sounds All Around,* Childrens Press, 1982.
Perkins, Al. *The Nose Book,* Random House, 1970.
Reiss, John J. *Numbers,* Macmillan, 1987.
Rice, Eve. *Goodnight, Goodnight,* Penguin Books, 1983.
Rockwell, Anne. *At Night,* Harper & Row, 1986.
Rylant, Cynthia. *Night in the Country,* Bradbury Press, 1986.

N

Oo

Oatmeal

❖ Make "Oatmeal Cookies."

Oatmeal Cookies

3 cups uncooked oatmeal	Preheat oven to 350°. Mix together the oil, sugar, water, egg, and vanilla in a bowl. Add the other ingredients and mix well. Drop the dough by teaspoonfuls on a cookie sheet sprayed with Pam. Bake for 12 to 15 minutes.
1 cup all-purpose flour	
1 tsp vanilla	
1/2 tsp baking soda	
3/4 cup vegetable oil	
1 cup firmly packed brown sugar	
1 egg	
1/2 cup sugar	
1/4 cup water	
raisins, chocolate chips, or chopped nuts (optional)	

❖ Have each child make a large letter O with glue on a sheet of construction paper. Then invite the children to sprinkle oatmeal on the glue. When the glue is dry, help children shake off the excess oatmeal to reveal an "Oatmeal O."

❖ Make oatmeal. Try one of the new instant flavored varieties that may be made by adding warm tap water. Invite the children to taste the oatmeal before it is cooked and then again after it is cooked. Discuss how raw and cooked oatmeal are alike and how they are different.

Octopus

❖ Read *My Very Own Octopus* by Bernard Most (see the unit book review). Help the children make an octopus from construction paper. Give each child a square piece of black construction paper (about 5" x 5"). Show children how to round the corners to make a circle. This will be the octopus' body. Then children may make the eight legs by cutting 1-inch strips from a piece of construction paper (about 4" x 8"). Suggest that children make the eyes from scraps of paper. Glue each child's octopus on a bulletin board covered with blue construction paper.

❖ Discuss where the octopus lives. Help the children name other animals that make their homes under water, such as jellyfish, oysters, clams, swordfish, whales, sharks, shellfish, shrimp, lobster, and so on.

Office

❖ Arrange for the children to visit the school office when it is not busy. Help the children identify and label the standard office equipment, such as typewriters, computers, staplers, rulers, pens, pencils, folders, telephones, telephone books, file cabinets, and desks.

❖ Set up an "Office Center" this week. Put a desk and standard office supplies that you might use in the center. For example, invite the children to use and experiment with paper, pads, pencils, pens, staplers, file folders, typewriters, and telephones.

Okra

❖ Cut off an end of an okra for each child. Have the children make a large letter O with an orange crayon on orange construction paper. Then invite the children to dip the cut end of the okra pieces in a plate of green tempera paint (or have them press the cut end of the okra pieces on a green ink pad) and stamp okra prints all along the crayon line to make an "Okra O." Make "Fried Okra" with the leftover okra.

Fried Okra

1 tsp salt
4 cups sliced okra
1 cup cornmeal
1 cup oil for frying

Cut the okra into little rounds and throw away the ends. Add the salt to the cornmeal and roll the okra in the mixture. Fry the okra in hot oil until golden brown. Drain on paper towels.

Olive

❖ Show the children some green olives and black olives. Help the children describe an olive using all of their senses. Point out that an olive has an oval shape. Show the children how to draw simple pictures of an olive. Stress drawing ovals. Then use the olives to make "Outstanding Olive Sandwiches."

Outstanding Olive Sandwiches

cream cheese	Use a doughnut cutter to cut the bread into O shapes. You may also use cookie cutters, jars, glasses, or cans with both ends cut off. Spread cream cheese on the bread slices. Slice olives and arrange on top of the cream cheese. Serve open-faced.
olives	
bread	

❖ Make construction-paper olives. Give each child a large rectangular piece of olive green construction paper for the olive and a much smaller rectangular piece of orange/red construction paper for the pimiento. Show the children how to round the corners of both rectangles to make an oval. Then have the children glue the orange/red oval on the tip of the green oval to make an olive.

Onion

❖ Hold up an onion for the children to see and ask them if they can identify it. Explain that an onion is a vegetable. Invite the children to name other vegetables. Encourage the children to describe the onion using all of their senses.

O

Then help children compare an onion to other familiar vegetables. Cut an onion into thick slices. Separate the rings to make circles of various sizes. Put white tempera paint in styrofoam meat trays and invite the children to dip the onion rings in the paint and use the rings to stamp O's all over a sheet of construction paper.

O-o-o-o!

❖ Cut a large letter O from construction paper and invite the children to stick hole reinforcers all over the O. Hole reinforcers are available with a gummed backing or a self-sticking backing.

❖ Many cereals are O-shaped. Select a nutritious O-shaped cereal. Have the children draw a large letter O with an orange crayon on a piece of construction paper. Invite the children to arrange the cereal along the crayon line to make a "Cereal O" and then eat the cereal when they are finished.

❖ Make cereal necklaces. Use an O-shaped cereal. For colored cereal that the children may eat, soak the cereal in a mixture of water and food coloring for about 30 seconds. Drain the cereal, spread it out on a cookie sheet, and bake for thirty minutes at 250°. Invite the children to use yarn or thin telephone cable wire to string the round cereal to make necklaces. Point out that the completed necklaces are also in the shape of an O.

❖ Make a circle chain. Give the children 12" x 12" squares of construction paper to cut into strips. Show the children how to staple or glue the ends of one strip together to make a circle. Then instruct children to slip the next strip through the circle and staple or glue the ends of that strip together to make another circle, and so on until all the strips are used. Point out that each stapled strip is in the shape of an O. Join all of the children's chains together to make one long chain. Then use the chain to decorate a door frame or as a bulletin-board border.

❖ Help the children make a list of foods that are shaped like an O.

❖ Challenge the children to make an O shape with their arms, fingers, legs, whole body, and mouth. Encourage the children to think of other ways that they might make an O shape, too.

Opposites

❖ Read *Over-Under* by Catherine Matthias, *Over, Under and Through* by Tana Hoban, *More Opposites* by Eric Hill, *Fast-Slow, High-Low: A Book of Opposites* by Peter Spier, and *Push, Pull, Empty, Full: A Book of Opposites* by Tana Hoban (see the unit book review). Use any cards or games in your classroom that show pictures of opposites. Hold up one card of a pair of opposites. Help the children identify the picture and then challenge them to name the opposite. Provide opportunities for the children to work individually or together in small groups to match pairs of opposite cards as well.

❖ Arrange one-half of a set of opposite cards along the chalkboard ledge. Then hold up the cards from the other half of the set, one card at a time, and invite the children to find the matching opposite cards on the ledge. When the children become comfortable and successful at matching cards, try just calling out the word or object without showing the children the picture cards, and ask the children to name the opposites. Use opposites such as little/ big, long/short, tall/short, slow/fast, go/stop, empty/full, fat/skinny, up/down, in/out, bottom/top, over/under, closed/open, above/below, front/back, right/left, on/off, day/night, hot/cold, run/walk, wet/dry, hard/soft, rough/ smooth, bad/good, loud/soft, clean/dirty, first/last, spoiled/fresh, and so on.

❖ Turn the lights on and off and then ask the children to call out the appropriate opposite words. Do the same with a flashlight, a mixer, or other items in your classroom that may be used to demonstrate "on" and "off."

❖ Help the children make a list of items that may be opened, such as doors, windows, gifts, boxes, letters, books, jewelry boxes, lunch boxes, umbrellas, scissors, jars, drawers, and so on. Invite the children to demonstrate opening and closing their mouths, arms, legs, fingers, hands, fists, and eyes. Teach the children the fingerplay "Open, Shut Them" from *Finger Frolics: Fingerplays for Young Children* by Liz Cromwell and Dixie Hibner (Partner Press, 1976).

Orange

❖ Give each child an orange. Point out that an orange is a fruit. Ask the children to name other fruits. Show the children how to draw a simple picture of an orange. Help the children describe their oranges using all of their senses, except taste. Then encourage children to add more details to their pictures, if they wish. Collect all of the oranges and use them to make freshly squeezed orange juice.

❖ Cut several oranges in half. Have the children draw a large letter O with a crayon on a large piece of construction paper. To make an "Orange O," invite the children to dip the cut end of an orange half in a plate of orange tempera paint and use it as a rubber stamp to make orange prints all along the drawn O.

❖   Cut an orange into thin slices. Give each child a slice to eat, being careful to leave the circular rind intact. Then suggest that children dip the round rinds in orange tempera paint and use them to make O prints on a sheet of construction paper.

❖   Make "Orange Balls."

Orange Balls

3/4 cup coconut
1 package vanilla wafers
1/2 cup concentrated frozen orange juice (without water added)
confectioners' powdered sugar

Crush the vanilla wafers. Add coconut and juice and mix together with your hands. Form the mixture into 1-inch balls. Roll the balls in sugar and then refrigerate.

❖   Help the children make a list of common items that are usually orange in color, such as jack-o'-lanterns, pumpkins, carrots, tangerines, and so on. Encourage the children to cut out pictures of orange items from magazines to make an orange collage.

❖ Put large dabs of red and yellow fingerpaint on pieces of fingerpaint paper and invite the children to smear the paint together to discover the color orange. Then encourage the children to use their index fingers to practice making O's in the paint. Have the children save their best drawn O's by transferring them to a sheet of yellow or white construction paper. Help the children gently position the sheet of construction paper over the fingerpainting, gently pat all over the paper, and then carefully peel off the construction paper to reveal the print underneath.

❖ Make orange fingerpaint pumpkins. Cut fingerpaint paper into a pumpkin shape. Invite the children to smear red and yellow fingerpaint all over their papers and then use their index fingers to draw detail lines on their pumpkins.

Outlet

❖ Take the children on a tour of your classroom to identify where all of the electrical outlets are located. (If you don't already have safety plugs in the unused outlets, ask the principal to supply you with the protectors.) Discuss some safety "Do's" and "Don'ts" involving outlets. Then help the children reword the "Don't" statements to make them "Do" statements. For example, "Don't put a cord under a carpet" might be reworded as "Always keep cords above a carpet," "Don't put too many plugs in an outlet," might become "Only put one plug in each outlet," "Don't use anything electrical near water" could be reworded as "Use electrical items away from water," and "Don't put fingers and pointed objects in an outlet" might become "Keep fingers and pointed objects out of outlets." Invite the children to make a safety poster for each rule. Show children how to draw a simple picture of an outlet to put on each poster as well.

Outside

❖ Take the children on a walk outside to collect straw, small sticks, leaves, and so on. When you return to the classroom, cut out a large letter O from construction paper and invite the children to glue their outside treasures on the O.

❖ Set up an obstacle course outside. Encourage the children to practice walking the course as you talk them through it. Set up the course so you may use directional words, such as "over" the swing, "under" the sliding board, "in, out, around" the hula hoop, "right" or "left" of the monkey bars, and so on. When the children have had ample opportunities to practice walking the obstacle course, challenge them to run through the course. Time each child with a stopwatch.

Oval

❖ Cut out a circle and an oval shape from construction paper. Discuss how a circle and an oval are alike and how they are different. Give each child a rectangular piece of construction paper. Show the children how they may make an oval shape by rounding the corners of their rectangles with scissors.

❖ Make several oval patterns of various sizes from cardboard. Help the children trace around the patterns on a sheet of construction paper. Then have the children cut out their ovals. Explain the word *overlap* to the children. Make a collage by overlapping the children's cut-out ovals. Invite interested children to trace around an oval pattern on white construction paper. Encourage the children to make several ovals that do not overlap. Then invite the children to paint or color the ovals.

Oyster

❖ Have each child make a large letter O with an orange crayon on a sheet of construction paper. Invite children to arrange oyster crackers along the crayon line to make an "Oyster O" and then eat the crackers when they are finished.

Food for Thought

Introducing children to a variety of foods is a wonderful way of reinforcing language concepts. The following foods all begin with the letter O and may be introduced at any time during this unit.

oatmeal, oatmeal cookies, okra, olives, omelets, onions, onion soup, orange juice, oranges, oyster crackers, oysters

Book Review

Children enjoy hearing good books read aloud. The books listed here are favorites of children and may be used to reinforce the letter O.

Hill, Eric. *More Opposites,* Price Stern Sloan, 1982.
Hoban, Tana. *Over, Under and Through,* Macmillan, 1986.
Hoban, Tana. *Push, Pull, Empty, Full: A Book of Opposites,* Macmillan, 1972.
Matthias, Catherine. *Over-Under,* Childrens Press, 1984.
Most, Bernard. *My Very Own Octopus,* Harcourt Brace Jovanovich, 1980.

Spier, Peter. *Fast-Slow, High-Low: A Book of Opposites,* Doubleday, 1972.

Pp

Paint

❖ Cut out a large letter P from white construction paper and invite the children to use a watercolor palette to paint the P colors of their choice. Explain about carefully rinsing the brush between paints to prevent the colors from getting muddy.

❖ Discuss the difference between painters and artists. Invite the children to role-play painters. Give each child a container of water and a paintbrush and invite him or her to paint P's on the chalkboard, outside on the side of a building, or on other dark surfaces where the water will show.

❖ Read *The Mystery of the Stolen Blue Paint* by Steven Kellogg (see the unit book review). Set up a "Painting Center." If you have an easel in your classroom, put an old shower curtain under the easel to minimize the mess. It is a good idea to put this center near running water to help with cleanup as well. Teach the children how to use the "Painting Center." Stress cleanup procedures and wearing paint shirts or smocks. Provide very large painting paper and red, blue, and yellow paint. Put a paintbrush in each paint container. Suggest that children paint P's, something pretty, and then finally a picture of their choice. One or two children at the "Painting Center" at a time is plenty.

❖ Help the children make a list of items that begin with the letter P. Invite each child to choose a favorite item from the list to paint on a poster-size sheet of construction paper. Encourage the children to lightly pencil in the pictures first (stress large) and then use paint to fill in the lines. Help the children label their pictures as well.

Pancake

❖ Read *Pancakes for Breakfast* by Tomie de Paola (see the unit book review). Ask the children if they eat pancakes for breakfast. Help the children make a list of other breakfast foods, such as grits, oatmeal, cereal, eggs, toast, muffins, sausage, bacon, orange juice, grapefruit, canteloupe, melon, and oranges.

❖ Invite the children to help plan a breakfast party. Invite parents and the principal as guests. Make pancakes from a mix or use frozen pancakes. Serve the pancakes with powdered sugar and jelly. Encourage the children to make placemats from construction paper. Suggest that children draw pictures on the placemats of their favorite story characters eating pancakes.

Paper Clip

❖ Cut out a large letter P from posterboard for each child in the classroom. Give each child a handful of paper clips and invite the children to slip the paper clips all along the edges of the P.

❖ Challenge interested children to attach as many paper clips together as possible to make a long chain.

Parachute

❖ Borrow a parachute from the physical education teacher. Invite the children to hold on to the outside edge of the parachute. Practice such concepts as circle to the left or to the right and put the parachute down on the ground or up in the air. Challenge the children to try to get under the parachute while they still hold on to the edge as well. Put Ping-Pong balls in the middle of the parachute and have the children make them "pop" by flapping the parachute up and down. Try beach balls, volleyballs, and foam balls, too.

Party

❖ Read *The Paper Party* by Don Freeman (see the unit book review). Sponsor a "People We Love" or "People Who Help Us" party. Invite adults in school who work with the class, parents, or another class as guests. Make pretty party hats from construction paper. To make a cone-shaped hat, cut out a circle with a diameter the width of the paper. Give each child a circle to decorate with polka dots. Then cut in from the edge of each circle to the center, bend the cut sides around to form a cone, and secure with glue or a staple. Show the children how to make a yarn or crepe-paper pom-pom to attach to the top. Help the children make a list of party foods to serve that begin with the letter P. Encourage the children to bring to school a small amount of his or her favorite P food, such as potato chips, peanuts, pretzels, punch, popcorn, peppermint candies, and so on to share the day of the party.

Pea

❖ Invite the children to shell raw peas. Keep the shells. Encourage the children to taste the peas raw and then cook the peas and encourage them to taste them cooked. Discuss how the raw and cooked peas are alike and how they are different. Teach the children the rhyme "Pease Porridge Hot" from *Wee Sing and Play*.

❖ Make a large letter P with glue on a sheet of construction paper and invite the children to arrange pea shells on the glue to make a "Pea P."

Peanut

❖ Sponsor a "Peanut Fest." Make "Perfectly Peanutty Peanut Butter" and then use it to make "Peanut Butter Cookies." Make "Peach-Peanut Patties" to spread on the cookies! Teach the children the fingerplay "A Peanut Sat on a Railroad Track" from *Wee Sing Silly Songs*. Invite the children to sing "Found a Peanut" from *Wee Sing Silly Songs* as well. This song is easy to learn and a class favorite. Prompt the children before each verse by asking, "And what comes next?" You'll be amazed at how quickly the children will learn the sequence.

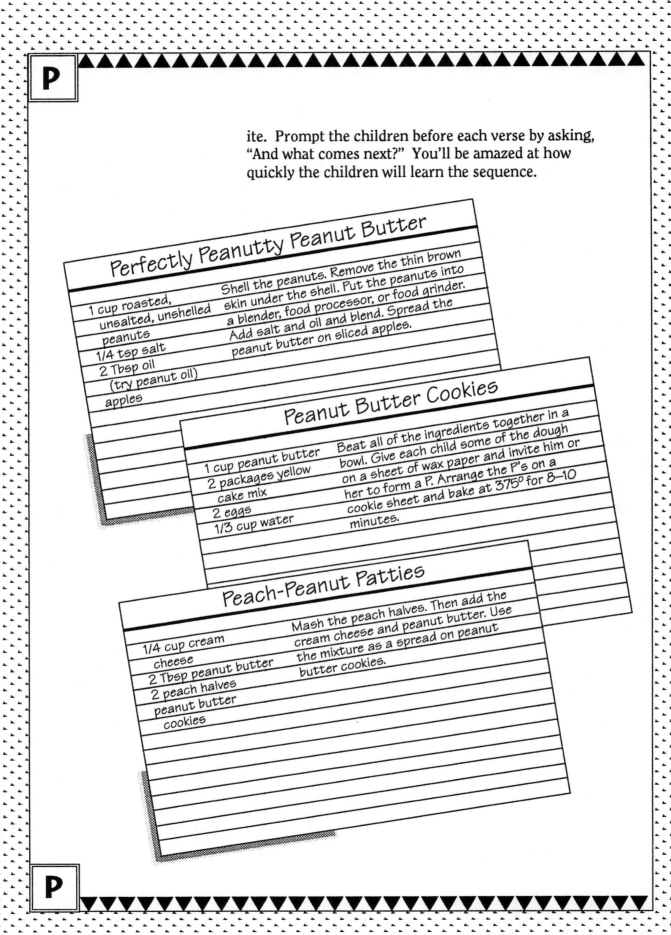

Perfectly Peanutty Peanut Butter

1 cup roasted, unsalted, unshelled peanuts	Shell the peanuts. Remove the thin brown skin under the shell. Put the peanuts into a blender, food processor, or food grinder. Add salt and oil and blend. Spread the peanut butter on sliced apples.
1/4 tsp salt	
2 Tbsp oil (try peanut oil)	
apples	

Peanut Butter Cookies

1 cup peanut butter	Beat all of the ingredients together in a bowl. Give each child some of the dough on a sheet of wax paper and invite him or her to form a P. Arrange the P's on a cookie sheet and bake at 375° for 8–10 minutes.
2 packages yellow cake mix	
2 eggs	
1/3 cup water	

Peach-Peanut Patties

1/4 cup cream cheese	Mash the peach halves. Then add the cream cheese and peanut butter. Use the mixture as a spread on peanut butter cookies.
2 Tbsp peanut butter	
2 peach halves	
peanut butter cookies	

❖ Boil raw (green) peanuts in salted water until the peanuts are somewhat soft. They will need to boil for an hour or two. Explain that these boiled peanuts are a Southern favorite.

❖ Invite the children to shell roasted peanuts in the shell. Save the shells. Have the children make a large letter P with a purple crayon on a sheet of construction paper. Give small groups of children a plastic lid filled with glue and invite them to dip peanut shells in the glue and arrange the shells along their crayon lines to make a "Peanutty P."

Pencil

❖ Encourage the children to practice making upper and lower case P's with a pencil on a bulletin board covered with white paper. Invite the children to fill the entire board with P's. Use a purple crayon to circle the best formed P's. Cut out a large letter P from white construction paper. Tack the P to the center of the bulletin board. Invite the children to use many different-colored pencils.

❖ Show the children how to draw a simple picture of a pencil. Then give each child a pencil. Help the children describe their pencils using all of their senses, except taste. Then encourage the children to add more detail to their original pencil pictures, if they wish.

❖ Read *If You Take a Pencil* by Fulvio Testa (see the unit book review). Discuss why we have pencils. Help the children make a list of other writing utensils, too, such as pens, crayons, and markers. Consider giving out purple and pink pencils for good behavior, good work, and so on.

Penguin

❖ Read *Penguins, Of All People!* by Don Freeman and *Pete the Penguin* by Jane Hammond (see the unit book review). Make penguins from construction paper. Give each child a rectangular piece of white construction paper for the body and a square piece of black construction paper for the head. Show the children how to round off the top two corners of the square. Hole reinforcers make nice eyes. Help the children trace around cardboard patterns on black construction paper for the wings. The beak may be made by folding a diamond-shaped piece of orange construction paper in half diagonally and then gluing one-half to the penguin's head. Suggest that children use paper scraps for feet.

Penny

❖ Cut out a large letter P from pink construction paper. Then invite the children to use a penny rubber stamp to make prints all over the P. Rubber stamps of the heads and tails of coins are inexpensive and may be purchased commercially.

❖ Use rubber stamps to fill a page with prints of all the different coins. Fill one page with the heads of all the coins and then fill another sheet with the tails of all the coins. Give each child a copy of both sheets and a handful of pennies with instructions to put a real penny on each of the penny stamps. After you have checked their work, invite the children to remove each penny from the sheet and then color the penny stamp with a purple crayon.

❖ Make a large letter P with a purple crayon. Give each child a handful of pennies to arrange on the purple crayon until the P is complete.

❖ Invite the children to sort a variety of coins (real or play money). Help the children sort the coins into like groups or into two more simple groups, such as pennies and not pennies. Discuss with the class how the penny is the same as the other coins and how it is distinctly different.

❖ Show the children how to fold a sheet of newsprint into fourths. Suggest that children open the paper and color along the fold lines with a purple crayon. Dictate a number from one to five or one to ten for the children to write in each section. Invite less experienced children to trace numbers. Give each child a handful of pennies and encourage him or her to count the appropriate number of pennies in each section. Have the children turn their papers over and dictate four new numbers.

❖ Play a game that teaches cooperation. Divide the class into small groups of three to four children. Give each group about fifteen pennies and a large bowl with a quarter or half-dollar in the bottom. Fill each bowl about half full with water and challenge the children in each group to take turns dropping pennies into the bowl. If one group completely covers the coin in the bottom of the bowl before they run out of pennies, that group wins. But if they don't cover the coin, the bowl wins.

People

❖ Make people paper dolls. Fold pink or purple paper into three sections accordion-style (the children can probably cut through about three thicknesses of paper easily). Cut out several girl and boy patterns from cardboard. Help the children trace around one of the patterns on the front cover of their folded papers. The arms, head, and legs must extend to the edges of the paper. Show the children how to cut out the dolls and then invite children to unfold their papers to reveal three dolls. Use the dolls as a nice bulletin-board border!

❖ Encourage the children to cut out pictures of people from magazines. Suggest that various ages and ethnic differences will enhance this activity. Invite children to glue the pictures on tagboard cards. Discuss each picture card. Ask the children to identify any pictures of community helpers. Ask the children to name each worker and the job the worker does. Then help the children sort the cards according to whether the picture is of a man, woman, girl, boy, or baby.

❖ Show the children how to draw a simple picture of a person. Label all the body parts as you draw them. Encourage more advanced children to add more details, such as eyebrows, eyelashes, lips, hands, knees, elbows, jewelry, clothes, and so on.

Peppermint

❖ Show the children a peppermint candy cane. Point out that usually peppermint candy is striped. Cut out several letter P patterns from cardboard. Help the children trace around a P on a sheet of white construction paper. Then help children use a ruler to make stripes. Invite the children to color every other stripe red to make a "Peppermint P."

Pets

❖ Read *Can I Keep Him?* by Steven Kellogg, *Crictor* by Tomi Ungerer, and *Pet Show!* by Ezra Jack Keats (see the unit book review). Invite each child to tell which animal he or she would most like to have as a pet and why. Discuss the pros and cons of keeping each animal the children name as a pet. Then help the children reach a consensus about the best animal to keep as a pet.

❖ Sponsor a "Picture-Perfect Pets" day. Invite the children who own pets to bring pictures of their pets to school to share with the rest of the class. Post the pictures on a bulletin board for all the children to enjoy.

❖ Read *Puppies Are Like That* by Jan Pfloog and *The Last Puppy* by Frank Asch (see the unit book review). Encourage children who have had experiences with puppies to share information with the rest of the class.

❖ Consider getting the class a pet if you don't already have one. You might borrow one for a short stay from another class or from one of the children in your classroom. Gerbils, hamsters, guinea pigs, fish, turtles, or rabbits make manageable pets. A class pet can be a wonderful experience for the entire class.

Pickle

❖ Invite the children to eat different kinds of pickles. Encourage children to try sweet and dill pickles, pickle relish, and so on. If possible, have some pickled peaches, pickled pig's feet, pickled eggs, pickled pears, pickled watermelon rind, and so on available for the children to taste. If you know someone who does a lot of canning and pickling, ask him or her to share some canned or pickled goods with the class. Encourage him or her to explain the pickling process, too.

❖ Explain to the children that pickles were once cucumbers. Bring some cucumbers and pickles for the children to taste. Discuss how the cucumber and pickle are alike and how they are different.

❖ Teach the children the nursery rhyme "Peter Piper" from *Wee Sing Nursery Rhymes and Lullabies*. Encourage the children to repeat each line of the rhyme after you. Start slowly and pick up speed as the children are able. Help the children identify all of the P words in each line, too.

Picnic and Park

❖ Arrange to take the class on a picnic. Have the picnic in a park, if possible. Invite the children to help plan and pack a lunch for the picnic. Plan a lunch with all P foods, such as peaches, potato chips, peanut butter sandwiches, plums, pretzels, pink lemonade, and pineapple pieces. Ask each child to contribute one item. Or you might ask each child to bring his or her own bag lunch for that day and pack one P food. Read *The Bears' Picnic* by Stan and Janice Berenstain to the children as they eat (see the unit book review).

❖ Read *When We Went to the Park* by Shirley Hughes, *The Park Book* by Charlotte Zolotow, and *Playgrounds* by Gail Gibbons (see the unit book review). Take the children to a nearby park. Ask the children to name all of the equipment there, such as slides, swings, merry-go-rounds, picnic tables, tires, climbing ropes, monkey bars or jungle gyms, ladders to climb across, tires to walk on and crawl through, and so on. When you return to the classroom, invite each child to share with the class his or her favorite piece of equipment.

Pig

❖ Teach the children the fingerplay "This Little Pig Went to Market" from *Wee Sing Nursery Rhymes and Lullabies*. Show the children how to draw a simple picture of a pig.

❖ Read *Pigs in Hiding* by Arlene Dubanevich, *Pigs Say Oink* by Martha Alexander, and *The Amazing Pig* by Paul Galdone (see the unit book review). Make several pig patterns from cardboard. Help the children trace around one of the patterns on pink construction paper. Ask parent volunteers to cut out the children's traced pigs (more experienced children may cut their own). Show the children how to glue small wadded-up pieces of pink tissue paper on their pigs and curl a pink pipe cleaner around their index fingers to form the pig's tail.

❖ Read *The Three Little Pigs* by Paul Galdone (see the unit book review). This is a wonderful story to tell the class from memory. Telling a story makes a good listening activity. When you finish, invite the children to draw pictures of their favorite parts of the story. Then encourage small groups of children to use their pictures to retell the story to the class. Some children may wish to act the story out as well.

Pineapple

❖ Show the children a fresh pineapple. Help children describe the fruit using all of their senses, except taste. Help the children name other fruits similar to pineapples as well. Encourage the children to discuss how the pineapple is alike and how it is different from other fruits. Cut a fresh pineapple for the children to sample.

❖ Make a P salad. Start with fresh pineapple or canned pineapple tidbits. Add chunks of canned or fresh peaches, pears, and plums. Sprinkle pecan pieces over the top. Serve the P salad on a place setting. Make "Pineapple Punch with Pizazz" to serve as a refreshment.

Pineapple Punch with Pizazz

1 can pineapple juice

1 large (2-liter) bottle ginger ale

pineapple sherbet or vanilla ice cream

Mix the juice and ginger ale. Pour into glasses and then add a scoop of sherbet to each glass.

Ping-Pong

❖ Teach the children to play "Ping-Pong Pass." Divide the class into two teams. Put each team on one side of a table. Place a Ping-Pong ball in the middle of the table. Each time the members of one of the teams blows the ball off the table on the opponent's side, that team earns a point. Five points wins the game.

Pink

❖ Cut pink construction paper into strips and ask the children to cut the strips into small squares. Have the children make a large letter P with glue on a sheet of construction paper. Invite the children to arrange the small pink squares along the glue line to make a "Pink P."

❖ Put a dab of red tempera paint into a small cup for each child. Add a dab of white tempera paint and invite the children to mix the two colors together with a paint-brush to discover pink. Suggest that children use their pink paint to paint P's on a large sheet of painting paper. Make pink lemonade to serve as a special treat.

Pizza

❖ Sponsor a "Pizza Party!" Make a pizza from scratch or a mix, buy a frozen pizza, or order out. Help the children make a list of their favorite pizza toppings, such as onions, green or black olives, extra cheese, pepperoni, bell peppers, mushrooms, and so on. Then ask each child to bring one of the toppings to school to add to a plain cheese pizza. Read *Curious George and the Pizza* by Margret Rey as the children eat (see the unit book review).

❖ Make individual pizzas. Use one side of a hamburger bun (one per child) as the pizza crust. Have a variety of toppings, too. Then invite the children to add a little tomato or prepared pizza sauce, cheese, and toppings of their choice. Show the children how to draw a simple picture of a pizza.

Plants

❖ Show the children four small plants. Point out that plants need air, water, soil, and light to survive. Explain that you are going to conduct an experiment for one week to find out if this is true. One plant will get no water, one plant will get no sunlight (put a box over this plant), one plant will be put in a pot with no soil, and the fourth plant will get water, soil, air, and light. At the end of one week discuss the results of the experiment with the class.

❖ On one half of a bulletin board, write "Animals" and on the other half write "Plants." Invite the children to cut out pictures from magazines to glue beneath each title. Discuss how plants and animals are alike. For example, both plants and animals need water. Discuss how they are different, too. Animals, for example, can move from place to place, but plants are secured to one place. Read *Plants in Winter* by Joanna Cole (see the unit book review).

Playdough

❖ Set up a "Playdough Center." Put out various colors of playdough, knowing that children will mix the colors! Otherwise, just put out one color at a time. (See page 76 for a recipe for making your own clay.) Invite the children to shape the playdough with cookie cutters, play knives, forks, spoons, plates, and other interesting items in the classroom. Monitor this center carefully after each group finishes to make sure the children are putting the tops back tightly on the playdough containers to prevent the dough from drying out.

❖ Give each child some playdough. Then encourage the children to mold the dough into items that begin with the letter P, such as pretzels, pigs, paddles, pencils, and pancakes. Invite the children to form the playdough into a letter P, too. Challenge children to make other letters of the alphabet as well.

Pocket

❖ Read *A Pocket for Corduroy* by Don Freeman (see the unit book review). Draw a pair of pants on a large sheet of purple or pink construction paper for each child to cut out or cut pants from white construction paper and invite the children to paint the pants either purple or pink. Give each child a library pocket to glue on the pants, too. Then encourage the children to cut out pictures of items from magazines that begin with the letter P to put in the pocket.

❖ Show the children a picture of a kangaroo. Focus the children's attention on the kangaroo's pocket. Explain that the kangaroo keeps its baby in the pocket until the baby is old enough to leave its mommy. Make an active bulletin board entitled "Pick-a-Pocket." Draw a picture of a kangaroo. Write upper case letters of the alphabet on small index cards to put in the kangaroo's pocket. Staple some library pockets to the bulletin board. Write the matching letters on the library pockets. Invite the children to take a card out of the kangaroo's pocket and place the card in the corresponding library pocket. More advanced children might be challenged to match upper case letters with lower case letters or even letters to pictures of the initial consonant sounds.

❖ Cut out a pocketbook pattern from cardboard and help interested children trace around the pattern on purple or pink construction paper folded in half. Align the bottom of the pocketbook along the fold line. Invite the children to cut out their pocketbooks and then cut out pictures of items that begin with the letter P from magazines to glue inside. When the pocketbooks are full of pictures, have the children fold it back in half and punch two holes at the top. String yarn through the holes to make a handle.

Police

❖ Discuss why we have police officers. Point out that police officers protect people, catch robbers, help people when they are in trouble, and so on. Read *Curious George Visits the Police Station* by Margret Rey and Allan J. Shalleck, *Police Officers: A to Z* by Jean Johnson, and *A Visit to the Police Station* by Dotti Hannum (see the unit book review).

❖ Make police puppets. Give each child a rectangular piece of blue construction paper for the body and a small square of construction paper for the head. Show the children how to round the corners of the square to make a circle for the face. Make a cardboard pattern for the hat (make a hat with a bill). Help the children trace around the pattern on blue construction paper and then invite them to cut out their own hat shape. Have the children fold the bill of the hat up to make it stand out. Next, have the children cut four strips of blue construction paper to make the arms and legs. Show the children how to fold each strip accordion-style and glue the arms and legs to the body. Encourage the children to add buttons, a star badge (gummed or adhesive backed), and facial features with scraps of paper. Some children may wish to use a crayon or marker to draw details on the police officer. Finally, tape or glue a popsicle stick or tongue depressor on the back of each puppet as a holder. Invite the children to use their puppets in a puppet theater.

Ponytail

❖ Sponsor a "Ponytail Day." Invite the children to bring to school any stuffed or rubber toy ponies they have at home. Some of these toy ponies have tails that may be combed. Encourage the children in your classroom who have long hair to wear a ponytail, if they wish. If possible, put your own hair in a ponytail, too! Ask the children to predict how ponytails got their name.

Pop

❖ Read *The Popcorn Book* by Tomie de Paola or *Popcorn* by Frank Asch (see the unit book review). Pop popcorn as a special treat.

❖ If possible, show the children popcorn-on-the-cob. Explain that popcorn grows on a cob just like sweet corn and field corn. Just for fun, invite the children to make a pretend popcorn tree. Draw a tree shape with limbs, but no leaves, for each child. Give small groups of children a plastic lid filled with glue. Then have the children dip popped kernels of popcorn in the glue and then put the popcorn "flowers" on the tree limbs.

❖ "Popples" are brightly colored stuffed animals and dolls that pop over and make something else, such as a pocketbook. Invite any children who have a Popple at home to bring it to school to demonstrate to the group. Read any of the Popples storybooks currently on the market as well.

❖ Teach the children to sing "Pop! Goes the Weasel" from *Wee Sing Children's Songs and Fingerplays*. Invite children to act out the song.

Potato

❖ Play "Hot Potato." Invite the children to sit in a circle on the floor. Give one child a potato. Explain that when you start to play some music, the children are to pass the potato around the circle as quickly as possible, as if the potato were very hot. When the music stops, the child left holding the potato is out and sits in the middle of the circle until another child is out and takes his or her place.

❖ Teach the children the choosing rhyme "Hot Potato" from *Wee Sing and Play* and then provide opportunities for the children to use the rhyme to choose who is to go first in line.

❖ Discuss the different ways that potatoes may be cooked. Children may think of mashed potatoes, baked potatoes, French fries, potato pancakes, and potato salad. Read *Potatoes Potatoes* by Anita Lobel and *The Great Potato Book* by Meredith and Thomas Hughes (see the unit book review). Then make "Mashed Potatoes" and "Baked Potatoes" for the children to taste.

Mashed Potatoes

6 medium potatoes
1/2 cup milk
1/4 tsp salt
3 Tbsp butter or margarine

Use any type of white potato. Peel and cube the potatoes. Boil until a fork goes through each potato easily (about 20–25 minutes). Mash the potatoes. Add butter and milk until the potatoes are the desired consistency. Add salt to taste.

Baked Potatoes

small, white potatoes
butter
lowfat sour cream

Pierce each potato with a fork. Bake the potatoes for approximately 1/2 hour at 350°. Cut potatoes in half and add a small amount of butter and lowfat sour cream to each half. Serve 1/2 potato to each child.

❖ Make potato prints with pink and purple tempera paint. Cut several potatoes in half. Use a sharp knife to cut out a P shape in each potato half. Be sure to cut the P backwards because the letter will be reversed when it is printed. Put pink paint and purple paint in styrofoam meat trays. Then invite the children to either dip the cut side of a potato in the paint or brush paint on the potato and then use the potato to print on paper. Suggest that children make pink potato prints on purple paper and purple potato prints on pink paper.

Present

❖ Wrap several small P presents, such as a penny, pencil, pack of paper, peppermint candy, small container of powder, small bag of pretzels, small puzzles, a purse, container of playdough, and so on. Each day, choose one present, give the children one or more hints, and invite children to guess what the present is. Give the present to the first child who guesses correctly. You might also use the little surprise packages as reinforcers for the week for exceptional work, good behavior, and so on.

Principal

❖ Arrange for the class to visit the principal in his or her office to find out what a principal does or ask the principal to come to your classroom. Encourage the principal to prepare a list of jobs that he or she does that start with the letter P. Invite the principal to be creative—give every child a purple pencil that says "From the Principal" on the side, print out a computer picture of a present for each child to color (personalized with the children's names on them) with the instructions that the present contains anything they want it to be, and so on. When you return to the classroom, encourage the children to draw a picture of the principal. Then, as each child dictates a sentence to you about what he or she has learned about the principal, write the sentences on the children's papers. Present the pictures to the principal as a thank-you note.

Pudding

❖ Sponsor a "Pudding Party." Make "Pumpkin Pudding." Wear pink and purple party hats. Cut off the bottom portion of white paper bags and give the children the top portions to color with pink and purple crayons or markers. To make a hat, gather one open end together tightly, tie with string or yarn, and fold up the open bottom edge. Have the children write P's all the way around the folded edge.

Pumpkin Pudding

1 cup canned pumpkin 1/4 tsp salt 1/2 tsp pumpkin spice 1 Tbsp honey 1 1/2 cups milk 1 package (3 3/4 oz) instant vanilla pudding	Mix together the pumpkin, salt, spice, and honey in a bowl. Gradually stir in the milk. Add the pudding and beat slowly for about 1 minute. Chill and serve.

❖ Invite the children to paint with pudding. Tape wax paper on each child's desk. Have the children wash their hands thoroughly and put on paint shirts, too. Spoon pudding on the wax paper and invite the children to smear the pudding all over the paper. Then suggest that they use their index fingers to practice making P's in the pudding.

Pumpkin

❖ Display a pumpkin in the classroom. Show the children how to draw a simple picture of a pumpkin. Help the children describe the real pumpkin using all of their senses, except taste, and then add more detail to their drawings.

❖ Cut a pumpkin in half and scrape away all the stringy parts with a blunt knife and large spoon. Invite each child to stick a hand inside the pumpkin and pull out a handful of the insides. Have the children separate the pumpkin seeds from all the stringy parts. Use the seeds to make "Pumpkin Seeds." Then cut the shell into several pieces. Put the pieces in a large cooking pot, fill with water, and cook on medium-high heat for 30-45 minutes. Add water as needed. The pumpkin is ready when it is soft. Cut off the skin and cool. Mash the pumpkin or put it through a food grinder, food processor, or blender. Encourage the children to eat the pumpkin like it is, then add some brown sugar or honey and pumpkin pie spice and invite the children to taste the pumpkin again. Use the leftover pumpkin to make "Pumpkin Puffs." Read *The Mystery of the Flying Orange Pumpkin* by Steven Kellogg and *Pumpkin Pumpkin* by Jeanne Titherington to the class as the children eat their pumpkin treats (see the unit book review).

Pumpkin Seeds

2 cups pumpkin seeds
1 tsp Worcestershire sauce
3 Tbsp melted margarine
1 tsp salt

Rinse the pumpkin seeds to remove the pulp. Boil the seeds in salted water for 10 minutes and then drain and dry. Blend the Worcestershire sauce, margarine, and salt. Then pour the mixture over the pumpkin seeds until the seeds are well coated. Spread the seeds on a baking sheet. Bake for 1–2 hours at 225°. Watch for burning.

Pumpkin Puffs

1 can pumpkin (or 6-8 oz fresh pumpkin, cooked and mashed)
3 cups flour
1 cup honey
1 tsp salt
4 tsp baking powder
2 tsp pumpkin pie spice
4 eggs
1/4 cup milk
1/2 cup butter
Pam spray or muffin liners
sugar (optional)

Mix together all of the ingredients in a large bowl. Spray a muffin tin with Pam and spoon the mixture into the muffin tin. Sprinkle with sugar, if desired. Bake at 400° for 20 minutes.

Puppets

❖ Set up a "Puppet Center." Put a variety of puppets in the center for children to play with. Encourage the children to bring puppets from home as well. Display your puppets on an old shoe rack. The rubber-coated square racks with places on all four sides for shoes are best. A puppet theater is easily made by using a tension rod, rope, or string between two posts and a curtain, or just a piece of cloth draped over the rod. The children may kneel behind the curtain and hold the puppets up over the top.

❖ If you have professional puppeteers in your community, make arrangements for your class to either go to one of their puppet shows or for the puppeteers to come visit your classroom and share their puppets with the children.

❖ Make simple puppets of familiar story characters, such as the pigs and the wolf in *The Three Little Pigs.* Draw your own simple characters or cut them from coloring books. Glue each picture to tagboard to make them sturdier. Glue a popsicle stick or tongue depressor to the back of each puppet. Invite the children to use the puppets to act out stories as you read or to retell their own stories.

Purple

❖ Make "Purple Cows." Ask the children why this drink is probably called a "Purple Cow." Then help the children discover what colors mix together to make purple. Put a large dab of blue fingerpaint and a large dab of red fingerpaint on sheets of fingerpaint paper. Invite the children to smear the paint together all over their papers to discover purple. Then encourage children to use their index fingers to practice making P's in the paint.

Purple Cows

grape soda
vanilla ice cream

Put one scoop of ice cream in each glass of grape soda.

❖ Ask the children to tear purple paper into strips and then tear the strips into small pieces. Have the children make a large letter P with glue on a sheet of construction paper. Invite children to arrange the torn pieces along the glue line to make a "Purple P."

❖ Read *The Purple Coat* by Amy Hest, *Paper, Paper Everywhere* by Gail Gibbons, and *Harold and the Purple Crayon* by Crockett Johnson (see the unit book review). Paint a small purple P on each child's pinky with tempera paint. Tempera paint washes off with water.

❖ Make purple popsicles. Pour grape juice into small paper cups and put the cups in the freezer. Put a stick in each cup when the popsicles are partially frozen. Invite the children to tear the paper cup from the frozen treats and enjoy. Encourage the children to save their popsicle sticks. Invite the children to work together in small groups of four and arrange their popsicle sticks to make some of the straight letters of the alphabet, such as A, E, F, H, I, K, L, M, N, T, V, W, X, Y, and Z. Some children may wish to make shapes with the popsicles sticks (squares, triangles, rectangles) and straight numbers (1, 4, 7) as well.

Puzzle

❖ Set up a "Puzzle Center." Put four to six wooden puzzles in the center and then change the puzzle choices daily. Swap puzzles with another teacher at your level to provide variety. Collect alphabet puzzles and puzzles that reinforce the categories you teach throughout the year, such as transportation, community helpers, foods, fruits, furniture, tools, and so on.

❖ Make puzzles. Draw and cut out two patterns on colored construction paper for each puzzle you make. Make puzzles of the basic shapes, such as a circle, oval, square, rectangle, triangle, and diamond, or use pictures cut from magazines or picture books. Cut one of the patterns into four to six pieces (you can always cut more pieces if these are too easy) and use the other pattern as the puzzle frame. Put each puzzle frame and its pieces in an envelope. Make a puzzle for each child in your classroom. When the children complete one puzzle, ask them to write their names on the outside of the envelope and trade puzzles with another child until they have completed all of the puzzles.

❖ Set up a "Peg Center." Pegboards come in all different sizes. Some have pegs as large as your thumbnail and few holes, while others have pegs the size of toothpicks with a hundred or more holes. If you are buying pegs and pegboards, buy some of all different sizes, depending on the maturity of your class. Encourage the children to do simple tasks at first, like filling every hole with a peg (working from left to right and top to bottom). Invite the children to use their pegs to make a letter P on the pegboard, too. Some children might try making letters, numbers, and shapes. Challenge more advanced children to make each row of pegs a different color and then to copy simple patterns.

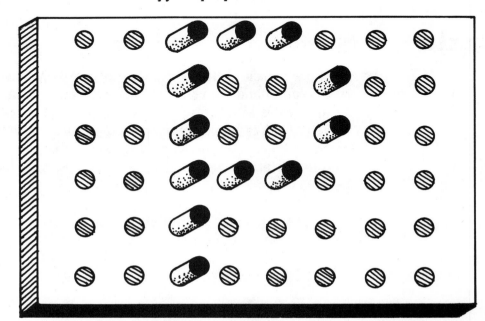

Food for Thought

Introducing children to a variety of foods is a wonderful way of reinforcing language concepts. The following foods all begin with the letter P and may be introduced at any time during this unit.

pancakes, papaya, Parmesan cheese, pasta, peaches, peanut butter, peanuts, pea pods, pears, peas, pea soup, pecan pie, pecans, pepper jelly, pepperoni, peppers, pepper steak, persimmons, pickled peaches, pickled pears, pickled pig's feet, pickles, pineapple, pineapple juice, pink lemonade, pinto beans, pistachios, pita pockets, pizza, plums, popcorn, popovers, pork, pork and beans, potato chips, potatoes, potato salad, pot pies, pot roast, pound cake, pretzels, prune juice, prunes, pudding, pumpernickel bread, pumpkin pie, pumpkins, pumpkin seeds, punch

Book Review

Children enjoy hearing good books read aloud. The books listed here are favorites of children and may be used to reinforce the letter P.

Ahlberg, Janet and Ahlberg, Allan. *Each Peach Pear Plum,* Penguin Books, 1986.

Alexander, Martha. *Pigs Say Oink,* Random House, 1981.

Asch, Frank. *Popcorn,* Parents Magazine Press, 1979.

Asch, Frank. *The Last Puppy,* Prentice Hall, 1983.

Baker, Bonnie J. *A Pear by Itself,* Childrens Press, 1982.

Berenstain, Stan and Berenstain, Janice. *The Bears' Picnic,* Beginner Books, 1966.

Cole, Joanna. *Plants in Winter,* Harper & Row, 1973.

Crews, Donald. *Parade,* Greenwillow Books, 1983.

de Paola, Tomie. *Pancakes for Breakfast,* Harcourt Brace Jovanovich, 1978.

de Paola, Tomie. *The Popcorn Book,* Holiday House, 1984.

Dubanevich, Arlene. *Pigs in Hiding,* Macmillan, 1983.

Freeman, Don. *A Pocket for Corduroy,* Penguin Books, 1978.

Freeman, Don. *Penguins, Of All People!,* Penguin Books, 1971.

Freeman, Don. *The Paper Party,* Penguin Books, 1977.

Galdone, Paul. *The Amazing Pig,* Houghton Mifflin, 1981.

Galdone, Paul. *The Three Little Pigs,* Houghton Mifflin, 1984.

Gibbons, Gail. *Paper, Paper Everywhere,* Harcourt Brace Jovanovich, 1983.

Gibbons, Gail. *Playgrounds,* Holiday House, 1985.

Hammond, Jane. *Pete the Penguin,* Warner Press, 1984.

Hannum, Dotti. *A Visit to the Police Station,* Childrens Press, 1985.

Hest, Amy. *The Purple Coat,* Macmillan, 1986.

Hoban, Tana. *Push Pull, Empty Full: A Book of Opposites,* Macmillan, 1972.

Hughes, Meredith and Hughes, Thomas. *The Great Potato Book,* Macmillan, 1986.

Hughes, Shirley. *When We Went to the Park,* Lothrop, 1985.

Johnson, Crockett. *Harold and the Purple Crayon,* Harper & Row, 1981.

Johnson, Jean. *Police Officers: A to Z,* Walker and Company, 1986.

Keats, Ezra Jack. *Pet Show!,* Macmillan, 1987.

Keats, Ezra Jack. *Peter's Chair,* Harper & Row, 1967.

Kellogg, Steven. *Can I Keep Him?,* Dial Books, 1976.

Kellogg, Steven. *The Mystery of the Flying Orange Pumpkin,* Dial Books, 1983.

Kellogg, Steven. *The Mystery of the Stolen Blue Paint,* Dial Books, 1982.

Lobel, Anita. *Potatoes Potatoes,* Harper & Row, 1984.

Pfloog, Jan. *Puppies Are Like That,* Random House, 1975.

Rey, Margret and Shalleck, Allan J. *Curious George Visits the Police Station,* Houghton Mifflin, 1987.

Rey, Margret. *Curious George and the Pizza,* Houghton Mifflin, 1985.

Rey, Margret and Rey, H. A. *Pretzel,* Harper & Row, 1984.

Testa, Fulvio. *If You Take a Pencil,* Dial Books, 1985.

Titherington, Jeanne. *Pumpkin Pumpkin,* Greenwillow Books, 1986.

Ungerer, Tomi. *Crictor,* Harper & Row, 1983.

Zolotow, Charlotte. *The Park Book,* Harper & Row, 1986.

Qq

Quack

❖ Read *Q Is for Duck* by Mary Elting and Michael Folsom (see the unit book review). Teach the children to sing "Six Little Ducks" from *Wee Sing Nursery Rhymes and Lullabies*. Review the sounds that sheep, cats, pigs, and other animals make.

❖ Have the children make a large letter Q with a pencil or crayon on a sheet of construction paper. Give each child a handful of small duck-shaped crackers to arrange along the pencil or crayon line to make a "Quackers Q." Invite the children to eat the crackers when the Q is finished.

❖ Play "Quack, Quack." Invite the children to stand in a circle. Designate one child to be "it" and stand in the middle. "It" is blindfolded and then stamps one foot loudly and says, "Go, ducks!" All of the ducks march around in a circle until "it" stamps his or her foot again and says, "Stop, ducks!" Everyone stops and "it" points to one child who then must say "Quack, quack." If "it" guesses who is speaking, that child becomes the next "it" and the game begins again. If "it" guesses incorrectly, the game continues until "it" guesses correctly.

Quarter

❖ Cut out a large letter Q from light-colored construction paper. Encourage the children to use a rubber stamp of a quarter to make quarter prints all over the Q.

❖ Make rubbings of quarters. Give each child a real quarter and a sheet of typing paper. Have the children put the typing paper over their quarters and then locate the quarters with their fingers. Suggest that children hold the quarters in place with one hand while they rub a crayon over the quarters with their other hand. Encourage the children to make a rubbing of their quarters (heads and tails) using the primary colors. Discuss the pictures on each side.

Queen

❖ Make queens from construction paper. Give each child a square piece of paper. Show the children how to round the corners to make a circle for the queen's face. Have the children turn a rectangular piece of colored construction paper sideways and snip V's out of the top to make a crown. Have the children cut strips of construction paper into small squares and use the small pieces to make hair and facial features.

❖ Find pictures of fairy-tale queens to show the children— the queen mother in *Sleeping Beauty,* the evil queen in *Snow White,* the Queen of Hearts in *Alice in Wonderland,* and so on. Discuss each queen and invite the children to name some other storybook queens as well. Ask the children if they know of any real queens. Explain that Queen Elizabeth is the Queen of England. Show the children how to draw a simple picture of a queen.

Question

❖ Play the "Question Game." Ask the children questions that may be answered with words that begin with the letter Q. For example, ask the children what Q word is a name of a coin (quarter), what Q word is a name for someone who is married to a king (queen), what Q word describes what a duck says (quack), and so on. Give the children who answer correctly a "quacker" (cracker) to eat.

❖ Show the children how to draw a question mark. Explain that a question mark is used at the end of a written question. Encourage the children to look through magazines and books to find some question marks. If you have a typewriter in your classroom, show the class the question mark on the keyboard.

Quick

❖ Discuss with the class what the word *quick* means. Ask the children to give examples of when it is appropriate to move very quickly and when it might be better to slow down and take your time. Just for fun, sponsor a "Quick

Party." Make "Quick-a-Bobs," "Quick Mint Shakes," and "Quick Treats" to serve as refreshments. Encourage the children to do everything quickly!

Quick-a-Bobs

pineapple chunks
cheese
ham (optional)

Cut the cheese and ham (if desired) into small chunks. Alternate the pineapple chunks, cheese chunks, and ham cubes on toothpick skewers. Experiment with other fruits as well. Help the children remove the toothpicks before eating their "Quick-a-Bobs."

Quick Mint Shakes

2 Tbsp chocolate syrup
1 cup cold milk
1 large scoop peppermint ice cream

Mix together all of the ingredients in a blender or with an eggbeater. Pour into a glass. Makes 1 serving.

Quick Treats

1 can salted
peanuts

1 medium box
raisins

1 bag popped
popcorn

Mix everything together in a bowl and
serve. Now, that's quick!

Quiet

❖ Play the "Quiet Game." Challenge the children to see
how long they can remain quiet. The child who remains
quiet the longest wins the game.

❖ Help the children make a list of as many examples as
possible of times when and where they were encouraged
to be quiet.

Quilt

❖ Read *The Josefina Story Quilt* by Eleanor Coerr (see the
unit book review). Ask the children if they have a quilt
at home that a parent or another member of the family
made. If possible, arrange for parents to bring the quilts
to school to show the class.

❖ Invite the children to draw a quilt. Give each child a
square sheet of large graph paper. Then encourage

children to color the squares different colors to make a pattern. Tape all of the individual squares together to make one large paper quilt.

Food for Thought

Introducing children to a variety of foods is a wonderful way of reinforcing language concepts. The following foods all begin with the letter Q and may be introduced at any time during this unit.

quiche, quince jelly, Quaker Oats

Book Review

Children enjoy hearing good books read aloud. The books listed here are favorites of children and may be used to reinforce the letter Q.

Coerr, Eleanor. *The Josefina Story Quilt,* Harper & Row, 1986.
Elting, Mary and Folsom, Michael. *Q Is for Duck,* Houghton Mifflin, 1980.
Zolotow, Charlotte. *The Quarreling Book,* Harper & Row, 1982.

Rabbit

❖ Show the children how to draw a simple picture of a rabbit. Give each child a cotton ball for the tail. Read *Mister Rabbit and the Lovely Present* by Charlotte Zolotow, *The Tale of Peter Rabbit* by Beatrix Potter, and *The Velveteen Rabbit* by Margery Williams (see the unit book review).

❖ Teach the children to sing "Little Cabin in the Woods" and "Little Peter Rabbit" from *Wee Sing Children's Songs and Fingerplays* and the song "Rabbit Ain't Got" from *Wee Sing Silly Songs*.

Radish

❖ Help the children plant radish seeds in a little plot outside or in individual milk cartons inside. They grow fast!

❖ Cut radishes in half with a sharp knife. Arrange the children into groups of four. Give each group a plastic lid filled with red tempera paint. Have each child draw a large letter R with a red crayon on a sheet of white construction paper. Then invite children to dip the radish halves in the red paint and use them like a rubber stamp to make radish prints all along the crayon line to make a "Radish R."

Radio

❖ Invite the children to listen to a radio this week during quiet time. Play a variety of different stations. Help the children make a list of the different radio programs. For example, radio programs provide people with news, weather, public announcements, music, talk-show interviews, call-in shows about issues, and so on.

❖ Show the children how to draw a simple picture of a radio.

Rain

❖ Ask the children if they have ever seen a rainbow. Encourage those children who have to describe a rainbow for the rest of the class. Ask when rainbows are usually seen as well. Read *Let's Paint a Rainbow* by Eric Carle and *A Rainbow of My Own* by Don Freeman (see the unit book review). Help the children draw rainbows on large sheets of construction paper (draw six color bands). Encourage the children to use the whole sheet! Then invite children to use tempera paint or watercolors to paint each color band a different color. Have the children paint the largest color band red, the next band orange, then yellow, green, blue, and finally purple. To check if the children know the primary colors, ask each child to describe his or her finished picture to you.

❖ Read *Rain Rain Rivers* by Uri Shulevitz, *Rain Drop Splash* by Alvin Tresselt, *The Rain Puddle* by Adelaide Holl, *Rain! Rain!* by Carol Greene, and *Peter Spier's Rain* by Peter Spier (see the unit book review). Teach the children the rhymes "Rain, Rain Go Away" and "It's Raining" from *Wee Sing Children's Songs and Fingerplays*. Invite the children to share what they do when it is raining and they want to go outside.

❖ Make rain gauges. Ask each child to bring a cylinder-shaped plastic container from home, such as a pill container (a pharmacist might give you enough for the class). Ask older students or parent volunteers to help each child make a gauge. Measure from the bottom and draw a line at every inch. Paint clear nail polish over the lines. Use a rubber band to fasten the container to a tongue depressor or popsicle stick. Take the children outside to an open space where the gauges will be left undisturbed. Have the children push the sticks on their gauges into the ground and then take the class outside to check the gauges every morning. Ask the children to decide if it has rained more or less than an inch during any twenty-four hour period.

Raisin

❖ Make "Rice and Raisin Pudding."

Rice and Raisin Pudding

3 cups cooked rice

2 small packages vanilla pudding

1/2 cup raisins

nutmeg (optional)

Make pudding according to package directions. Then add the rice and raisins. Sprinkle with nutmeg, if desired.

❖ Give each child a sheet of construction paper and a handful of raisins. Use a red crayon to draw a large letter R on each child's paper. Then have the children arrange the raisins along the red crayon line to make a "Raisin R." Invite the children to make "Right-on Raisin Snack" with their raisins when they are finished.

Right-on Raisin Snack

Mix together all of the ingredients and serve. Serves 1 to 2 children.

2 tsp raisins
1 tsp peanuts
1 tsp sunflower
  seeds
1 tsp coconut
1 Tbsp carob chips

Read

❖ Help the children make a list of items that are read. For example, people read newspapers, books, magazines, TV guides, signs, billboards, letters, recipes, menus, and so on. Invite the children to ask their parents and other members of their families what they read and then see if they can add more reading materials to the list.

❖ Set up a "Reading Center." Feature books with R words in the title for the children to browse through (see the unit book review). Ask the school librarian if you might borrow some *Ranger Rick* magazines for your center as well.

❖ Write a letter home to parents encouraging them to read to their children this week. Make out slips of paper for parents to record the names of books and authors of the books they read to their children. Make a red caterpillar head from construction paper and tape it to a wall in the classroom. Then invite the children to add a circle to the caterpillar for each book their parents read to them. Encourage the children to help the caterpillar grow all the way around the classroom!

Recipe

❖ Ask each child to dictate how to make his or her favorite food. Record the children's exact words as they dictate to you. Accept whatever the child says. Have each recipe typed on a white sheet of paper and invite the children to add illustrations. Compile all of the pages to make a class recipe book. Make a copy for each child to take home as a gift for their mothers or fathers. You might title the recipe book "Really Remarkable Recipes."

❖ If you have done a lot of cooking with the children and they have a vague idea of what goes into a cake or cookies, put out many different cake and cookie ingredients, such as flour, butter, sugar, oil, vanilla, raisins, milk, chocolate, nuts, baking soda, eggs, and peanut butter. Invite the children to make up a recipe. Or ask each child to bring in one ingredient to make a cake or cookies and use whatever the children bring. Invite each child to add one ingredient to make a class concoction, or divide the class into teams and have each team work with an aide or adult volunteer. Write down each ingredient the children want to add so the class will have a written record of the recipe when they are finished. Encourage the children to give their recipe a name, too.

Record Player

❖ Teach each child to use the record player in your classroom and then provide opportunities for the children to practice with an old record. Ask the children to sign their names on a large R cut from tagboard when they have demonstrated that they can turn the machine on and off, adjust the volume, place the needle on and take the needle off the record without scratching it.

❖ Encourage the children to bring their favorite records from home this week (write a letter home asking for parental permission). Then invite children to listen to the records during quiet times. Play songs that have words beginning with the R sound.

Rectangle

❖ Discuss how rectangles and squares are alike and how they are different. Point out that a rectangle and a square both have four sides and four corners, but all the sides are the same length on a square. Hold up examples of squares and rectangles and ask the children to decide if each is a rectangle or a square. Encourage children to provide reasons for their decisions, too. Once the children are comfortable and successful at differentiating between squares and rectangles, cut out and laminate different-sized squares and rectangles from construction paper for sorting into two piles.

❖ Provide opportunities for the children to practice drawing rectangles. Use the following sequential instructions: 1) left side, top to bottom, 2) right side, top to bottom, 3) top, left to right, 4) bottom, left to right. Picking up their pencils after each stroke will help children make square corners.

❖ Show the children how to cut rectangles from ovals of any size by cutting off the oval's sides, top, and bottom. Make a collage with the children's rectangles.

❖ Cut out cardboard patterns of rectangles in different sizes. Help the children trace around the patterns on large sheets of construction paper. Suggest that children use watercolors or tempera paint to paint the different rectangles.

❖ Cut out a large rectangle from red posterboard and put it on the floor. Set building blocks out on a table and invite the children to select all of the rectangle blocks to arrange around the outside edges of the rectangle on the floor. Remove the posterboard to reveal a large rectangle made from the blocks. Have the children count the number of sides and corners. Mix up the blocks and challenge small groups of children to assemble the shape once more.

Red

Red

❖ Make red rings. Give each child a large red button with two holes. Thread a red pipe cleaner through the two holes in the button and then use the pipe cleaner to wrap the ring around the child's finger. Sponsor a "Red Day." Invite every child to wear the red ring and some red clothing. Encourage the children to bring something from home that is red as well. Cut out several R's from red construction paper for anyone who forgets. Make sure to wear something red yourself! Make "Really Raspberries," a red gelatin with raspberries added, to serve as a special treat.

Really Raspberries

1 package raspberry Jell-O
1 package frozen raspberries
Cool Whip (optional)

Fix Jell-O according to the directions on the package. Fold in the raspberries and pour the mixture into a dish. Chill. Serve plain or with a tablespoon of Cool Whip on each serving.

❖ Have the children tear red construction paper into small pieces. Then invite children to make a large letter R with glue on a sheet of construction paper and arrange the small pieces of paper on the glue line to make a "Red R."

317

❖ Read *Ed's Red Bed* by Francis H. and Joyce M. Wise and *Red Riding Hood* by James Marshall (see the unit book review). Ask the children to name as many red items as possible. For example, Santa Claus' suit, valentines, fire engines, roses, candy canes, lipsticks, fingernail polish, and apples are usually red. Then ask the children to either draw the items they name or find pictures of red items in magazines to cut out. Make a red collage with the pictures.

❖ Play "Red Rover." Divide the class into two teams with at least five players on each team. Invite the players on each team to hold hands and face the opposing team. One team starts the game by saying "Red Rover, Red Rover, send (name of a child on the other team) right over." The identified child must run over to the opposing team and try to break through the clasped hands of any two children on that team. If the child breaks through, he or she brings someone from that team back. If the child doesn't break through, he or she must stay on the opposing team's side. Each team takes a turn calling "Red Rover." The team with the most children when time is called, wins the game.

❖ Read *Rudolf the Red-Nosed Reindeer* by Robert L. May (see the unit book review). Show the children how to draw a simple picture of Rudolf with a red nose. Suggest that children color the nose red, smear glue over the nose, and then sprinkle red glitter over the glue.

❖ Collect roll-on deodorant bottles. Children may share a bottle if you don't have enough for each child. Clean the bottles and then fill them with red tempera paint. Have each child make several large R's with a pencil on a large sheet of construction paper or painting paper. Then invite children to go over each R with the roll-on bottle to make "Rollin' Rs."

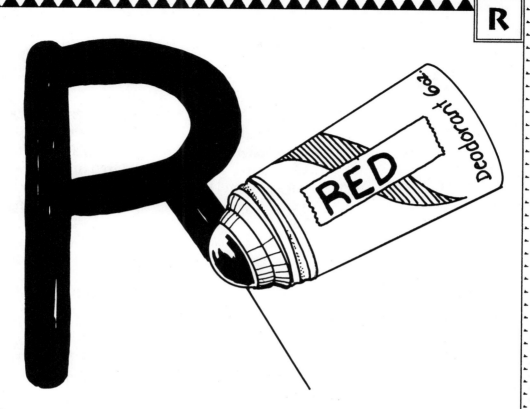

Refrigerator

❖ Discuss why we have refrigerators. Ask the children to identify the parts of a refrigerator—freezer, meat drawer, crisper, and so on. Help the children make a list of what food items might be kept in each compartment, too. Have the children fold a white sheet of typing paper in half to look like a refrigerator. Ask them to write "R Is for Refrigerator" on the outside cover. Encourage the children to glue a picture of a refrigerator on the cover as well (from newspaper ads or catalogs). Suggest that children cut out pictures from magazines of food items that might be kept in refrigerators and glue the pictures on the inside of the folded paper.

❖ Discuss with your class the danger of playing in old refrigerators. Explain that children may get locked inside by mistake where there is no air to breathe. Encourage the children to report to an adult any abandoned refrigerators with the doors still on.

Ribbon

❖ Give each child a length of ribbon and a piece of rick-rack to cut into small pieces. Have each child draw a large letter R with a red crayon on a piece of construction paper. Instruct the children to trace over the R with glue and then arrange the ribbon and rickrack pieces along the glue line to make a "Ribbon and Rick-rack R."

Rice

❖ Cook some brown rice. Add a dash of salt and a dab of butter. Invite the children to taste the rice plain and then use the rice to make "Remarkable Riceburgers." Serve with root beer.

Remarkable Riceburgers

2 Tbsp cooked brown rice	Mix together all of the ingredients in a small bowl. Form the mixture into a patty and fry in a buttered pan. Makes 1 patty.
1/2 tsp chopped parsley	
2 tsp grated carrot	
dash salt and pepper	
dash garlic powder	
1 tsp flour	
2 tsp beaten egg	
soy sauce (optional)	
butter	

❖ Have each child make a large letter R with glue on a sheet of red construction paper. Give each child a handful of rice to sprinkle over the glue. When the glue is dry, help the children carefully shake off the excess rice to reveal a "Rice R."

Right

❖ Encourage the children to write R's with a red crayon all along the right side of every paper they work on this week.

❖ Tie a red ribbon on the right wrist of each child to help him or her remember which is the right hand. Help the children practice using right and left directions by inviting them to do "The Hokey Pokey" from *Wee Sing and Play* and "Looby Loo" from *Wee Sing Children's Songs and Fingerplays*. Use left-right directions or just use right directions for less experienced children. Teach the children the fingerplay "Right Hand, Left Hand" from *Wee Sing Children's Songs and Fingerplays* as well.

Robot

❖ Ask the children if they know what a robot is. Explain that robots are machines that can do many things for people. Read *Get Ready for Robots!* by Patricia Lauber (see the unit book review). Ask the children to decide what they would like to have a robot do for them, such as make their bed, clean their room, rake or clean the yard, do their homework, and so on. Invite the children to walk with stiff legs, like a robot.

❖ Encourage any children who have robot computer toys at home to bring them to school to share with the rest of the class. Show the children how to draw a simple picture of a robot.

Rock

❖ Collect rocks. Invite the children to bring rocks from home, too. Help the children sort the rocks by color and size. Invite the children to choose one rock that is most like themselves. Then encourage children to show their rocks to another child and share with that person how their rocks are like them. For example, a child might pick a particular rock because it is the smallest rock in the pile and that child is the smallest child in his or her family.

❖ Buy small aquarium rocks. (One bag will be enough for several years of projects.) Have the children make a large letter R with glue on a sheet of heavy paper or cardboard. Then invite children to arrange some of the small aquarium rocks on the glue line to make a "Rocky R."

❖ Read *A First Look at Rocks* by Millicent E. Selsam and Joyce Hunt (see the unit book review). Make "Rocky Road." Discuss how this recipe might have gotten its name (it looks like rocks in a road).

Rocky Road

1 package miniature marshmallows	Spray a baking pan with Pam. Arrange the marshmallows in a single layer on the bottom of the pan. Melt the chocolate chips and peanut butter in a pan over low heat. Stir until melted and then pour the mixture over the marshmallows. Cool in the refrigerator for 30 minutes. Then cut into small squares for serving.
1 cup crunchy peanut butter	
2 cups chocolate chips	
Pam	

Rose

❖ Read *The Rose in My Garden* by Arnold Lobel (see the unit book review). Have roses in your classroom this week, or ask if any families in your class grow roses that they might be willing to share with the children.

❖ If possible, help the children plant a rose bush outside one of your classroom windows. Contact a local garden club for a donation.

❖ Teach the children to sing and act out "Ring Around the Rosey" from *Wee Sing Children's Songs and Fingerplays*. This is a good time to review the words *up* and *down*. On the last verse, either say, "We all fall down" and have the children fall down, or say, "All hands up" and have the children put their hands and arms way up in the air.

Rub

❖ Cut out several R's from sandpaper. Have the children close their eyes and feel the sandpaper R. Invite children to trace over the R with their fingers, too. Have the children make rubbings of the R by positioning typing paper over the sandpaper R, finding and holding the R with one hand, then rubbing a crayon over the paper. The children should see an R appear on their papers. Invite the children to make rubbings of other textures in the classroom. Plastic lace doilies and textured floor or ceiling tiles also make good rubbings.

Rubber

❖ Help the children make a list of items that are made from rubber. Then read *From Rubber Tree to Tire* by Ali Mitgutsch (see the unit book review).

❖ Invite the children to paint an R with rubber cement on shiny paper, like fingerpaint paper. When the rubber cement is completely dry, have the children paint their entire sheet with red paint. The children may rub off the rubber cement to reveal an R when the paint has dried. (You may wish to try this activity first because some papers work better than others.)

Ruler

❖ Give a ruler to each child in the class. Use rulers that only have the inch markings, if you have a choice, but use whatever you have in the classroom. Help the children practice measuring objects to the nearest inch.

❖ Encourage the children to use a ruler with a pencil or crayon to practice making straight lines all over a sheet of paper. Then invite the children to use their rulers to make lines all over a large R cut from a large sheet of light-colored construction paper.

Run

❖ Sponsor relay races. Divide the class into teams of four or five. Invite the team members to line up. At your signal, have the first person in line run to a target and back and tag the next child in line. The first team to have all its members complete the race wins.

❖ Set up an obstacle course either outside or in the gym. Invite the children to practice running the course each day this week. Time each child with a stopwatch. Encourage the children to improve their times.

❖ Begin each day this week by inviting the children to run short distances with you outside on nice days and in the gym on other days. If you run inside, play music for the children to run to. Emphasize form instead of speed. Ask the physical education teacher for running tips.

Food for Thought

Introducing children to a variety of foods is a wonderful way of reinforcing language concepts. The following foods all begin with the letter R and may be introduced at any time during this unit.

radishes, rainbow sherbet, raisin bread, raisins, raspberries, raspberry sherbet, red cabbage, red grapes, red lettuce, relish, rhubarb, ribs, rice, rice cakes, Rice Krispies, ricotta cheese, Ritz crackers, roast, romaine lettuce, rutabaga, rye bread, rye crackers

Book Review

Children enjoy hearing good books read aloud. The books listed here are favorites of children and may be used to reinforce the letter R.

Carle, Eric. *Let's Paint a Rainbow,* Putnam Publishing Group, 1982.

Freeman, Don. *A Rainbow of My Own,* Penguin Books, 1978.

Galdone, Paul. *Rumpelstiltskin,* Houghton Mifflin, 1985.

Greene, Carol. *Rain! Rain!,* Childrens Press, 1982.

Holl, Adelaide. *The Rain Puddle,* Lothrup, 1965.

Lauber, Patricia. *Get Ready for Robots!,* Harper & Row, 1987.

Lionni, Leo. *Let's Make Rabbits,* Pantheon, 1982.

Lobel, Arnold. *The Rose in My Garden,* Greenwillow Books, 1984.

Marshall, James. *Red Riding Hood,* Dial Books, 1987.

May, Robert L. *Rudolf the Red-Nosed Reindeer,* Longman Trade, 1983.

Mitgutsch, Ali. *From Rubber Tree to Tire,* Carolrhoda, 1986.

Potter, Beatrix. *The Tale of Peter Rabbit,* Dover Press, 1972.

Selsam, Millicent E. and Hunt, Joyce. *A First Look at Rocks,* Walker and Company, 1984.

Shulevitz, Uri. *Rain Rain Rivers,* Farrar, Straus and Giroux, 1969.

Spier, Peter. *Peter Spier's Rain,* Doubleday, 1982.

Tresselt, Alvin. *Rain Drop Splash,* Lothrop, 1946.

Williams, Margery. *The Velveteen Rabbit,* Avon Books, 1987.

Wise, Francis H. and Wise, Joyce M. *Ed's Red Bed,* Wise Publishing, 1974.

Zolotow, Charlotte. *Mister Rabbit and the Lovely Present,* Harper & Row, 1977.

Ss

Salt

❖ Stir salt with a piece of colored chalk. Press down while you stir and invite the children to watch the salt turn colors. Have each child make a letter S with glue on a sheet of construction paper. Then invite children to sprinkle some of the colored salt over the glue. When the glue is dry, help the children gently shake off the excess salt to reveal a "Salty S." After a couple of days, when the "Salty S" is thoroughly dry, invite the children to close their eyes and feel the shape of the S with their fingers.

❖ Read *From Sea to Salt* by Ali Mitgutsch (see the unit book review). Help the children make a list of foods that are salty, such as potato chips, peanuts, corn chips, pretzels, saltines, and so on. Point out that it is not a good idea to eat a lot of salty foods. Encourage the children to taste their food first before adding salt.

Same

❖ Prepare index cards with either two like or two unlike shapes, colors, numbers, or alphabet letters glued on each card. Hold up the cards one at a time and ask the children if the items on the cards are the same. Encourage the children to give reasons for their answers.

❖ Make sock patterns from heavy cardboard. Help the children trace around the patterns on sheets of construction paper. Invite each child to make two pairs of socks. Then instruct the children to color two socks the same and two that are different.

Saw

❖ Use a saw to demonstrate sawing a board in half. Invite the children to take turns sawing. Point out what sawdust looks like. Help the children name other tools, such as a drill, screwdriver, hammer, wrench, and pliers.

❖ Collect sawdust from a lumber mill or from someone who works with wood. Have the children make a large letter S with glue on a sheet of construction paper. Then invite the children to sprinkle some sawdust over the glue. When the glue is dry, help the children shake off the excess sawdust to reveal a "Sawdust S." Use the leftover sawdust to make "Sawdust Clay." Objects made with the sawdust clay may be painted with tempera paint when dry. Suggest that children try making S's with the clay.

Sawdust Clay

9 cups sawdust
8 cups flour
3 Tbsp salt
water
1 1/2 Tbsp powdered tempera paint (optional)

Mix together the sawdust, salt, and flour. Add small amounts of boiling water until the mixture is a stiff, flaky, adhesive dough. Add more sawdust if the dough becomes sticky. Makes about 18 balls about the size of an orange. The dough takes about a week to thoroughly dry when it is exposed to the air.

329

Scarecrow

❖ Make a scarecrow. Cut a hat pattern from heavy cardboard and help the children trace around the pattern on wallpaper samples. Invite the children to cut out their own hat shapes. Show the children how to round the corners on a pink square to make a round face shape. Have the children add facial features with scraps of construction paper, crayons, or markers and then glue the hat on the head shape. Cut a body pattern from heavy cardboard and help the children trace around that pattern on construction paper. Invite the children to cut out the shape, glue the head on the body, and glue straw pieces on the back for hands and feet. Glue the scarecrows on popsicle sticks or tongue depressors. If you have plants growing in the classroom, you might put some of the scarecrows in the planters.

❖ Make a scarecrow. Stuff a pair of pants with newspaper and tie each leg with string. Authentic scarecrows are stuffed with straw and you should use straw if you have it. Stuff a shirt with newspaper or straw and tie the arms with string. Tie or sew the pants and shirt together. Stuff the top of a pair of pantyhose with newspaper or straw to make the head. Use construction-paper scraps to make facial features. Then tuck the head into the neck of the shirt. Add an old wig or curled construction paper strips for hair and top with an old straw hat. Hang the scarecrow on a nail or place it in a chair and wait for the children to notice! When they do, discuss where a scarecrow might be found and why.

School

❖ Discuss why children come to school. Encourage the children to ask their parents to share some of their school experiences with the children. Invite the children to tell the rest of the class about some of those experiences. Ask the children to predict what might happen if a bear were to come to their school. Then read *The Berenstain Bears Go to School* by Stan and Janice Berenstain (see the unit book review).

❖ Discuss the origin of your school name, the mascot, school colors, and so on. On a nice day, take the children outside and invite them to draw a picture of the school.

❖ Call out the name of school items and invite the children to locate the items in the classroom. Start with a stapler, staples, crayons, pencils, chalk, books, a dictionary, pens, writing paper, construction paper, scissors, pencil erasers, the chalkboard, chalkboard erasers, rulers, a yardstick, a globe, glue or paste, paint, a paintbrush, watercolors, and so on. Tape a label on each of the items as the children locate them. Leave the name labels on all week to give the children opportunities to see each word and use their knowledge of initial consonant sounds to read each word.

❖ Make an S pattern from heavy cardboard. Help the children trace around the S on construction paper. Invite each child to cut out his or her own S and then use a stapler to staple all over the S shape.

❖ Arrange for the children to visit the school secretary. Encourage the secretary to explain to the children what the job entails. Help the children learn the secretary's name, too. Set up a "Secretary Center" this week. Put a desk in the center, along with paper, a typewriter, pencils, stapler, telephone, and other secretarial supplies that you might have.

Screen

❖ Find or buy screening. Screens from old windows and scraps from construction sites work well. Cut the screening into different size S's. Give each child an S and invite him or her to position a sheet of typing paper over the S, hold the S in place with one hand, and rub a crayon over the paper. The children will see a letter S begin to appear on their papers. Encourage the children to make several rubbings using different size S's and different colored crayons as well.

❖ Splatter-paint some S's. Cut out several different size S's from tagboard. Cover each child's desk with a newspaper. Have the children wear paint shirts. Help each child position the S's on a sheet of construction paper and then put the paper in a shallow box. Put a screen over the box and show the children how to dip a toothbrush into tempera paint and splatter the paint over the S's by brushing paint over the screen. Invite the children to try rubbing a popsicle stick back and forth over the toothbrush to splatter the paint, too. Lift the S's from the paper and throw them away. When the paper is dry, each child will have a page filled with S's.

Scribble

❖ Encourage the children to use all of the colors in their crayon box to scribble on a sheet of typing paper or a sheet of white construction paper. Cut out several S patterns from heavy cardboard. Invite the children to trace around an S pattern on their scribble drawing with a black crayon or black magic marker.

Sea

❖ Read *Life in the Sea* by Eileen Curran, *Starfish* by Edith T. Hurd, *Three by the Sea* by Edward Marshall, or *Harry by the Sea* by Gene Zion (see the unit book review). Help the children make a list of as many words associated with the sea as possible that begin with the letter S, such as starfish, sand dollar, sea gulls, seashells, sailboat, sun, sand, sailfish, submarine, sea horse, swordfish, surfboard, and swimsuit. If you live close to a seashore, plan a field trip to the beach to collect some of the S items.

❖ Invite the children to use pasta shaped like seashells to make an S. First, have the children make a large letter S with glue on a dark blue sheet of construction paper. Then invite children to arrange the seashell macaroni on the glue to make a "Seashell S."

❖ Make a sand tray by filling a large rubber container with play sand. Play sand is available in many toy stores or at a gravel or sand company. Put an assortment of spoons, cups, colanders, shovels, funnels, and so on in the sand tray for pouring and digging.

❖ Have the children make a large letter S with glue on a sheet of construction paper. Then invite children to sprinkle sand over the glue. When the glue is dry, help the children carefully shake the excess sand off to reveal a "Sandy S." After a few days, when the sand is completely dry, encourage the children to close their eyes and feel the shape of the S with their fingers.

Seeds

❖ Invite the children to taste sunflower seeds. Buy the seeds in the shell so children may crack the shells and eat the seeds inside. Ask the children to keep the shells. Then have children make a large letter S with glue on a sheet of construction paper and arrange the sunflower shells on the glue to make a "Sunflower Shell S."

❖ Teach the children to sing "The Seed Cycle" from *Wee Sing and Play*. Collect seeds all week. Ask parents to contribute apple, watermelon, pumpkin, orange, grapefruit, and canteloupe seeds. Discuss how the different types of seeds are alike and how they are different. Help the children plant some of the seeds and see what happens. Have the children make a letter S with glue on a sheet of construction paper. Then invite children to arrange some of the seeds on the glue to make a "Seedy S." Read *All About Seeds* by Susan Kuchalla and *How a Seed Grows* by Helene J. Jordan (see the unit book review).

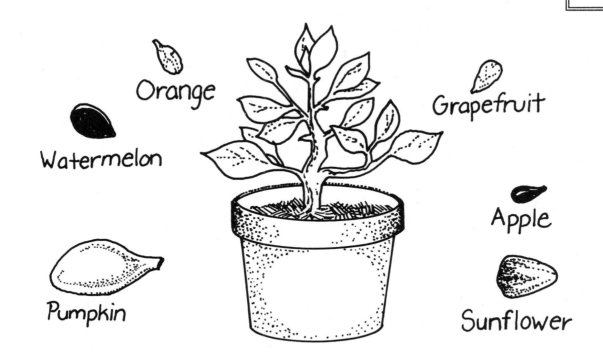

Orange

Grapefruit

Watermelon

Apple

Pumpkin

Sunflower

Senses

❖ Help the children name the five senses. Encourage children to tell what each sense does, too. Read *Rand McNally Question Books: The Senses* by Kathie B. Smith and Victoria E. Crenson (see the unit book review).

❖ Help the children make a list of good smelling things and bad smelling things. Invite the children to add more items to the lists all week. Read *Smelling* by Richard L. Allington and Kathleen Krull and *Smelling* by Henry Pluckrose (see the unit book review). Use stickers that children may scratch and smell as well.

❖ Hide string, blunt-tip scissors, stones, rubber spiders, straws, sponges, sticks, or any other items that begins with the letter S, in a "secret sack." Use a cloth bag. Invite the children to feel the hidden item through the bag and then try to guess what the item is. Stress that children have to use their sense of touch to guess.

Six and Seven

❖ Read *Seven Little Monsters* by Maurice Sendak and *Snow White and the Seven Dwarfs* by Wanda Gag (see the unit book review). Ask the children to name all of the seven dwarfs—Sleepy, Sneezy, Happy, Doc, Dopey, Grumpy, Bashful—and tell why they think each dwarf got his name.

❖ Play "Heads Up, Seven Up." Choose seven children (count as you pick 1-2-3-4-5-6-7) to come to the front of the classroom. When you say, "Heads down, seven around," the children sitting at desks must put their heads down on their desks (no peeking). Then instruct each of the seven children up front to walk around the room, tap one child lightly on the head, and then quickly return to the front of the classroom. When a child has been tapped, ask him or her to raise a hand so he or she doesn't get tapped more than once. When seven children have been tapped say, "Heads up, seven up" and all the children may raise their heads. The tapped children stand up and each gets one guess to name which child (of the seven children up front) tapped them. If a child guesses correctly, he or she exchanges places with the child up front. If not, the child sits back down. The game continues after all seven tapped children have had their chance to guess.

❖ Make a cardboard pattern of a 7 for the children to trace around and then cut out. Have the children use a hole punch to punch a hole in the tops of their sevens. Then invite each child to count out seven paper clips. Show the children how to open the paper clips to make an S. Help children hook the paper clips together and then hook the clips to the top of the 7. Hang the 7's from the ceiling.

❖ Encourage the children to practice making 7's, first on the chalkboard and then on paper. Have each child fold a sheet of newsprint into fourths. Suggest that children use a crayon to trace along the fold lines. Ask the children to write a 7 in each section and then count stickers, sticks, sunflower seeds, or some other S object into each section. Encourage the children to turn their papers over, use a crayon to trace over the fold lines, and then write a 6 in each section. Invite the children to glue six stars in each section.

❖ Encourage the children to practice making 6's using the directional words "down and curl." Invite the children to make 6's on the chalkboard first, then on unlined newsprint, and finally on lined paper. Discuss with the children how a 6 and a 9 are alike and how they are different.

Skip, Skate, Stomp, Spin, and Stand

❖ Teach skipping to those children who have not perfected the skill. Use the instructions, "Step, hop," alternating feet. Teach the children to sing "Skip to My Lou" from *Wee Sing and Play*. Invite the children to skip with a partner as they sing.

❖ Ask the children if they have ever gone ice skating. Encourage those children who have to describe the experience for the others. Then invite the children to pretend to skate. Have the children put their hands behind their backs and pretend to skate across ice. If possible, arrange for the children to take a field trip to an ice-skating or roller-skating rink and try it out.

❖ Invite the children to stomp their feet while sitting down in a chair and then standing up. Then challenge children to spin all the way around on one foot and then on the other. Encourage the children to practice standing on one foot and then the other as well. See who can stand on one foot for the longest time. Then teach the children to sing and act out "This is the way we slide across the ice" (or skip together, spin around, stomp our feet, stand on one foot) to the tune of "Here We Go 'Round the Mulberry Bush."

❖ Play "Simon Says" using directions that begin with the letter S, such as "Skip to me and back," "Slide to the side," "Spin around two times," "Spin around on one foot," "Stomp your feet six times," "Stand on one foot for seven seconds," and "Pretend to skate across the ice."

Smile

❖ Use smiley-face stickers or a smiley-face rubber stamp this week as a reward for good behavior, good work, and so on.

❖ Ask the children to name things that make them smile and things that make them sad, too. Give each child two circles. Encourage the children to draw a happy face on one of the circles and a sad face on the other. Glue the circles back-to-back with a popsicle stick or tongue depressor in-between. Each day, ask the children if they are happy or sad and invite them to hold up the happy face or the sad face. Encourage children to share why they feel happy or sad.

Snow

❖ Read *The Snowy Day* by Ezra Jack Keats (see the unit book review). Make "Special Snow." Put a piece of waxed paper on each child's desktop and then drop some of the homemade snow on the paper. Or, just put the snow on the desktops. (It'll do a nice job of cleaning!) Invite the children to smear the snow all over and use their index fingers to practice making S's. Discuss how the special snow is the same and how it is different from real snow.

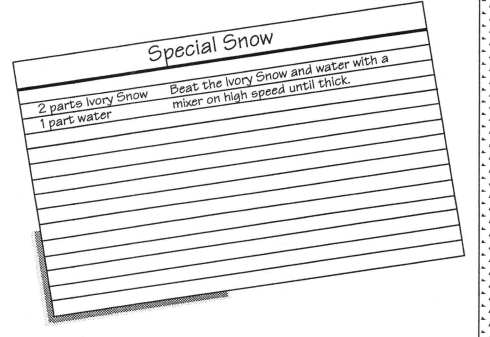

Special Snow

2 parts Ivory Snow   Beat the Ivory Snow and water with a
1 part water   mixer on high speed until thick.

❖ Teach the children the fingerplay "Chubby Little Snowman" from *Wee Sing for Christmas* and the song "I'm a Little Snowman" from *Wee Sing Children's Songs and Fingerplays*. Sing the words of the song several times throughout the day. Sometimes sing the song very softly, sometimes loudly, and then other times sing in a moderate voice to reinforce the concepts soft and loud. Once the children learn the song, leave out phrases as you sing and invite them to fill in the correct words.

❖ Make snow pictures. Invite the children to draw a snowperson with white chalk on black or dark blue construction paper. Spray the finished pictures with hair spray to prevent the chalk from smearing. Ask the children to help make "Snowballs," a coconut candy that looks like snowballs, to serve as a special treat. Discuss how these snowballs are the same and how are they different from real snowballs.

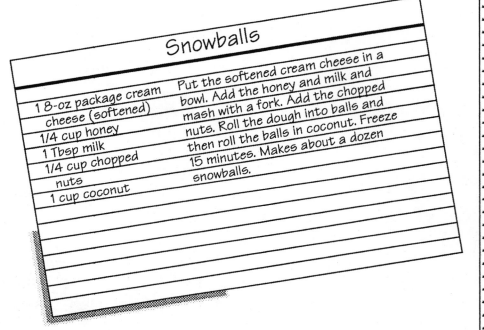

Snowballs

1 8-oz package cream cheese (softened)	Put the softened cream cheese in a bowl. Add the honey and milk and mash with a fork. Add the chopped nuts. Roll the dough into balls and then roll the balls in coconut. Freeze 15 minutes. Makes about a dozen snowballs.
1/4 cup honey	
1 Tbsp milk	
1/4 cup chopped nuts	
1 cup coconut	

❖ Show the children how to draw a simple picture of a snowperson. Then invite children to make a snowperson from construction paper. Give the children three square sheets of white construction paper, each square progressively smaller. Show the children how to make the squares round by rounding the corners. Facial features, arms, buttons, and a hat may all be made by cutting scraps of colored construction paper. Glue the snowpeople to sheets of black or dark blue construction paper. Cut a sponge into small pieces and attach a clothespin to each sponge. Invite the children to dip the clothespin sponges into white tempera paint and then dab the sponges on their papers wherever they want snow.

Sort and Sequence

❖ Set up a "Sorting Center" this week. Each day, set out different items for the children to sort by size—small, medium, and large. Use wooden beads, buttons, coins, pencils, straws cut in three different sizes, tagboard shapes cut in three different sizes, and so on. You might also invite the children to sort different size nuts, screws, and washers as well.

❖ Give each child a handful of crackers that come in several small sizes within one box. Have the children sequence the crackers from smallest to largest and then from largest to smallest. Invite the children to eat their crackers after you have checked their work.

❖ Cut a set of five to seven straws, or make sets of squares, circles, and so on in different sizes, for the children to sequence from large to small or small to large. Put each sequencing set in an envelope. Encourage the children to sequence the items in one envelope, have an adult check their work, write their names on the outside of the envelope, and then trade envelopes with another child until they have done all of the sequencing sets.

Soup

❖ Ask the children to name as many different kinds of soup as possible, such as tomato, cream of mushroom, minestrone, clam chowder, oyster stew, vegetable beef, chicken noodle, chicken and rice, French onion, and so on. Invite the children to vote on their favorite soups. Graph the results.

❖ Read *Stone Soup* by Marcia Brown (see the unit book review). Make "Stone Soup"—a version of vegetable soup. Ask each child to bring one vegetable from home for the soup. Add three bouillon cubes to represent the stones. Heat the soup and then invite the children to enjoy eating!

Stone Soup

3 bouillon cubes
any vegetables (potatoes, carrots, turnips, tomatoes, mushrooms, onions, celery, cauliflower, or cans of corn, peas, or beans)

Rinse and clean each fresh vegetable. Chop the vegetables into chunks. Mix together all of the ingredients and put them in a large pot. Add water to cover the vegetables and cook on medium low heat for 1–2 hours or until the vegetables are soft.

Spaghetti

❖ Encourage the children to taste uncooked spaghetti. Cook the spaghetti noodles, add a small dab of butter, and invite the children to taste the noodles once again. Discuss how the cooked spaghetti and uncooked spaghetti are alike and how they are different.

❖ Teach the children to sing "On Top of Spaghetti" from *Eye Winker Tom Tinker Chin Chopper* by Tom Glazer (Doubleday, 1973).

❖ Cook spaghetti and drain. Pour a little oil over the noodles to keep them from sticking together. Give the children one string of spaghetti at a time and invite them to make an S with each string on a paper plate (the plate needs to be thick so the sides won't curl when the spaghetti dries).

Sparkle

❖ Make a pattern of the letter S from heavy cardboard. Help the children trace around the pattern on any color construction paper. Invite the children to cut out their own S's. Give each child a paintbrush and some glue in a plastic lid. Have the children paint a line down the middle of the S and then drop individual sequins on the glue to make a "Sequined S."

❖ Ask the children to name some items that are usually silver in color (aluminum foil, jewelry, cans, faucets). Give each child a strip of aluminum foil. Point out that aluminum foil is silver in color. Have the children tear the foil into small squares. Then invite children to make a large letter S with glue on a sheet of construction paper and arrange the silver pieces on the glue to make a "Silver S." Some children may wish to sprinkle silver glitter on the glue instead.

❖ Teach the children to sing "Twinkle Twinkle, Little Star" from *Wee Sing Children's Songs and Fingerplays*. Show more advanced children how to make a star with one stroke. Other children may make a six-pointed star by drawing two triangles, one on top of the other. Have the children draw stars with glue on colored construction paper and then sprinkle glitter over the glue. Or, suggest that children paint the stars with a mixture of 1/2 cup liquid starch, 2 cups of salt, 1 cup water, and powdered tempera paint. Have the children cut out their stars and put them on a bulletin board covered with black or dark blue paper. Title the bulletin board "Twinkle Twinkle Little Stars."

Spider

❖ Read *Be Nice to Spiders* by Margaret B. Graham and *The Very Busy Spider* by Eric Carle (see the unit book review). Invite each child to make a spider. Cut out the spider's body in an hourglass shape from black construction paper. Give each child a spider body and a piece of black construction paper. Have the children cut the black piece of construction paper into eight strips for the spider legs. Show the children how to fold each leg in half and then fold up both ends of each strip about 1/2 inch. Have the children glue the legs to the spider's body—four legs on each side. Hang the spiders from the ceiling with black yarn or from a spider's web made by weaving black yarn together. Attach the yarn to the chalkboard and a door frame, or another wooden structure, with small nails or tacks.

❖ Sponsor a "Sing-Along." Teach the children to sing "Eentsy Weentsy Spider" from *Wee Sing Children's Songs and Fingerplays*. Sing other songs that the children have learned this year as well. Invite each child to choose a favorite song for the class to sing.

❖ Encourage the children to use clay to make a spider and other creatures that begin with the letter S. For example, children may make snakes by rolling clay and a snail may be made by rolling a snake length into a coil. Encourage the children to try making the letter S with a snake-length piece of clay as well as other letters of the alphabet, numbers, and shapes (especially squares).

Square

❖ Give each child a square piece of tagboard. Invite children to feel around the edge of the square. Discuss how many sides the square has and how many corners, too. Point out that all the sides are equal or the same.

❖ Cut out a large square from tagboard and put it on the floor. Set building blocks on a table and invite the children to select all of the square blocks. Have the children place the square blocks all around the outside edges of the tagboard square on the floor. After the blocks are placed, pick up the tagboard to reveal the square shape of the blocks. Help the children count the sides and corners. Then mix up the blocks and challenge the children to recreate the square without the tagboard model.

❖ Cut sponges into 2-inch square pieces. Have the children dip the sponges in tempera paint and use the sponges to print on large pieces of paper, trying not to let any of the squares touch one another. When the paper is filled with square prints, cut the prints apart. Invite the children to cut out as many of the sponge prints as they wish. Use the cut-out squares to make a large letter S on a bulletin board.

❖ Cut out squares, circles, rectangles, and triangles of different sizes from heavy cardboard. Put one shape in a "secret sack"—a cloth bag works best. Invite children to feel the shape through the bag and then guess whether the shape is a square or not a square. Children who know all of the shapes may be challenged to guess the actual shape.

❖ Give each child several circles of different sizes and show them how they may cut off the rounded sides of each circle to make a square. Arrange all of the children's squares on a sheet of paper to make a collage. Overlap the squares for a more interesting design.

❖ Help the children trace around several different-sized square patterns on sheets of white construction paper. Suggest that children use crayons, markers, watercolors, or tempera paint to color each square a different color.

❖ Have the children practice making squares as you draw models on the chalkboard and talk them through it. Use the following directional instructions: 1) Left side, top to bottom, 2) right side, top to bottom, 3) the top, left to right, and 4) the bottom, left to right. Asking the children to pick up their pencils after every new stroke will help them make nice sharp corners.

❖ Make a cake or another dessert in a square pan. Stress cutting the treats into squares.

Squirt

❖ Invite the children to use squirt bottles filled with water to spray sheets of clean white paper (fingerpaint paper works best). Next, have children cut up pieces of colored tissue paper or crepe paper and use the pieces to make a design on their damp papers. Then have children squirt water all over the paper again. The colors will run and make an abstract design. When dry, most of the crepe paper or tissue paper will peel off. The paper may be cut into the shape of a large star to make "Super Stars."

❖ Fill three or four spray bottles with watered-down tempera paint in a primary color, such as, red, blue, and yellow. Set up a clothesline outside and clothespin large sheets of white paper on the line. Then invite the children to spray paint the white paper with two or three different colors. The colors will run together and drip to make lovely abstract designs. Designate one area for spraying (have one child spray at a time) and another area for drying.

Stick

❖ Take the children outside on a nice day and have them gather small sticks from the playground. Cut out a large letter S from construction paper. Invite the children to put little dabs of glue on the S and then place a stick on each dab of glue. Continue until the S is covered with sticks.

❖ Play "Pick-Up Sticks." This game may be purchased at most toy stores, or make your own sticks. Soak toothpicks or popsicle sticks in water mixed with food coloring. Soak five sticks in four or five different colors or use colored toothpicks. Remove the sticks to dry. Invite each child to choose a color and then say the color out loud. Have one child hold all the sticks straight up in his or her hand and then drop the sticks on the floor. The children then take turns seeing who can pick up their colored sticks first without moving any of the other sticks. If they move another stick, they lose their turn. The first child to pick up all of his or her colored sticks wins.

❖ Divide the class into small groups of four. Give each child a popsicle stick. Encourage the children in each group to work together and share their popsicle sticks to make as many straight letters of the alphabet as possible—A, E, F, H, I, K, L, M, N, V, W, X, Y, and Z. Some groups may wish to make numbers and shapes.

Stop

❖ Make a stoplight from construction paper. Give each child a red, yellow, and green square of construction paper and a black rectangle and triangle. Show the children how to round the corners of each square to make a circle. Encourage the children to identify each shape. Ask the children if they know in which order the lights are arranged on a stoplight. If possible, ask the children to check this out and report back to you the following day. Then invite children to glue the circles on the rectangle in the correct order—red on top, yellow in the middle, and green on the bottom. Have the children glue the triangle on top.

❖ Discuss what each light on a stoplight means. Explain that the lights are meant to give directions for cars, trucks, and bikes, as well as for pedestrians. Show the children how to draw a simple picture of a stoplight. Encourage children to color their pictures, too.

❖ Play "Red Light." Choose one child to be "it." Invite all the other children to line up at the back of the classroom. Have "it" put his or her head down on a desk, cover his or her eyes, and say "green light." The children at the back of the classroom may then walk or run forward, but when "it" says "red light" and raises his or her head, the children must freeze. If "it" sees any children move as he or she looks up, those children must start over again. The first child to touch "it" becomes the next "it" and the game starts again. Make "Stoplight Stoppers" for the children to enjoy after the game.

Stoplight Stoppers

rectangular crackers or wafers	Spread peanut butter on each cracker. Then arrange the candy pieces to look like a stoplight (see illustration).
red, yellow, and green candy pieces	
creamy peanut butter	

❖ Play "Stop and Go." Invite the children to move in time to music. When the music begins, encourage the children to go or move according to the movement you describe, such as skip, run, crawl, and so on. When the music stops, the children must stop.

❖ Make a stop sign. Cut out several hexagon patterns. Help the children trace around one of the hexagon patterns on red construction paper. Invite each child to cut out a hexagon shape from the red construction paper. Make patterns for the letters S-T-O-P and help the children trace around these letters on white construction paper. Ask adult helpers or older students to help the children cut out the letters. Then have the children glue the white letters on their red hexagon to spell "STOP." Give each child a popsicle stick or tongue depressor to glue on the back for the pole.

Stranger

❖ Discuss with the children what to do if a stranger offers them candy or a ride. Stress that children should always say "No," or ask their parents for permission first. Read *Never Talk to Strangers*: *A Book About Personal Safety* by Irma Joyce or *The Berenstain Bears Learn About Strangers* by Stan and Janice Berenstain (see the unit book review).

❖ Contact the public relations division of the local police department. They often present programs about abduction prevention for young children. If possible, arrange for a presentation at your school.

Strawberry

❖ Help the children name as many berries as possible, such as blueberries, blackberries, boysenberries, raspberries, and strawberries. Ask the children which berry begins with the letter S. Have some fresh strawberries in the classroom for the children to taste. Use the leftover strawberries to make "Sensational Strawberry Sundaes" and "Strawberry Slushes." Invite the children to use straws to drink their slushes.

Sensational Strawberry Sundaes

strawberry ice cream
fresh strawberries
Cool Whip (optional)

Put a scoop of ice cream in a bowl. Mash fresh strawberries to pour on top of the ice cream. Add 1 Tbsp Cool Whip to the top, if desired. Garnish with a whole fresh strawberry.

Strawberry Slushes

4 limes
2 cups strawberries
4 tsp sugar
2 cups ice

Squeeze the limes. Put the lime juice, strawberries, sugar, and ice into a blender. Blend and then pour the slush into serving glasses.

Street

❖ Take the children on a walk to the closest street sign. Read the sign. Explain that street signs are placed where two streets intersect or meet. Encourage the children to learn the name of the street where their school is located.

❖ Teach each child the number and name of the street where he or she lives. Write each street name on a tagboard strip. Pin the strips on a bulletin board. Write each child's address on a strip of paper. Give the children their address strips and then encourage them to pin the strips under the appropriate "street signs" on the bulletin board.

❖ Watch "Sesame Street" on television this week if it is appropriate for your class.

String

❖ Make string paintings. Cover an area with newspapers or an old shower curtain. Put tempera paint in small cups. Have the children wear paint shirts and invite each child to hold one end of a piece of string with one hand and push the rest of the string into the paint with a popsicle stick or tongue depressor. The children may then pull the string all over sheets of paper until there is no paint left on the string. Encourage the children to try a second color and even a third color to make various abstract designs. Have the children use a new string for each color. The children may also fold a sheet of construction paper in half, open the paper up, and place a string saturated with paint on one side of the paper with the unpainted end of the string hanging out. Have the children refold the paper, put easy pressure on the paper, and slowly pull the string out.

Children may vary this procedure by using two strings with two different colors or three strings with three different colors.

❖ Collect colored straws to make necklaces. Have the children cut the straws into pieces. Invite the children to use yarn or string with tape wrapped around one end to string short pieces of straw. Encourage children who cut longer pieces of straws to use telephone cable wire to string their necklaces. Some children may wish to string thread spools on shoestrings or string beads according to bead pattern cards. Bead patterns show a two-dimensional picture of beads. The child is encouraged to select matching beads to string in the same sequence shown on the card. Bead pattern cards may be purchased commercially or you may make your own.

Stripe

❖ Cut out a large letter S from white construction paper for each child in your classroom. Show the children how to use a ruler to make stripes on their S. Or, have the stripes already drawn on the S's. Invite the children to color or paint each stripe a different color. Help the children make a list of striped items. For example, zebras, peppermints, and candy canes are all striped. Identify anyone in the room who is wearing stripes. If possible, wear something striped on the day you plan to discuss this word. Invite the children to wear something striped the next day. Give the children a stick of fruit-striped chewing gum. Discuss which fruit each color represents.

❖ Read *Dots, Spots, Speckles, and Stripes* by Tana Hoban (see the unit book review). Use a sharp knife to cut V's along one side of several different colored, peeled crayons. Invite the children to hold one of the crayons sideways and pull the cut side across the paper to make stripes. Encourage the children to experiment making different colored stripes to fill their papers. Then give children an S pattern to trace around on their papers with a black crayon or marker. Invite more advanced children to cut out their traced S to reveal a "Striped S."

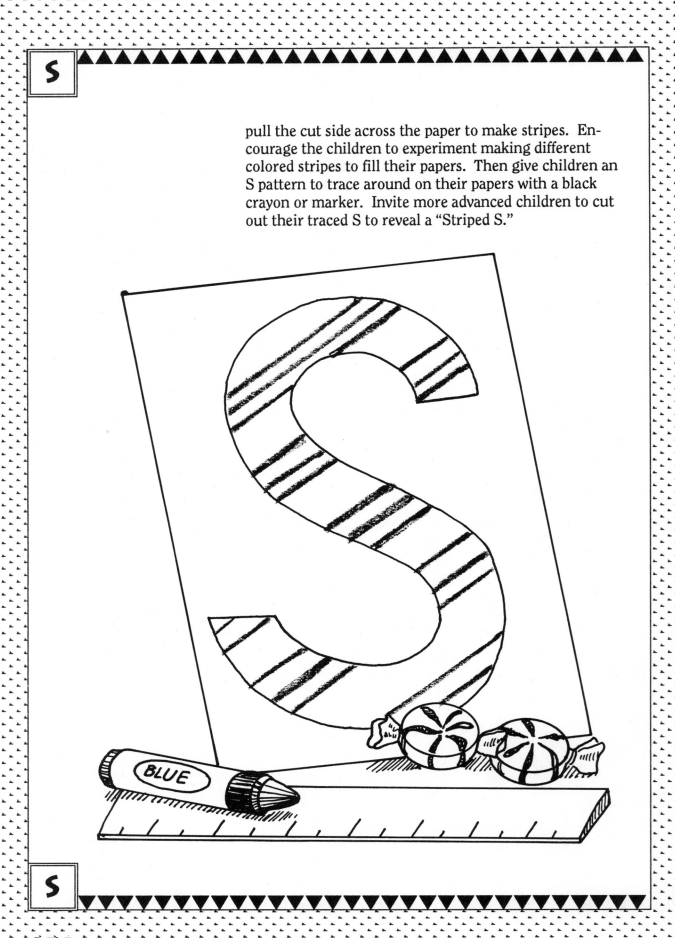

Sugar

❖ Read *From Beet to Sugar* by Ali Mitgutsch (see the unit book review). Help the children make a list of foods that contain a lot of sugar, such as cake, candy, colas, and cookies. Ask the children how they feel when they have eaten too much sugar. Point out that too much sugar may make them feel sick, give them headaches, cause cavities, and so on. Encourage each child to name at least one snack food they like that does not contain processed sugar (apples, oranges, peanuts, cheese, milk, grapes, raisins). Then suggest that children eat more of these foods at snacktime.

Sun and Sleep

❖ Read *Sun Up, Sun Down* by Gail Gibbons, *Wake Up, Sun* by David Harrison, *Shine, Sun!* by Carol Greene, and *Skyfire* by Frank Asch (see the unit book review). Invite the children to paint pictures of the sky and the sun. First, have the children paint a large piece of white construction paper with blue tempera paint. While the blue is drying, have them paint a paper plate yellow. Suggest that children cut strips of yellow construction paper for sunbeams. Instruct the children to then glue the paper-plate sun and the yellow sunbeams on the blue paper.

❖ Help the children make a list of all the exciting things they like to do on a sunny day. Write each activity on a separate strip of paper and then pin the strips to the bulletin board. Invite each child to take one of the strips off the bulletin board and glue it on a sheet of paper. Then encourage each child to draw an accompanying picture. Show the children how to draw a simple picture of the sun to include in their pictures as well. Discuss why people wear sunglasses. Invite the children to wear sunglasses to school for one day.

❖ On a sunny day, take the children outside and discuss how the sun makes shadows. Encourage the children to make their shadows longer and shorter. Then ask children to try and run faster than their shadows or to make their shadows go backwards. Ask the children to see if they can move just one part of their shadows. Invite the children to play "Shadow Tag." Choose one child to be "it." Explain that "it" must try to step on another child's shadow. If successful, that child becomes the next "it."

❖ Show the children how to draw a simple picture of a sunset. Point out that the sun goes down at the end of a day. Ask the children what happens when the sun goes down. Read *Dr. Seuss's Sleep Book* by Dr. Seuss, *Sleepy People* by Mary B. Goffstein and *Sleep Is for Everyone* by Paul Showers (see the unit book review). Invite the children to draw pictures of their own faces showing what they look like when they are very sleepy. Help the children compare pictures and look for similarities between the pictures, too. For example, many children might have drawn closed eyes.

Supermarket

❖ Read *Supermarket Magic* by Jack Kent or *The Supermarket* by Anne and Harlow Rockwell (see the unit book review). Help the children make a list of foods that begin with the letter S that are found in the supermarket, such as sugar, salt, spaghetti, strawberries, sausages, salmon, salami, sardines, shrimp, sauerkraut, spinach, squash, saltines, sunflower seeds, and syrup. If possible, take the children to the supermarket to do this activity!

Food for Thought

Introducing children to a variety of foods is a wonderful way of reinforcing language concepts. The following foods all begin with the letter S and may be introduced at any time during this unit.

salad, salami, Salisbury steak, salsa, saltines, sandwiches, sardines, sauerkraut, sausage, scallions, seafood, seeds, sesame seeds, shrimp, slaw, snow peas, sorbet, soup, sour cream, soy sauce, spaghetti, spinach, squash, steak, stew, stir-fry, strawberries, string beans, stuffing, succotash, summer sausage, sunflower seeds, sushi, sweet and sour sauce, syrup, Swiss steak

Book Review

Children enjoy hearing good books read aloud. The books listed here are favorites of children and may be used to reinforce the letter S.

Allington, Richard L. and Krull, Kathleen. *Smelling,* Raintree Publications, 1980.

Anglund, Joan W. *Spring Is a New Beginning,* Harcourt Brace Jovanovich, 1963.

Asch, Frank. *Skyfire,* Prentice Hall, 1984.

Berenstain, Stan and Berenstain, Janice. *The Berenstain Bears Go to School,* Random House, 1978.

Berenstain, Stan and Berenstain, Janice. *The Berenstain Bears Learn About Strangers,* Random House, 1986.

Brown, Marcia. *Stone Soup,* Live Oak Media, 1987.

Carle, Eric. *The Very Busy Spider,* Putnam Publishing Group, 1984.

Curran, Eileen. *Life in the Sea,* Troll Associates, 1985.

de Paola, Tomie. *The Quicksand Book,* Holiday House, 1977.

Gag, Wanda. *Snow White and the Seven Dwarfs,* Putnam Publishing Group, 1938.

Gibbons, Gail. *Sun Up, Sun Down,* Harcourt Brace Jovanovich, 1987.

Goffstein, Mary B. *Sleepy People,* Farrar, Straus and Giroux, 1979.

Graham, Margaret B. *Be Nice to Spiders,* Harper & Row, 1978.

Greene, Carol. *Shine, Sun!* Childrens Press, 1983.

Harrison, David. *Wake Up, Sun,* Random House, 1986.

Hoban, Tana. *Dots, Spots, Speckles, and Stripes,* Greenwillow Books, 1987.

Hurd, Edith T. *Starfish,* Harper & Row, 1962.

Jordan, Helene J. *How a Seed Grows,* Harper & Row, 1960.

Joyce, Irma. *Never Talk to Strangers: A Book About Personal Safety,* Western Publishing, 1985.

Keats, Ezra Jack. *The Snowy Day,* Penguin Books, 1962.

Kent, Jack. *Supermarket Magic,* Random House, 1978.

Kuchalla, Susan. *All About Seeds,* Troll Associates, 1982.

Marshall, Edward. *Three by the Sea,* Dial Books, 1981.

Mayer, Mercer. *Just Me and My Little Sister,* Western Publishing, 1986.

McGovern, Ann. *Stone Soup,* Scholastic, 1986.

Mitgutsch, Ali. *From Beet to Sugar,* Carolrhoda Books, 1981.

Mitgutsch, Ali. *From Sea to Salt,* Carolrhoda Books, 1985.

Pluckrose, Henry. *Smelling,* Watts, 1986.

Rockwell, Anne and Rockwell, Harlow. *The Supermarket,* Macmillan, 1979.

Ross, Tony. *Stone Soup,* Dial Books, 1987.

Sendak, Maurice. *Seven Little Monsters,* Harper & Row, 1977.

Seuss, Dr. *Dr. Seuss's Sleep Book,* Random House, 1962.

Showers, Paul. *Sleep Is for Everyone,* Harper & Row, 1974.

Smith, Kathie B. and Crenson, Victoria E. *Hearing,* Troll Associates, 1987.

Smith, Kathie B. and Crenson, Victoria E. *Rand McNally Question Books: The Senses,* Macmillan, 1986.

Smith, Kathie B. and Crenson, Victoria E. *Smelling,* Troll Associates, 1987.

Smith, Kathie B. and Crenson, Victoria E. *Tasting,* Troll Associates, 1987.

Smith, Kathie B. and Crenson, Victoria E. *Thinking,* Troll Associates, 1987.

Smith, Kathie B. and Crenson, Victoria E. *Touching,* Troll Associates, 1987.

Wandelmaier, Roy. *Stars,* Troll Associates, 1985.

Webb, Angela. *Sand,* Watts, 1987.

Zion, Gene. *Harry by the Sea,* Harper & Row, 1965.

Tt

Tea

❖ Sponsor a "Tea Party" on Tuesday at 10:00. Have the children bring dress-up clothes to school. Have some extra dress-up clothes for children who forget. Serve iced tea with "Terrific Triangle Toast."

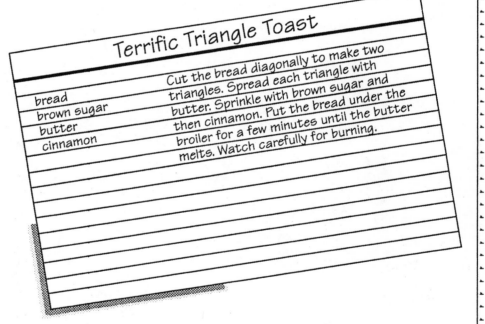

Terrific Triangle Toast

bread	Cut the bread diagonally to make two triangles. Spread each triangle with butter. Sprinkle with brown sugar and then cinnamon. Put the bread under the broiler for a few minutes until the butter melts. Watch carefully for burning.
brown sugar	
butter	
cinnamon	

❖ Teach the children to sing "I'm a Little Teapot" from *Wee Sing Children's Songs and Fingerplays*. Then teach the children the song with motions. Make a teapot pattern from heavy cardboard. Help the children trace around the pattern on a sheet of construction paper and invite each child to cut out a teapot. Help the children write a poem. Give each child a typewritten copy to glue on the teapot. Finally, give each child a teabag to staple to the teapot. This makes an especially nice greeting card for a parent or relative.

❖ Have each child make a large letter T with glue on a sheet of construction paper. Then invite the children to open a teabag and sprinkle the tea leaves over the glue. When the glue is dry, help children carefully shake off the excess tea leaves to reveal a "Tea Leaves T."

Teacher

❖ Ask the children to imagine what school might be like if there were no teachers! Read *My Teacher Sleeps in School* by Leatie Weiss, *Arthur's Teacher Trouble* by Marc Brown, and *The Day the Teacher Went Bananas* by James Howe (see the unit book review).

❖ Encourage each child to draw a picture of you.

❖ Help the children make a list of all the duties that you perform as a teacher. Choose different children to be the pretend teacher this week. At the end of the week, ask children to discuss what it felt like to be the teacher.

Teeth

❖ Review with the children the proper way to brush their teeth. Ask the children to show you what they remember by teaching them to sing "This Is the Way We Brush Our Teeth" (sung to the tune of "The Mulberry Bush") from *Wee Sing Children's Songs and Fingerplays*. Read *The Tooth Book* by Theodore Le Sieg, *Arthur's Tooth* by Marc

Brown, *Little Rabbit's Loose Tooth* by Lucy Bate, and *The Wobbly Tooth* by Nancy E. Cooney (see the unit book review).

Telephone

❖ Help each child learn his or her telephone number from memory. If a child does not have a telephone, have him or her memorize the number of a close relative or neighbor. Send a note home with each child asking parents what telephone number they would prefer you teach their child.

❖ Discuss why we have telephones. Make a telephone pattern in two parts on heavy cardboard—one part for the receiver and the other part for the base of the telephone. Help the children trace around the patterns on black construction paper. Invite each child to cut out his or her own patterns. Have the children connect the receiver to the base by punching a hole in the end of the receiver and another hole in the bottom right-hand corner of the base. A length of black yarn should then be tied to the holes. Give each child a square sheet of white construction paper and have him or her round the corners to make a circle. Children may then punch holes around the outer edge of their circles (don't worry about how many). Glue the circle on the front of the telephone base to make a dial. Some children may be able to write their own telephone numbers on the telephone as well.

❖ Save an old telephone book. Help the children locate the names that begin with the letter T. Tear those pages out and invite the children to cut the pages into strips and then the strips into small squares. Have the children make a large letter T with glue on a sheet of construction paper and then arrange the telephone-page pieces along the glue line to make a "Telephone T."

❖ Encourage children to play with the toy telephones in the classroom. Invite the children to bring toy telephones from home as well. Sometimes a local telephone company will give you some telephones that cannot be repaired. Explain that the telephones will be used in your classroom.

Television

❖ Show the children how to draw a simple picture of a television set. Ask the children to compare their televisions at home with the television you show them how to draw. You might then draw rabbit ears or even a VCR on top depending upon your children's experiences.

❖ Ask the children if they spend time watching TV with their families. Ask the children what their favorite TV shows are, too. Help children make a list of other activities they might do with their families if they didn't have a TV. Then read *The Day the TV Broke* by Roni S. Denholtz and *The Berenstain Bears and Too Much TV* by Janice and Stan Berenstain (see the unit book review).

❖ Watch "Sesame Street" with the children at school this week or some other program appropriate for your class. Suggest appropriate programs for the children to watch at home in the afternoons, too. Then send a note home to parents asking their help in encouraging their children to watch only the programs you list. Include the day, time, and channel for each program you suggest. Give the children a small treat, such as "I'm Terrific!" stickers, if their parents send back a note verifying that they watched the prescribed programs each day. Encourage the parents and children to continue watching quality TV programs together.

Ten

❖ Provide lots of opportunities for the children to count out ten of a variety of objects. Show the children how to fold a sheet of newsprint into fourths. Have the children unfold the papers and then use a crayon to trace over the fold lines. Encourage the children to write the number 10 in each square. Explain that a 10 is written by drawing a stick and then a circle. Give small groups of children four piles of four different objects (torn paper scraps, tinfoil squares, pieces of tissue, tree bark pieces, and so on). Invite the children to count out ten of each item and then place the items on each section of their papers. Teach the children to sing "Ten in a Bed" from *Wee Sing Silly Songs*. You might change the song to

"Ten in a Section" and invite the children to manipulate the objects in one of their paper sections as they sing the song.

❖ Practice counting to ten as a group this week. Have the children count all of their fingers first. Use flash cards, too. Show the children flash cards in both sequential and then random order. Give each child a set of index cards numbered from one to ten with instructions to sequence the cards. Encourage each child to stand and recite to ten from memory when he or she is ready.

❖ See if the class can think of ten ways to use their bodies to make a T. Suggest that children use their fingers, arms, and feet to make individual T's. Encourage children to work together with a partner as well (two children may lie down perpendicular to one another).

Tent

❖ Invite the children to share what they know about tents, how tents are used, and any experiences they might have had with tents. Point out that tents are used today for camping, in circuses, at funerals, weddings, and so on. Show the children pictures of a tent.

❖ Set up a tent this week in which the children can play. You may also make a tent by draping a sheet over a table. Invite children to take turns doing some of their work inside the tent, too.

❖ Show the children how to draw a simple picture of a circus tent.

Throw, Tickle, Tiptoe, Turn, and Touch

❖ Sponsor a "Throwing Tournament." Invite the children to throw beanbags at a target, such as a trash can. If you have a Velcro dart game that uses Velcro balls instead of darts, invite the children to compete in that game as well.

❖ Put an old tire or inner tube on the floor and have the children practice jumping in and out of it. Practice walking, hopping, crawling through and running around the tire as well.

❖ Play "Simon Says" using commands with words that begin with the letter T. For example, you might say, "Walk on your tiptoes," "Tickle somebody else," "Turn all the way around," "Turn to the left or right," "Crawl under the table," and "Touch your toes, teeth, and thumb."

❖ Teach the class to play "Tag." Choose one child to be "it." "It" chases the other children until he or she tags a child. The tagged child then becomes "it" and the game continues.

Tic-Tac-Toe

❖ Make a large tic-tac-toe on the chalkboard. Divide the class into two teams. Ask one child at a time from each team a "T" question, such as "I'm thinking of the number in a pair" (two) and "I'm thinking of what you may use to blow your nose" (tissue). Make the clues as complicated or as simple as appropriate for your class. The child who answers correctly gets to put an "X" or an "O" on the chalkboard grid for his or her team. The first team to get tic-tac-toe wins. Invite the children to play tic-tac-toe in pairs as well.

Tie

❖ Encourage the children to practice tying and untying their shoes. Ask parents to work on this skill at home, too. Tie a colorful ribbon around the children's index fingers when they can successfully tie their shoes.

❖ Cut out a T for each child from sturdy paper or cardboard. Punch holes on each side of the T's. Thread a long piece of yarn through one of the holes from the front of the T and out through the hole on the opposite side. Align the ends of the yarn by pulling them straight up and making any necessary adjustments and then tie the yarn in a knot. Make sure there is enough yarn left from the knot to tie into a bow. Give each child one of the prepared T's. Invite the children to tie a bow. Invite more advanced children to tie more than one bow.

Time

❖ Discuss time in general. Ask the children what time they get up in the morning, eat lunch, get out of school, get home from school, eat supper, go to bed, and so on. Times, of course, will vary. Ask the children how they know what time it is. Point out that clocks, watches, and the sun all help us to tell what time it is. Read *What Time Is It, Mrs. Bear?* by Julia Killingback (see the unit book review).

❖ Discuss the days of the week. Give children an opportunity to say the days of the week in order. Point out that two days of the week begin with the letter T. Ask the children to name those two days, Tuesday and Thursday. Each day you go over the calendar, reinforce the concepts, Today is _____ and Tomorrow is _____. Read *Today Was a Terrible Day* by Patricia R. Giff or *The Tomorrow Book* by Doris Schwerin to reinforce these concepts as well (see the unit book review).

❖ Sponsor a "Terrific Tuesday" share day. Encourage each child to bring something from home that begins with a T to share with the class. Help the children make a list of possible items, such as a tea bag, a tulip, a box of tissue, a play telephone, a telephone book, play tools, a stuffed toy turtle, a toothbrush, a toy train, and so on.

Tissue

❖ Cut colored tissue paper into small pieces. Give each child some tissue-paper pieces and a sheet of white construction paper. Pour liquid starch (or use white glue thinned with water) into a container and invite the children to dip a wide brush in the starch and paint a T on their papers. Have the children arrange the small tissue pieces on the starch. The children may overlap the pieces of tissue. Suggest that children paint the top part of the T and arrange the tissue on it first and then paint the vertical part so the starch will not dry out.

❖ Explain that it is both healthy and polite to use a tissue to blow your nose or to wipe your mouth. Discuss how a tissue is different and how it is the same as construction paper or newsprint. Give each child a tissue. Have the children tear the tissues into small pieces. Invite the children to make a large letter T with glue on a sheet of dark construction paper and then arrange the torn tissue along the glue line to make a "Tissue T."

Tongue

❖ Invite the children to try saying some tongue twisters. Use *Timid Timothy's Tongue Twisters* by Dick Gackenbach or *Faint Frogs Feeling Feverish and Other Terrifically Tantalizing Tongue Twisters* by Lilian Obligado as a resource for finding lots of good tongue twisters (see the unit book review). Teach the children to say "Betty Botter" and "Peter Piper" from *Wee Sing Nursery Rhymes and Lullabies* as well.

❖ Give each child two tongue depressors. Ask the children if a doctor has ever used a tongue depressor to look at the back of the children's throats. Have the children make a T with the two tongue depressors. Then encourage the children to work together with a partner and share tongue depressors to make the letters A, E, F, H, I, K, L, M, N, V, W, X, Y, and Z. Have the children make the numbers 1, 4, and 7, too.

❖ Read *Tasting* by Richard L. Allington and Kathleen Krull, *Tasting* by Henry Pluckrose, and *A Tasting Party* by Jane B. Moncure (see the unit book review). Sponsor a "Tasting Party." Invite the children to taste "Tuna Tasties" and "Taco Popcorn."

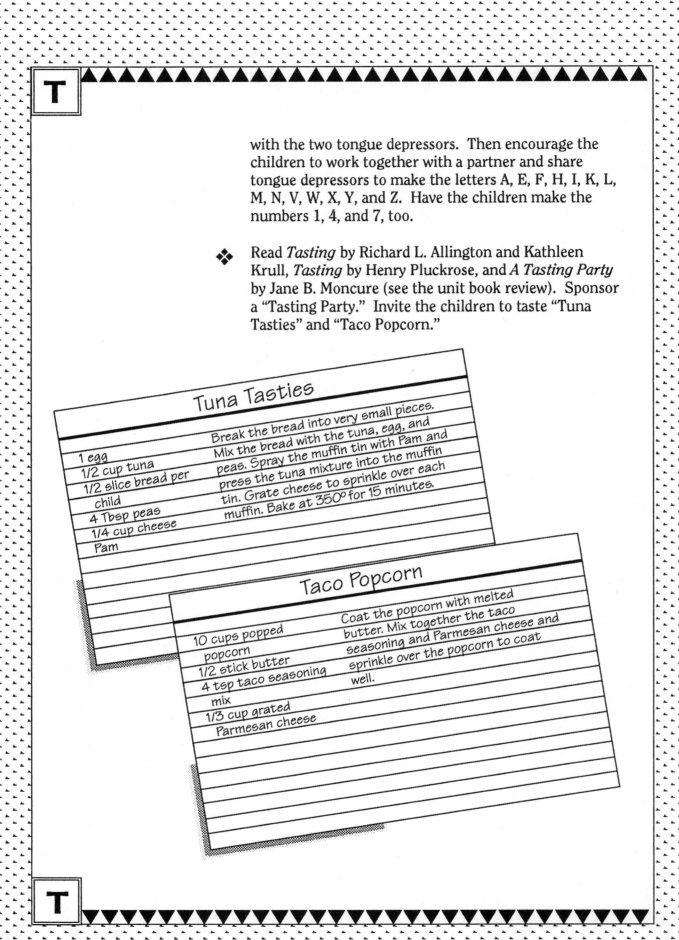

Tuna Tasties

1 egg
1/2 cup tuna
1/2 slice bread per child
4 Tbsp peas
1/4 cup cheese
Pam

Break the bread into very small pieces. Mix the bread with the tuna, egg, and peas. Spray the muffin tin with Pam and press the tuna mixture into the muffin tin. Grate cheese to sprinkle over each muffin. Bake at 350° for 15 minutes.

Taco Popcorn

10 cups popped popcorn
1/2 stick butter
4 tsp taco seasoning mix
1/3 cup grated Parmesan cheese

Coat the popcorn with melted butter. Mix together the taco seasoning and Parmesan cheese and sprinkle over the popcorn to coat well.

Tools

❖ Read *Toolbox* by Anne Rockwell, *Tool Book* by Gail Gibbons, *Tools* by Ken Robbins, and *My Very First Book of Tools* by Eric Carle (see the unit book review). Set up a small "Tool Center." Put a small hammer, some large nails, scrap wood, screws, a screwdriver, wrench, and pliers in the center. Provide opportunities for the children to experiment in the center.

❖ Bring a variety of tools from home to show the children. Certainly the children will recognize a saw, a hammer, and a screwdriver. Bring tools, such as a rake and hoe to show the children, too. Explain the use of each tool and demonstrate how to use each tool, if possible. Ask the custodian to come visit your classroom and show the children some tools and how they are used.

Toys

❖ Ask each child to draw a picture of his or her favorite toy or invite the children to bring toys to school to share. Then invite the children to share reasons why these toys are their favorites.

Trace

❖ Provide tracing paper for children to place over pictures of triangles, trees, turtles, trains, and any other pictures they might like to trace. You might also have children trace horizontal and vertical lines, their names, and alphabet letters, too.

Transportation

❖ Divide a bulletin board into three columns. Title the columns "Land," "Air," and "Sea." Invite the children to cut out pictures of transportation vehicles from magazines and then place the pictures under the appropriate headings.

❖ Use any language picture cards for transportation that you have in your classroom as flash cards to help children recognize airplanes, hot-air balloons, vans, fire engines, tractors, motor homes, ambulances, tugboats, police cars, mail trucks, station wagons, buses, jeeps, trains, trucks, canoes, ships, boats, helicopters, cabs, motorcycles, bicycles, tricycles, big wheels, scooters, spaceships, and so on.

❖ Make truck and car tracks. Give each child a large sheet of construction paper, a paint shirt, and an area covered with newspaper. Provide an assortment of small toy cars and trucks. Invite the children to choose a vehicle and then describe how they think their particular car or truck might be used. Put a small dab of paint in a contrasting color on each child's paper and have the children run their little cars or trucks back and forth through the paint to make tracks. If desired, try a second dab of paint on the same paper and even a third dab of another color.

❖ Read *Curious George and the Dump Truck* by Margret Rey, *Trucks* by Byron Barton, *Trucks* by Gail Gibbons, *Truck* by Donald Crews and *The Truck Book* by Harry McNaught (see the unit book review). Encourage the children to fill a bulletin board with pictures of cars and trucks they cut out from magazines.

❖ Read *Trains* by Byron Barton, *Freight Train* by Donald Crews, and *Trains* by Gail Gibbons (see the unit book review). Make a train. Help each child trace around a rectangle pattern on bright construction paper. Invite the children to cut out their own rectangles. Give each child two squares of brown or black construction paper and then show the children how to round the corners to make circles. These will be the wheels for the boxcars. Cut out an engine and caboose from construction paper to tack on a bulletin board. Give each child a numbered index card to glue on their boxcars. Then invite children to place their cars in order to make a number train on the bulletin board. Teach the children to sing "The Train" from *Wee Sing Children's Songs and Fingerplays*.

Trees and Triangles

❖ Get permission to plant a tree in the school yard. A local garden club may be willing to donate a tree for the class to plant. This is an especially good activity around Arbor Day, which is celebrated at different times of the year in different parts of the country.

❖ Make triangle patterns of different sizes from heavy cardboard. Help the children trace around the patterns on different shades of green construction paper or red, yellow, brown, and orange paper in the fall. Invite the children to cut out the triangles. Then have children draw grass or a hill on a sheet of white or light blue construction paper and then add the traced triangles for trees.

❖ Read *A Tree Is Nice* by Janice M. Udry and *Discovering Trees* by Douglas Florian (see the unit book review). Show the children how to draw a simple picture of a tree. If possible, take the children outside to an area that has trees. Encourage the children to hug a tree. Then help the children describe what a tree feels like. When you return to the classroom, encourage the children to add more details to their tree pictures. Display the finished drawings on a bulletin board with the title "T Is Tree-mendous."

❖ Make several triangles from tagboard. Ask the children to feel around the outside edges of the triangles with their fingers. Discuss how many sides and corners there are in a triangle. Discuss how a triangle is the same and how it is different from a square and a rectangle.

❖ Give the children five small squares and five small rectangles cut from scraps of construction paper. Show the children how to make the rectangles into triangles by cutting on the diagonal. (*Diagonal* will probably be a new word for some children, so teach the word using the definition "opposite corners," and draw diagonal lines on the chalkboard. You might have the children draw diagonal lines on pre-drawn squares and rectangles on the chalkboard to make sure they understand the concept before you use paper.) Cut patterns for the letter T from heavy construction paper. Help the children trace around a T pattern on construction paper and then invite children to cut out the traced T. Invite the children to glue their ten triangles on their T's.

Tulip

❖ Read *The First Tulips in Holland* by Phyllis Krasilovsky (see the unit book review). Show the children how to draw a simple picture of a tulip.

❖ Make tulip patterns from heavy cardboard. Help the children trace around four patterns on brightly colored construction paper. Invite children to cut out the traced tulips. Suggest that children staple each tulip to a straw or green pipe cleaner to make a stem. Make a garden by cutting a cardboard egg carton into thirds. Give each child one-third—a section of four individual egg containers. Have the children turn the sections over and paint the bottoms green or brown with tempera paint. After the paint is dry, the children may push the stems through the bottoms of the carton.

Turtle

❖ Arrange to keep some live turtles in the classroom for the children to observe. Turtles are inexpensive and make easy class pets. Show the children how to draw a simple picture of a turtle.

❖ Make paper-plate turtles. Have the children paint the bottoms of two heavy paper plates green. Cut patterns for the head, tail, and four legs from heavy cardboard. Help the children trace around the patterns on green construction paper and then invite children to cut out the traced turtle parts. When the painted paper plates are dry, have the children put the two plates together with the painted sides showing, stuff the middle with newspaper, and then staple the plates together with the head, tail, and legs attached between the plates. Children may use a black magic marker to make designs on the top shell. Read *Little Turtle's Big Adventure* by David Harrison aloud to the children and their turtles (see the unit book review).

Two

❖ Read *My Two Book* by Jane B. Moncure (see the unit book review). Make patterns for the letter T from heavy cardboard. Help each child trace around the pattern two times on light-colored construction paper and then invite them to cut out the two traced T's. Suggest that the children write 2's all over the T's.

❖ Help the children practice making 2's by using the directional instructions "around and over" as you draw several 2's on the chalkboard. Invite small groups of children to make 2's on the chalkboard as they repeat the instructional words. When the children are making correctly formed 2's on the chalkboard, give them a sheet of newsprint. Have children fold the sheet into fourths, open the paper, and write a 2 on each section, back and front. When the children are ready, encourage them to work on lined paper.

❖ Encourage the children to cut out a variety of 2's from magazines and the grocery section of the newspaper. Then invite children to make a large letter T with glue on a sheet of construction paper and arrange the 2's along the glue line to make a "Two's T."

❖ Discuss with the children that a pair is two of something. Help the children make a list of as many items that come in pairs as possible. For example, socks, shoes, mittens, gloves, earrings, feet, hands, pants, and twins all come in pairs.

Type

❖ Look for an old typewriter in your school that the children might use. Make sure the ribbon is clean and show the class how to put paper in the typewriter. Put the keys in the "caps lock" position. Provide opportunities for each child to type T's, the ABC's, words that begin with the letter T that they copy from an alphabet bulletin board, or other words they might have memorized, such as color or number words, or the names of other children in the class.

Food for Thought

Introducing children to a variety of foods is a wonderful way of reinforcing language concepts. The following foods all begin with the letter T and may be introduced at any time during this unit.

taco, Tang, tangerine, tapioca, toast, tofu, tomato, tomato juice, tomato soup, tortilla, tostado, Triscuits (wheat crackers), tuna, turkey, turnips

Book Review

Children enjoy hearing good books read aloud. The books listed here are favorites of children and may be used to reinforce the letter T.

Allington, Richard L. and Krull, Kathleen. *Tasting,* Raintree Publishing, 1980.

Barton, Byron. *Trains,* Harper & Row, 1986.

Barton, Byron. *Trucks,* Harper & Row, 1986.

Bate, Lucy. *Little Rabbit's Loose Tooth,* Crown, 1975.

Berenstain, Stan and Berenstain, Janice. *The Berenstain Bears and Too Much TV,* Random House, 1984.

Brown, Marc. *Arthur's Teacher Trouble,* Little, Brown and Company, 1986.

Brown, Marc. *Arthur's Tooth,* Little, Brown and Company, 1986.

Carle, Eric. *My Very First Book of Tools,* Harper & Row, 1986.

Cooney, Nancy E. *The Wobbly Tooth,* Putnam Publishing Group, 1981.

Crews, Donald. *Freight Train,* Penguin Books, 1985.

Crews, Donald. *Truck,* Penguin Books, 1985.

Denholtz, Roni S. *The Day the TV Broke,* Jan Productions, 1986.

Florian, Douglas. *Discovering Trees,* Macmillan, 1986.

Gackenbach, Dick. *Timid Timothy's Tongue Twisters,* Live Oak Media, 1989.

Galdone, Paul. *The Teeny-Tiny Woman,* Ticknor & Fields, 1986.

Gibbons, Gail. *Tool Book,* Holiday House, 1982.

Gibbons, Gail. *Trains,* Holiday House, 1987.

Gibbons, Gail. *Trucks,* Harper & Row, 1981.

Giff, Patricia R. *Today Was a Terrible Day,* Penguin Books, 1984.

Harrison, David. *Little Turtle's Big Adventure,* Random House, 1985.

Howe, James. *The Day the Teacher Went Bananas,* E. P. Dutton, 1984.

Killingback, Julia. *What Time Is It, Mrs. Bear?*, William Morrow and Company, 1985.

Krasilovsky, Phyllis. *The First Tulips in Holland*, Doubleday, 1982.

Le Sieg, Theodore. *The Tooth Book*, Random House, 1981.

Mayer, Mercer. *Terrible Troll*, Dial Books, 1981.

McNaught, Harry. *The Truck Book*, Random House, 1978.

Moncure, Jane B. *A Tasting Party*, Childrens Press, 1982.

Moncure, Jane B. *My Two Book*, Child's World, 1985.

Obligado, Lilian. *Faint Frogs Feeling Feverish and Other Terrifically Tantalizing Tongue Twisters*, Penguin Books, 1983.

Pluckrose, Henry. *Tasting*, Watts, 1986.

Rey, Margret. *Curious George and the Dump Truck*, Houghton Mifflin, 1984.

Robbins, Ken. *Tools*, Macmillan, 1983.

Rockwell, Anne. *Toolbox*, Macmillan, 1974.

Schwerin, Doris. *The Tomorrow Book*, Pantheon, 1984.

Udry, Janice M. *A Tree Is Nice*, Harper & Row, 1987.

Weiss, Leatie. *My Teacher Sleeps in School*, Penguin Books, 1985.

Uu

Umbrella

❖ Show the children an umbrella on a rainy day. Discuss what umbrellas are used for. Read *My Red Umbrella* by Robert Bright, *The Yellow Umbrella* by Henrik Drescher, and *Umbrella* by Taro Yashima (see the unit book review). Show the children how to draw a simple picture of an umbrella. Invite children to color their umbrellas, too.

❖ Make umbrellas. Cut a pattern for the top of the umbrella from tagboard. Help the children use the pattern to trace two umbrella tops (one for the front and one for the back) on colorful sheets of construction paper or on wallpaper samples. You might trace the umbrella top on white construction paper and invite the children to use watercolors to paint the umbrellas as well. Have the children cut out their traced umbrella tops. Then show children how to shape a pipe cleaner into a J shape to make a handle or cut out construction-paper handles.

Under

❖ Provide opportunities for the children to practice following "under" directions, such as:

Inside Directions	**Outside Directions**
Get under an umbrella. Crawl under the table. Crawl under your desk. Put your hands under your chin. Put your hands under your book. Put your hands under your desk. Put your hands under the floor. (Just checking!) Put your pencil under your chair. Hide your pencil under your hands.	Walk under the slide. Crawl under a swing. Crawl under the jungle gym. Stand under a tree. Put a leaf under your foot.

❖ Stack several large colored blocks in a random pattern. Use each color only once. Then ask questions like "Which block is under the red?" or "Which block is under the blue?" Give each child a set of blocks. Instruct the children to put the red block under the blue block, and so on.

❖ All week, have the children draw a line across the top of their papers from left to the right. Invite the children to do all their work under the line. Stress the word *under*.

❖ Sponsor "over" and "under" relay races. Divide the class into two teams. Have team members form two straight lines. Give the first child in each line a ball. First, time the teams passing the ball under their legs to the next person in line until the ball reaches the end of the line. Next, time the teams passing the ball over the head of one child and then under the legs of the next child alternating until the ball reaches the last child in line. Stress the words *over* and *under*.

Unicorn

❖ Ask the children if they know what a unicorn is. Point out that a unicorn is a make-believe animal. Find a picture of a unicorn to show the class. Unicorns are often used on posters. Invite children who have stuffed animal unicorns at home to bring them to school to share with the rest of the class.

❖ Discuss how a unicorn is like a horse and how it is different. Make a "Unicorn Snack."

Unicorn Snack

1 cup peanut butter	Beat together all of the ingredients and drop by teaspoonfuls onto a cookie sheet.
1 package yellow cake mix	Bake at 375° for 8–10 minutes.
2 eggs	
1/3 cup water	

Uniform

❖ Play the "Uniform Game." Help the children make a list of people who wear uniforms—for example, doctors, police officers, security guards, bus drivers, mail carriers, waitresses and waiters, firefighters, nurses, pilots, flight attendants, sports players, soldiers, delivery persons, fast-food chain employees, priests, rabbis, ministers, judges, forest rangers, train engineers or conductors, cooks and chefs, umpires, and so on. Discuss what each person does. Role-play several of the uniformed people for the class and encourage the children to guess which person you are.

❖ Find pictures of as many uniformed people as possible. Glue the pictures on tagboard cards. Use the cards as flash cards to help children learn to identify each worker. Encourage the children to learn what each uniformed person does as well.

❖ Invite the children to make a collage of pictures of uniformed people. Suggest that children cut out pictures from magazines and then glue the pictures on construction paper in a U shape.

Up and Down

❖ Make "Pineapple Upside-Down Cake."

Pineapple Upside-Down Cake

| 1 can (16 oz) pineapple slices (or use 6-7 peach halves) yellow cake mix 1 stick margarine 1 cup brown sugar | Preheat the oven to 350°. Melt the margarine and pour it into a cake pan. Sprinkle brown sugar over the margarine. Arrange the pineapple on the brown sugar. Prepare the yellow cake mix and pour the batter over the pineapple. Bake for 35–40 minutes. Cool for 5 minutes and then invert the cake onto a serving plate. Let the cake stand for 1 minute before removing the pan. |

❖ Teach the children to sing "The Noble Duke of York" from *Wee Sing and Play.* Then read *Great Day for Up!* by Dr. Seuss (see the unit book review).

Us

❖ On a sheet of newsprint or construction paper, have each child draw a self-portrait. Invite the children to cut out their portraits. Arrange the pictures on a bulletin board so they spell out the word "Us." Discuss the word *us*.

Food for Thought

Introducing children to a variety of foods is a wonderful way of reinforcing language concepts. The following foods all begin with the letter U and may be introduced at any time during this unit.

upside-down cake

Book Review

Children enjoy hearing good books read aloud. The books listed here are favorites of children and may be used to reinforce the letter U.

Andersen, Hans Christian. *The Ugly Duckling,* Troll Associates, 1979.

Bright, Robert. *My Red Umbrella,* William Morrow and Company, 1985.

Drescher, Henrik. *The Yellow Umbrella,* Bradbury Press, 1987.

Seuss, Dr. *Great Day for Up!,* Random House, 1974.

Yashima, Taro. *Umbrella,* Penguin Books, 1958.

Zolotow, Charlotte. *The Unfriendly Book,* Harper & Row, 1975.

Vacation

❖ Invite the children to share with the rest of the class one favorite place where they have vacationed with their families. Explain that family outings to visit local parks and visits to other family members' homes are vacations, too. Read *The Bears' Vacation* by Stan and Janice Berenstain or *The Popples' Vacation* by Peggy Kahn (see the unit book review).

Valentines

❖ Help the children make a class alphabet book with old valentines. Collect as many different valentines as possible. Put all of the valentines out on a table for the class to see. Have the children find one valentine to glue on a page for each letter of the alphabet. For example, a valentine with an airplane or animals might be glued on the "A" page, valentines with a baby, balloons, or bunnies could be glued on the "B" page, and so on. Encourage the children to use their imaginations! Use extra valentines to make a wonderful border for an alphabet bulletin board or as a border to display work children have completed while working on the letter V.

Body V's

❖ Show the children how they might use their bodies to make a letter V. Invite the children to spread two fingers apart, put their arms together at the elbows, and spread their legs apart. Two children lying on the floor at angles to each other may also make a V. Encourage the children to experiment making V's in other ways as well.

Vanessa and Veronica

❖ Help the children think of as many names as possible that begin with the letter V. Suggest Vanessa, Veronica, Victoria, Vicky, Vivian, Vera, Vida, Valerie, Vanna, Velvet, Venus, Verna, Violet, Virginia, Van, Vance, Vernon, Vick, Victor, Vincent, and Virgil. Invite the children to say each name and listen for the V sound. Read *Veronica* and *Veronica and the Birthday Present*, both by Roger Duvoisin (see the unit book review).

Vanilla

❖ Sponsor a "Vote on Vanilla" party. Set out bite-size samples of vanilla wafers, vanilla ice cream, vanilla frosting, vanilla pudding, vanilla milk shake, and vanilla yogurt. Invite the children to taste each of the treats and then vote on their favorite. Make ballots with the word *vote* and a symbol for each of the foods. Encourage the children to make a mark beside their choices and then drop the ballots in a ballot box. Graph the results.

Make several packages of instant vanilla pudding. Have the children wash their hands. Cover each desk with wax paper, put globs of pudding on the wax paper, and invite the children to fingerpaint with the pudding. Have the children make V's in the pudding and other letters, numbers, and shapes, too. Encourage the children to clean up when they are finished!

Vegetables

❖ Make "Very Vegetable Soup." Ask each child to furnish one vegetable from home. Have the children name and then taste each vegetable raw before adding it to the soup.

Very Vegetable Soup

3 bouillon cubes
any fresh vegetables
(potatoes, carrots,
tomatoes, mushrooms,
onions, celery,
cauliflower, turnips,
cabbage, and cans
of corn, peas, beans,
mushrooms, and stewed
tomatoes)

Rinse and clean the vegetables.
Cut each vegetable into cubes and
place in a large pot. Add water to
cover the vegetables. Add the
bouillon cubes and cook over
medium-low heat for 1-2 hours or
until the vegetables are soft.

❖ If you have food picture cards in your classroom, invite the children to sort the cards into two categories, such as "Vegetables" and "Not Vegetables" or "Fruits" and "Vegetables." Then use the cards as flash cards.

❖ Have the children cut out pictures of vegetables from magazines to make a collage. Help the children glue the pictures on a large sheet of construction paper in a V shape. Plan a class field trip to a produce market, if possible, so the children may see a variety of fresh vegetables.

❖ Read the school lunch menu for the week aloud to the children. Ask children to identify all of the vegetables.

❖ Discuss with the children how their bodies need vitamins to grow and that the food they eat gives them the needed vitamins. Make "Veggie Vitamins."

Veggie Vitamins

1 Tbsp oil	Heat the oil in a frying pan or a wok, if available, at medium heat. Add the vegetables and stir-fry for 3-5 minutes. Add a small amount of soy sauce, if desired.
4 cups fresh vegetables (1/2-inch zucchini or squash slices, 1/4-inch carrot slices, 1/2-inch pepper strips, individual broccoli or caulifiowerets, sliced mushrooms)	
soy sauce (optional)	

❖ Read *The Giant Vegetable Garden* by Nadine B. Westcott (see the unit book review). Consider planting a vegetable garden. Speak with an experienced gardener in your area for advice on what to plant, when to plant, and how to prepare the soil.

Velvet

❖ Buy a roll of violet velvet ribbon. Discuss with the children that *violet* is another word for the color purple.

The words *violet* and *purple* are written on many primary crayons. Check your class crayons and point this out if your crayons are so marked. Give each child a piece of the ribbon to cut into little squares. Invite the children to make a large letter V with glue on a sheet of construction paper and then arrange the ribbon pieces along the glue line to make a "Violet Velvet V."

❖ Ask someone who sews to save scraps of velvet and other materials for the class. Glue pieces of velvet, corduroy, wool, cotton cloth, and other textured materials on tagboard cards. Ask the children to pick out the velvet pieces, first by just using their sense of sight, and then with their eyes closed, using their sense of touch.

Vest

❖ Wear a vest to school. Invite each child to try it on. Discuss how a vest is like a sweater or coat and how it is different. Encourage children who have vests to wear them to school on a designated day.

Video

❖ Discuss what a VCR (video cassette recorder) is. If you have a VCR in your classroom, or have access to a VCR, arrange to show a videotape for the children's enjoyment. The *Wee Sing* video tapes, *Wee Sing Together: A Magical Musical* and *King Cole's Party: A Merry Musical Celebration,* are especially good for young children.

❖ If your school has a video camera, arrange to have the children videotaped. Help the class prepare a song with motions, a simple dance, or another special presentation. Or, videotape the children saying their ABC's. Replay the tape on TV so the children may see and hear themselves.

Violets

❖ Brighten up your room with real violets. Ask someone who grows violets if he or she might be willing to share several different types with the class for the day. Draw a variety of vases on a large sheet of construction paper. Invite the children to draw stems in the vases first and then encourage them to draw a violet on each stem.

Violin

❖ Ask the children if any of them play the violin. If so, invite those children to play their violins for the rest of the class. Ask a high school strings teacher or a violinist from a local musical group to come visit your classroom and demonstrate how a violin is played.

Volleyball

❖ Invite the children to hit a balloon back and forth over a lowered volleyball net or a string across the classroom. Invite interested children to practice hitting a volleyball back and forth over a standard volleyball net. Teach more advanced children to play volleyball.

Food for Thought

Introducing children to a variety of foods is a wonderful way of reinforcing language concepts. The following foods all begin with the letter V and may be introduced at any time during this unit.

vanilla extract, vanilla yogurt, veal, vegetable juice, vegetables, vegetable soup, Velveeta cheese, venison, Vienna sausages, vinaigrette dressing, vinegar

Book Review

Children enjoy hearing good books read aloud. The books listed here are favorites of children and may be used to reinforce the letter V.

Berenstain, Stan and Berenstain, Janice. *The Bears' Vacation,* Beginner Books, 1968.

Duvoisin, Roger. *Veronica,* Knopf, 1961.

Duvoisin, Roger. *Veronica and the Birthday Present,* Knopf, 1971.

Kahn, Peggy. *The Popples' Vacation,* Random House, 1987.

Westcott, Nadine B. *The Giant Vegetable Garden,* Little, Brown and Company, 1981.

Wallpaper

❖ Invite the children to look through a book of wallpaper samples, choose a pattern they particularly like, and then tear the page from the book. (Places that sell wallpaper will often give away old books when they are finished with them.) Ask the children to cut their page into strips. Encourage children to exchange some of their strips with other classmates so each child will have a variety of patterns. Have the children cut their strips into small squares. Invite children to make a large letter W with glue on a sheet of construction paper and then arrange the wallpaper pieces along the glue line to make a "Wallpaper W."

Walnut

❖ Show the children how to crack a walnut. Invite the children to taste the meat of the nut. Use the rest of the nuts to make "Wonderful Walnut Waffles" and "Waldorf Salad." Put the shells in a paper bag and use a hammer to crush them into smaller pieces. Have the children make a large letter W with glue on a sheet of construction paper. Invite children to sprinkle the walnut pieces over the glue. When the glue is dry, help children carefully shake off the excess shells to reveal a "Walnut W."

Wonderful Walnut Waffles

frozen waffles (1 double waffle may be cut to serve 4 small children)

powdered sugar

fresh fruit

walnuts

Toast waffles in toaster, microwave, or oven until they are brown and warm. Top each with powdered sugar and fruit. Sprinkle with walnuts.

Waldorf Salad

2 cups apples

2 cups celery

1/4 cup mayonnaise

1/4 cup walnuts

nutmeg (optional)

Wash and cut the apples into cubes, with or without the peel. Wash and cut the celery into cubes. Put the apples and celery into a bowl. Add mayonnaise and nuts and mix well. Sprinkle nutmeg over the top, if desired.

Water

❖ Read *Water Is Wet* by Penny Pollock (see the unit book review). Fill a sand tray or a large container with water and invite the children to use sand buckets, cups, pitchers, measuring cups and spoons, funnels, sponges, nesting cups, and so on to play with the water. If possible, plan to do this activity outside. Put an old shower curtain underneath the tray and have the children wear waterproof paint shirts.

❖ Make several patterns of the letter W from heavy cardboard. Help the children trace around the patterns on sheets of white construction or drawing paper. Invite the children to cut out their own W and then paint it with watercolors. Remind the children to wash their brushes in clean water between colors to keep the paints and palette from becoming muddy.

❖ Ask the children to demonstrate wiping their shoes when coming into a room from outside. Discuss why they should wipe their shoes. Put a welcome mat at your classroom door on which the children may wipe their shoes when they come in. If there are other mats in another part of the school, point these out to the class and discuss why they are there as well. If the other mats have the word "Welcome" on them, point out the W to the children. Praise the children each time they remember to wipe their shoes.

Watermelon

❖ On a nice day, cut and slice a watermelon outside for the class to enjoy. Plant some of the seeds and invite the children to see what happens. Give small handfuls of the rest of the seeds to the children. Encourage the children to work together in small groups of three. Suggest that one child in each group make a large letter W with a pencil on a sheet of construction paper. Have another child in the group trace over the pencil line with glue. Have the third child arrange the watermelon seeds along the glue line to make a "Watermelon W."

❖ Show the children how to draw a simple picture of a watermelon slice.

❖ Make watermelon pictures. Encourage each child to use a full sheet of construction paper. Show the children how to round the corners at the bottom with their scissors to make the paper the shape of a watermelon slice. Give the children strips of green, white, and red construction paper. Have the children cut the green strips into little pieces and then glue the pieces along the bottom to make one row of green snips. Next, have children do the same to make a row of white snips. Finally, invite children to fill in the rest with red snips. A few single black snips may be added on top of the red for seeds.

Weather

❖ Make a "Weather Wheel." Give each child a strip of white paper folded into three 1-inch squares. In one square, have the children draw a sun to represent a sunny day. In the next square, ask children to draw a cloud to represent a cloudy day, and in the last square, have children draw a cloud with raindrops falling down to represent a rainy day.

You may have the children draw other pictures to suit your weather during the time of year you are studying this letter as well. For example, you might want to add a snowperson to represent a snowy day if you are studying this letter during winter, and so on. Have the children cut each square apart and glue the squares on a large paper plate. Add an arrow cut from construction paper with a brad. Encourage the children to use the plates every morning to discuss the weather. Invite each child to turn the arrow to the appropriate weather picture to represent the day. If you have a commercially-made weather wheel or weather indicators for your calendar, use them as well.

❖ Read *The Weather* by Claude D'Ham and *Sam Cat: A Book About Weather* by Gillinan Humphries and Francis Thatcher (see the unit book review). Discuss the day's weather each morning. Encourage the children to discuss what they should wear each day to school depending on that day's weather as well. Give the children clothing catalogs and invite them to cut out pictures of clothing that they might wear each day.

Weave

❖ Weave with paper. Have the children fold a sheet of construction paper in half the long way and make cuts along the fold about every 2 inches from the fold to within 1 inch of the outside edge. Caution the children not to cut all the way across. Ask the children to cut a contrasting color of construction paper into strips. Have the children open their folded sheets of paper. Review the concepts "over" and "under" and then show children, in small groups, how to use the strips to weave through the paper.

Week

❖ Review the number of days in a week with the class. Have the children count the seven days on a calendar using their fingers. Practice saying the days of the week in order, too. Write each of the days of the week on tagboard flash cards. Use the flash cards both in sequential order and randomly.

❖ Discuss each day of the week. Point out the beginning letter of each day. On Wednesday, have a special sharing day. Invite each child to show and tell about one item that begins with the letter W. Help the children brainstorm a list of W words beforehand to give them some ideas for what they might bring. For example, suggest a whistle, wand, wire, watch, wooden block, walnuts, a book about a worm, and so on.

❖ Make several sets of index cards with a day of the week on each card. Encourage the children to take one set of index cards and place them in order. More advanced children may be able to copy or write the days of the week and learn to spell each day orally as well.

Weigh

❖ Bring a bathroom scale to school to weigh each child in your room. Show the children how to read the big numbers and then count the single marks to figure out their own weight. (Be aware that scales are sometimes marked in 2's and should not be used unless the child has been taught to count by 2's.) Invite the children to practice weighing each other until they can figure out the weights (this should only be tried with those children who can count to 100). Encourage the children to memorize their own weights.

❖ A balance scale is fun and can reinforce the concepts "heavy" and "light." Find an assortment of items and ask the children to first decide which is heavier by just looking and then by weighing. Another good activity is to put an item on one side of the balance and then invite the children to put beans on the other side. By counting the beans, the children find out how many beans different items weigh.

Whale

❖ Read *The Whale Who Wanted to Be Small* by Gill McBarnet and *Dale the Whale* by Bob Reese (see the unit book review). Show the children how to draw a simple picture of a whale.

Wheels

❖ Read *Big Wheels* by Anne Rockwell, *Wheels* by Byron Barton, and *The Box with Red Wheels* by Maud and Miska Petersham (see the unit book review). Sponsor a "Wonderful Wednesday Wheel Day." Encourage the children to bring anything from home with wheels—toy cars, toy trains, pull toys, and so on to share with the class.

❖ Show the children how to draw a simple picture of a wagon with wheels. Then teach the children to sing "Old Brass Wagon" from *Wee Sing and Play*.

Whistle, Wink, Whisper, and Walk

❖ Collect whistles of different types and invite the class to experiment blowing each one. (Outside!) Encourage the children to bring whistles from home as well. Discuss when it is okay to use a whistle. Use a whistle this week to call the children in from the playground.

❖ Invite each child to demonstrate his or her whistle. Encourage children who can't whistle to practice whistling. Read *Whistle for Willie* by Ezra Jack Keats (see the unit book review).

❖ Explain that a wink is a quick open and shut movement of one eye. Show the children how to draw a simple picture of a wink. Invite children to practice winking by rapidly closing and opening both eyes (which is really blinking). Then encourage children to try the left eye and then the right.

❖ Have each child practice whispering. Discuss when it is good to whisper, too. Point out that it is usually a good idea to whisper in the library, when another person is sleeping, and when telling a secret.

❖ Challenge the children to walk a straight line taped or drawn on the floor. For a real challenge, take the children to the gym and see if they can walk a balance beam. Vary your walking instructions. For example, you might ask the children to walk heel-to-toe behind a leader, walk backwards, walk sideways leading with the left foot and then the right, walk to music, walk fast and then slow, walk on tiptoes, and so on.

❖ If possible, take the children for a short walk each day. Encourage the children to look for any W words (you might plant some along your trail). Teach the children to sing "Walking Walking" from *Wee Sing Children's Songs and Fingerplays*. Then suggest that children sing the song as they walk. Stress that walking is good, healthy exercise. When you return to the classroom, read *I Can Take a Walk* by Shigeo Watanabe and *Walking Is Wild, Weird and Wacky* by Karen Kerber (see the unit book review).

White

❖ Help the children make a list of items that are usually white, such as the moon and stars, snow, rice, vanilla ice cream, a dove, and so on. Point out items in the classroom that are white as well. Invite the children to cut out pictures from magazines of items that are white and then use the pictures to make a giant letter W on a bulletin board.

❖ Ask for permission for the children to write on the school sidewalk with chalk. Then give each child a piece of white chalk and a small separate space and invite the children to draw W's and white items. Use a hose to wash the chalk away, or perhaps the rain will do the job for you.

Wild

❖ Read *Where the Wild Things Are* by Maurice Sendak (see the unit book review). Then give the children an assortment of scrap construction paper. Demonstrate tearing the paper to make a "wild" thing. Encourage each child to use his or her imagination to make a "wild" thing by tearing pieces of construction paper.

❖ Make "Wild and Wonderful Dip." Try dipping wheat crackers.

Wild and Wonderful Dip

1/2 cup cottage cheese
1/2 cup plain yogurt
1/4 onion
1 tsp celery salt
crackers or vegetables
(carrots, turnips,
mushrooms, cucumbers,
radishes, cauliflower)
1/2 tsp horseradish or
3 shakes Tabasco
(optional)

In a bowl, mix the cottage cheese, yogurt, and salt. Add grated onion. Wash, peel, and cut the vegetables of your choice or use crackers for dipping. For a real "wild and wonderful" taste, add horseradish or Tabasco.

Winter

❖ Read *Winter* by Richard L. Allington and Kathleen Krull, *Winter* by Nancy M. Davis, and *Winter Is Here!* by Jane B. Moncure (see the unit book review). Discuss how winter is different and how it is the same as summer. Invite the children to make a collage of pictures cut from magazines of winter items. Glue pictures of coats, jackets, earmuffs, toboggans, gloves, mittens, boots, long pants, and sweaters on a bulletin board covered with white paper.

Wire

❖ Cut W's of different sizes from wire screening. Old window screening will work, or hunt for scraps of wire screening around a construction site. Have the children position a sheet of typing paper over a wire W. Suggest that children hold the W in place with one hand and then rub a crayon over the paper on the place where the W is located. The children will soon see a W appear on their papers. Invite the children to use different colors and different sized W's to create interesting designs.

❖ Give each child a piece of wire about six to eight inches long. Use thin, single pieces of telephone cable wire. Encourage the children to bend their wires to make a W. Some children may wish to try making different letters of the alphabet with the same piece of wire as well.

Witch

❖ Ask the children to explain what a witch is. Point out that witches are not real, but make-believe. Ask the children if all witches are bad. Then read *Humbug Witch* by Lorna Balian, *Witches Four* by Marc Brown, *A Woggle of Witches*

by Adrienne Adams, and *Tilly Witch* by Don Freeman (see the unit book review). Show the children how to draw a simple picture of a witch.

❖ Teach the children to sing "Ten Little Witches" to the tune of "Ten Little Indians" from *Wee Sing Children's Songs and Fingerplays*. Play "Old Mother Witch." Invite the children to hold hands and form a circle. Choose one child to be the witch and stand in the middle of the circle. The children in the circle chant "Old Mother Witch fell in a ditch, picked up a penny and thought she was rich." At the word *rich,* the children drop hands and run, with the witch trying to catch them. The first child caught becomes the new witch and the game starts over.

❖ Make a witch's wand. Cut out two white construction-paper stars for each child. Invite the children to paint each star with black, green, or purple tempera paint, or cut the stars from colored construction paper. Show the children how to roll up a sheet of newspaper to make a stick and staple the stars to either side. Suggest that children add green or gold glitter, if desired.

Wood

❖ Ask the children to help identify the items in your classroom that are made from wood. Discuss how wood comes from trees. Cut out pictures from magazines of items made from wood and glue them to a large sheet of construction paper. Invite the children to add more pictures to fill the sheet and make a collage.

❖ Gather a supply of scrap wood pieces. (Sometimes a lumberyard will donate wood scraps to schools.) Give small groups of children some scraps of wood, a hammer, and nails. (This will have to be closely supervised!) Invite children to practice nailing pieces of wood together. Some children may actually make something, but the important lesson is just to give the class an opportunity to experience the materials. Challenge the groups and ask them to try nailing four pieces of wood together to form a W.

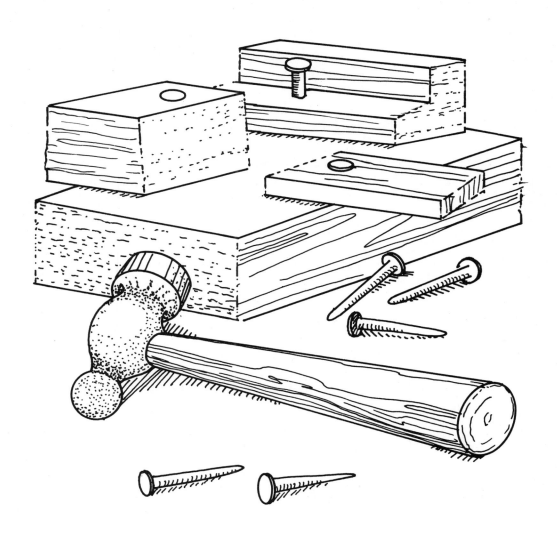

❖ Give each child four popsicle sticks or four tongue depressors. Discuss how these are made from wood. Then ask the children to shape the sticks into a W. Encourage children to try to form numbers and shapes and other straight letters, such as A, E, F, H, I, K, L, M, N, T, V, X, Y, and Z as well.

Workers

❖ Invite the children to give their opinions about why people work, the kinds of work that the children's parents do, the children's chores and responsibilities, work the children would like to do when they are adults, and so on.

❖ Help the children identify workers at school, such as the custodian, the principal, the librarian, lunchroom workers, the nurse, secretaries, bus drivers, and teachers. Discuss each person's job. Use your camera to make your own set of flash cards of people who work at school to help the children learn each person's name and job title.

❖ Review community workers, such as firefighters, police officers, grocers, and so on. Read *Richard Scarry's What Do People Do All Day?* by Richard Scarry and *Things People Do* by Anne Civardi (see the unit book review). Use any community helpers flash cards you may have to help the children learn to recognize each type of worker.

Worm

❖ Teach the children to sing "Nobody Likes Me" from *Wee Sing Silly Songs*. Then invite the children to eat gummy worms!

❖ Read *Where Is Willie Worm?* by Demi and *The Big Fat Worm* by Nancy Van Laan (see the unit book review). Invite the children to make wiggly worms. Cut a cardboard egg carton in half the long way to make strips of six consecutive sections. Give each child a strip with the instructions to turn the carton over and paint the bottom brown or green with tempera paint. When the paint is dry, show the children how to add spots for eyes and attach pipe cleaners for the antennae.

❖ If you have an appropriate place to go, get a small shovel and take the class on an excursion to dig for earthworms. An adult who fishes might be willing to give you some pointers on where to dig. Invite the children to keep the worms and study them for a day and then return them to the ground.

Food for Thought

Introducing children to a variety of foods is a wonderful way of reinforcing language concepts. The following foods all begin with the letter W and may be introduced at any time during this unit.

waffles, Waldorf salad, walnuts, water chestnuts, watercress, watermelon, wax beans, weiners, wheat germ, Wheaties (cereal), whole wheat bread, wild rice, Worcestershire sauce

Book Review

Children enjoy hearing good books read aloud. The books listed here are favorites of children and may be used to reinforce the letter W.

Adams, Adrienne. *A Woggle of Witches,* Macmillan, 1985.

Allington, Richard L. and Krull, Kathleen. *Winter,* Raintree Publications, 1981.

Balian, Lorna. *Humbug Witch,* Abingdon, 1965.

Barton, Byron. *Wheels,* Harper & Row, 1979.

Brown, Marc. *Witches Four,* Parents Magazine Press, 1980.

Civardi, Anne. *Things People Do,* Usborne-Hayes, 1986.

Davis, Nancy M. *Winter,* DaNa Publications, 1986.

Demi. *Where Is Willie Worm?,* Random House, 1981.

D'Ham, Claude. *The Weather,* Playspaces, 1975.

Freeman, Don. *Tilly Witch,* Penguin Books, 1978.

Humphries, Gillinan and Thatcher, Francis. *Sam Cat: A Book About Weather,* Childrens Press, 1984.

Keats, Ezra Jack. *Whistle for Willie,* Penguin Books, 1977.

Kerber, Karen. *Walking Is Wild, Weird and Wacky,* Landmark Editions, 1985.

McBarnet, Gill. *The Whale Who Wanted to Be Small,* Ruwanga Tradition, 1986.

Moncure, Jane B. *Winter Is Here!,* Child's World, 1975.

Petersham, Maud and Petersham, Miska. *The Box with Red Wheels,* Macmillan, 1949.

Pollock, Penny. *Water Is Wet,* Putnam Publishing Group, 1985.

Reese, Bob. *Dale the Whale,* Childrens Press, 1983.

Rockwell, Anne. *Big Wheels,* E. P. Dutton, 1986.

Scarry, Richard. *Richard Scarry's What Do People Do All Day?,* Random House, 1968.

Sendak, Maurice. *Where the Wild Things Are,* Harper & Row, 1988.

Van Laan, Nancy. *The Big Fat Worm,* Knopf, 1987.

Watanabe, Shigeo. *I Can Take a Walk,* Putnam Publishing Group, 1985.

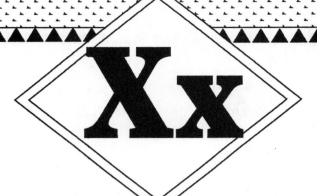

X Marks the Spot

❖ Read *Xavier's Fantastic Discovery* by Lucinda McQueen (see the unit book review). Give each child one sheet of 1-inch graph paper. Show the children how to draw an X in each of the squares by first drawing a diagonal line from the top right corner of the square to the opposite corner, and then a diagonal line from the top left corner of the square to the opposite corner. Invite the children to practice making exact X's on the graph paper. For fun, work with small groups of children and help them cross-stitch over their X's. Use yarn and plastic needles.

❖ Arrange a "Treasure Hunt." Leave clues in three to six different places. For example, start with a clue that reads "Go to the closet that has a mop, broom, and vacuum cleaner." The children then decide where to go. In this case, they would go to the custodian's closet for the next clue. Prearrange for a big red X to mark the correct spot—"X marks the spot." The clues may send the children all over the school finding the X's.

❖ Invite the children to play Tic-Tac-Toe. Teach the children in pairs or have them play in teams on the chalkboard.

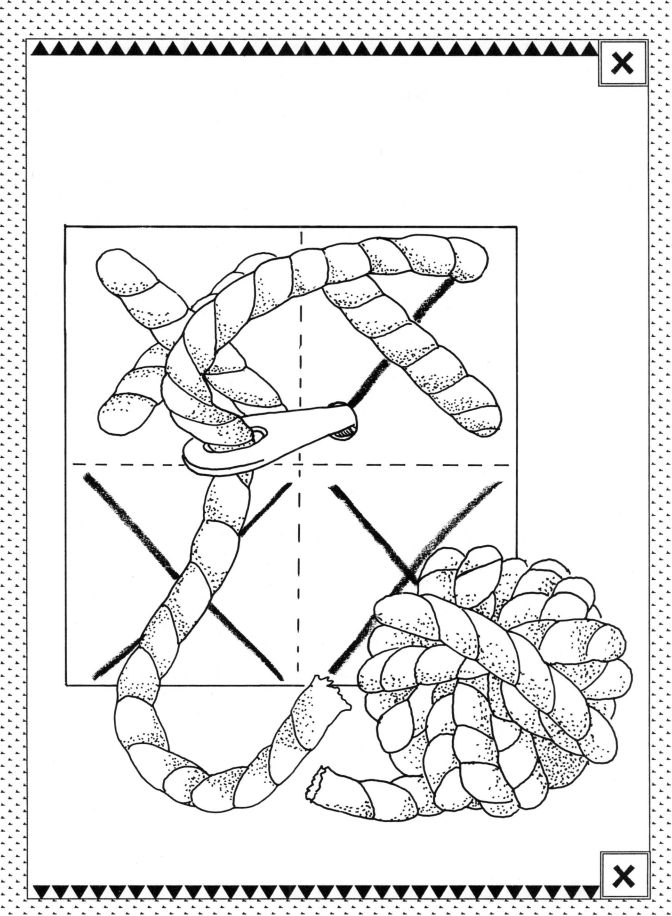

X-ray

❖ Ask your doctor and dentist for some old X-rays. Show the X-rays to the children. Explain that doctors and dentists use X-rays to check for broken bones or to see the inside of the body or teeth. Invite children who have had X-rays taken to share their experiences with the rest of the class.

❖ Draw a simple X-ray with white chalk on black construction paper. Explain that you can see bones on an X-ray and that you are going to draw some bones that you might see in an X-ray of the body. Draw each body part on the chalkboard and then wait for the children to draw that body part on their papers. Start with the head, then the neck and body, then shoulders, arms and fingers. Have a small red heart cut from construction paper to give each child. Invite the children to glue the heart on the right side of their skeleton drawings, under the shoulder. Then continue drawing the ribs and pelvis, and finally the legs, feet, and toes.

❖ Serve the children hot cross buns. Teach the children to sing "Hot Cross Buns" from *Wee Sing Nursery Rhymes and Lullabies.*

Xylophone

❖ Ask the music teacher or a band member to come visit your classroom and show the children how to play a xylophone. Encourage the children to each play one or two notes. Encourage any children who may have small xylophones at home to bring them to school to share with the rest of the class.

Food for Thought

Introducing children to a variety of foods is a wonderful way of reinforcing language concepts. The following food begins with the letter X and may be introduced at any time during this unit.

hot cross buns

Bibliography

Children enjoy hearing good books read aloud. The book listed here is a favorite of children and may be used to reinforce the letter X.

McQueen, Lucinda. *Xavier's Fantastic Discovery*, Parker Brothers, 1984.

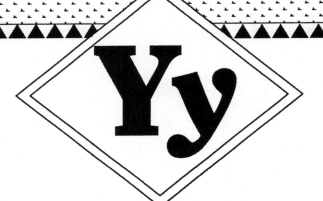

Yacht

❖ Show the children a picture of a yacht. Ask children if they know what this type of boat is called. Explain that a yacht is used for racing and pleasure. Make a yacht pattern from tagboard. Help the children trace around the pattern on yellow construction paper. Then invite children to cut out their yachts and add circles for the portholes with a black crayon. The children may then paint blue water on a large sheet of white construction paper with watercolors or tempera paint. When the paint is dry, have the children glue their yachts on the paper.

Yams

❖ Invite the children to try fried yams. They're yummy! Ask the children if they have ever eaten sweet potatoes. Explain that sweet potatoes and yams taste very much alike. Make "Yum-Yum Yams" as a special treat.

Yum-Yum Yams

	Drain the yams and arrange them in the
2 cans yams	bottom of a baking pan sprayed with
2 apples (peeled	Pam. Add a layer of apple slices. Sprinkle
and sliced)	the margarine, sugar, and nuts on top.
5 Tbsp brown	Sprinkle nutmeg over the casserole. Bake
sugar	at 350° for 30 minutes.
3 Tbsp margarine	
1/4 cup chopped	
walnuts (or pecans)	
Pam	
1/4 tsp nutmeg	

Yarn

❖ Make yellow yarn mobiles. Put white glue in an open bowl and invite the children to dip the yellow yarn in the glue, using a popsicle stick, spoon, or tongue depressor to saturate the yarn completely, except for the end the child is holding. Then have the children arrange the yarn on waxed paper in interesting designs. Ask children to bend the end of the yarn to use as a hanger and cut off the end they were holding since it has no glue on it. When the glue is thoroughly dry, remove the mobiles from the waxed paper and hang them in a window or from the ceiling.

❖ Make yarn Y's. Make a Y pattern from heavy cardboard. Help the children trace around the pattern on yellow construction paper. Invite the children to cut out their own Y's. Give each child several pieces of yarn in different colors to cut into small pieces. Invite the children to work together in small groups. Cover the work area with wax paper and then give each group a small cup of glue. Have the children brush glue on the yellow construction paper Y and then remove the Y from the wax paper to another area to drop their pieces of yarn on the glue. Encourage the children not to touch the glue as they are dropping the yarn or their hands will get sticky and the yarn will stick to their hands.

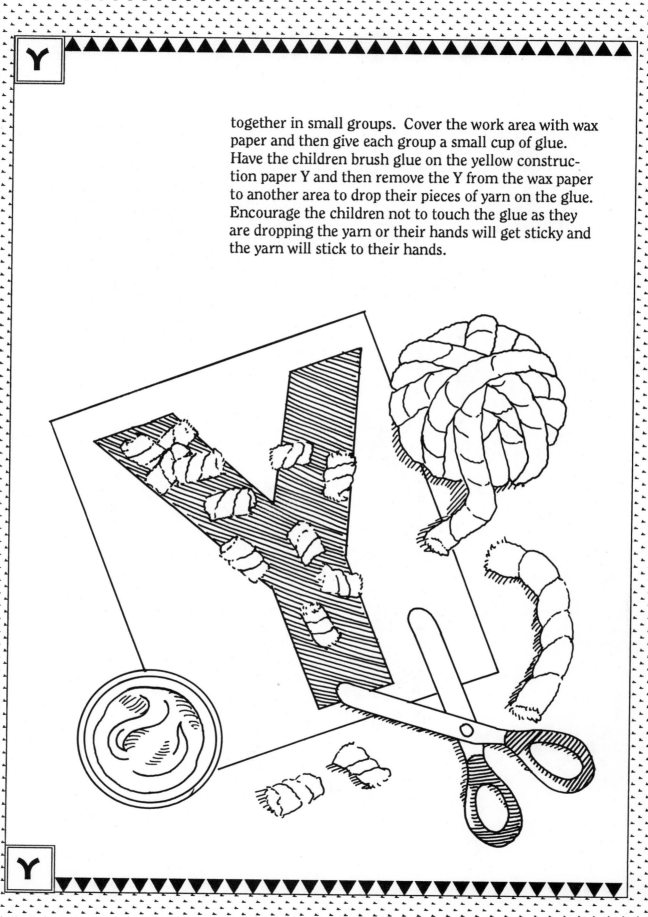

Year and Yesterday

❖ Ask the children how long a year is. Explain that some events only happen once a year. For example, the children have one birthday each year, Thanksgiving and other holidays only occur once a year, they attend a different grade in school each year, and so on. Encourage the children to name other events that happen once a year as well. Point out that New Year's Eve marks the end of a year. Teach the children to say and write the current year.

❖ Each day as you discuss the calendar, repeat "Today is _____" and "Yesterday was _____."

Yell, Yawn, and Yodel

❖ Sponsor a yelling contest. Take the children outside and invite them to yell "Yippee!" "Yeah!" "Yes!" "Yoo-hoo!" "Yesiree!" and "Yahoo!" Award a simple prize to the child who yells the loudest.

❖ Invite each child to pretend to yawn. Ask the children when they usually yawn. Point out that yawning may mean they are tired or bored. Encourage the children to keep track of the times when they yawn.

❖ Teach the children the yodeling song "Once an Austrian Went Yodeling" from *Wee Sing Silly Songs*. Then arrange for the children to sing the song for the children in another classroom.

Yellow

❖ Read *The Big Yellow Bus Is a Good Friend of Mine* by William S. Bradshaw, Jr. (see the unit book review). Make yellow books. Invite each child to fold a piece of yellow construction paper in half to form a book. Then suggest that children cut out pictures from a magazine of yellow items to glue inside their books. Encourage the children to draw and color items that are yellow, too. For example, they might draw a lemon, lollipop, moon, flower, banana, baby duck, pear, and so on.

Yogurt

❖ Invite the children to eat yummy yellow yogurt, either lemon or banana flavor. Then use any flavor yogurt to make "Yogurt Yummies."

Yogurt Yummies

2 cups yogurt
1 1/2 cups orange juice
1 tsp vanilla
popsicle sticks

Mix together the yogurt, orange juice, and vanilla. Pour the mixture into small paper drinking cups. Put the cups in the freezer. Put a popsicle stick in each cup after the mixture is partially frozen. Makes 6–8 servings.

Food for Thought

Introducing children to a variety of foods is a wonderful way of reinforcing language concepts. The following foods all begin with the letter Y and may be introduced at any time during this unit.

yams, yogurt, yolk

Book Review

Children enjoy hearing good books read aloud. The books listed here are favorites of children and may be used to reinforce the letter Y.

Bradshaw, Jr., William S. *The Big Yellow School Bus Is a Good Friend of Mine,* Webb-Newcomb,1981.

Lonie, Al-ling. *Yeh Shen: A Cinderella Story from China,* Putnam Publishing Group, 1982.

Marshall, James. *Yummers, Too,* Houghton Mifflin, 1986.

Oppenheim, Joanne F. *You Can't Catch Me!,* Houghton Mifflin, 1986.

Seuss, Dr. *Yertle the Turtle and Other Stories,* Random House, 1985.

Stevenson, James. *Yuck!,* William Morrow and Company, 1987.

Zz

Zero

❖ Make Z patterns from heavy cardboard. Help the children trace around the Z on sheets of colored construction paper. Have the children cut out their own Z's. Then invite children to arrange hole reinforcers all over the Z.

❖ Explain that zero comes before the number one on the number line. Invite the children to practice making zeros and writing the numbers 0 through 10 on the chalkboard. When children are ready, encourage them to do the same thing first on paper with lines and then on paper without lines.

❖ Have the children make a large zero on a sheet of construction paper. Give each child a handful of cereal shaped like a zero to arrange on the drawn zero until the circle is complete. Invite the children to eat the "zeros" when they are finished.

Zigzag

❖ Purchase different colors and sizes of rickrack, or have someone who sews save scraps for you. Point out how the rickrack makes a zigzag pattern. Invite the children to practice walking in a zigzag line. Ask different children to have a turn being the leader. Give each child a strip of the rickrack and ask him or her to cut it into smaller pieces. Have the children make a large letter Z with glue on a sheet of construction paper. Invite children to arrange the zigzag pieces along the glue line to make a "Zigzag Z."

❖ Borrow several pairs of pinking shears. Show the children how pinking shears cut in a zigzag pattern. Cut strips of colored construction paper using the pinking shears and give each child a strip to cut into small squares. Have the children make a large letter Z with glue on a sheet of construction paper. Invite children to arrange the small zigzag squares along the glue line to make a "Zigzag Z."

Zinger

❖ Make a zinger. Give each child a piece of string about 10 inches long, two 6-inch squares of tin foil, and a cotton ball. Encourage children to use their imaginations to create something—anything they would like. Then invite the children to show and tell about their zingers!

Zinnia

❖ Invite the children to help plant zinnias outside in a small plot or use individual milk cartons to plant individual flowers. A cleaned sand or water table also makes a nice indoor flower plot. When the flowers bloom, use them to make beautiful flower arrangements to brighten your classroom.

Zip

❖ Read *Zippity Zap! A Book About Dressing* by Harriet Ziefert (see the unit book review). Show the children a large jacket that has a front zipper that separates. A small adult windbreaker will do fine. Invite the children to put the jacket on and zip it up. Work individually with children having trouble. Show the children how to draw a simple picture of a zipper.

❖ Give each child a ziplock bag. In each bag, put large dabs of red and blue, red and yellow, red and white, blue and yellow, black and white, or black and orange tempera or fingerpaint that may be mixed together to make a new color. Put one color in one corner of the bag and the other color in the opposite corner. Then invite the children to zip their bags together and mash the two colors to make a new color. Open one corner of the bag and have the children squeeze their new colors on a plastic container lid. They may then use the new colors to paint Z's.

❖ Put thick tempera paint into ziplock bags. Fill the bags about one-fourth full of paint. Press out as much air as possible and then close the bags tightly. Give each child a bag. Invite the children to spread the paint out evenly in their bags and then use their index fingers to draw Z's (like a "magic slate"). They may erase by rubbing the palms of their hands over the bags to even out the paint. Some children may wish to try making other letters, numbers, and shapes as well.

Zip Code

❖ Explain that zip codes are five-part numbers that help postal workers separate the mail for quick delivery. Encourage each child to memorize his or her own zip code. Save some letters with clearly written zip codes on them. Show the letters to the children and ask the children to identify where the zip code is on each letter. Invite the children to read the numbers, too.

Zoo

❖ Read *Who in the Zoo?* by Wilma Shore, *Zoo* by Jan Pienkowski, *Curious George Visits the Zoo* by Margret Rey and Allan J. Shalleck, and *Zoo* by Gail Gibbons (see the unit book review). If there is a zoo nearby, arrange for the children to visit.

❖ Use picture cards of zoo animals as flash cards this week. Arrange the cards along the chalkboard ledge and then ask the children to name the animals that have two legs, four legs, webbed feet, feathers, hairy bodies, and so on. Encourage the children to sort the animals into groups that swim, fly, walk, run fast, and so on. Add other animal

cards and challenge the children to sort the cards into two groups, such as "Animals and Zoo Animals," "Zoo Animals and Pets," or "Zoo Animals and Not Zoo Animals."

❖ Explain that some zoo animals are kept in cages. Help the children make animal cages. Have the children first cut four strips of paper for the frame of the cage (a top and bottom and two sides). Show the children how to glue the pieces on a sheet of construction paper. Suggest that children draw a zoo animal of their choice inside the cage and then cut three more strips of paper to glue on the cage for bars.

❖ Read *Greedy Zebra* by Mwenye Hadithi (see the unit book review). Show the children how to draw a "Z-zebra." Make Z patterns from heavy cardboard. Help the children trace around the pattern on a sheet of white construction paper. Instruct the children to add a circle for an eye and stripes with a crayon. (A zebra really has dark brown stripes, not black!) Ears, a mane (using zigzag Z's), a tail, and legs may be drawn with a crayon to complete the "Z-zebra."

Zucchini

❖ Show the children a zucchini and ask them if they know what it is. Explain that zucchini is a vegetable that may be eaten in a number of different ways. Make "Zowie Zucchini Muffins," fry zucchini slices, and make zucchini bread for the children to taste.

Zowie Zucchini Muffins

1/2 cup zucchini
1 egg
1 Tbsp vegetable oil
1/4 tsp honey
1/4 tsp grated
   lemon peel
3/4 cup flour
1/2 tsp baking
   powder
dash salt
1/4 tsp cinnamon

Grate the zucchini. Mix together all of the ingredients. Pour the mixture into a muffin tin sprayed with Pam or use muffin liners. Bake for 20 minutes at 400°.

❖ Give each child a ziplock bag. Invite children to practice zipping and unzipping the bag. Ask each child to choose a number between one and ten. Then help him or her count out that number of zucchini spears to put in the bag. Make "Zippy Dip with Zucchini" and invite the children to dip their zucchini spears in the mixture and eat.

Zippy Dip with Zucchini

zucchini
2 cups cottage
cheese
milk
1/2 cup mayonnaise
salad dressing mix

Wash the zucchini and cut it into short spears. Add the milk to the cottage cheese and mix until the mixture is smooth. Add mayonnaise and the dry dressing mix. Chill.

Food for Thought

Introducing children to a variety of foods is a wonderful way of reinforcing language concepts. The following foods all begin with the letter Z and may be introduced at any time during this unit.

Zesta (saltines), zucchini, Zweiback (teething cookie)

Book Review

Children enjoy hearing good books read aloud. The books listed here are favorites of children and may be used to reinforce the letter Z.

Gibbons, Gail. *Zoo,* Harper & Row, 1987.

Hadithi, Mwenye. *Greedy Zebra,* Little, Brown and Company, 1984.

Pienkowski, Jan. *Zoo,* David and Charles, 1985.

Rey, Margret and Shalleck, Allan J. *Curious George Visits the Zoo,* Houghton Mifflin, 1985.

Shore, Wilma. *Who in the Zoo?,* Lippincott, 1976.

Ziefert, Harriet. *Zippity Zap! A Book About Dressing,* Penguin Books, 1984.

Z